THE DEVIL'S BEST TRICK

THE DEVIL'S BEST TRICK

HOW THE FACE OF EVIL DISAPPEARED

RANDALL SULLIVAN

Atlantic Monthly Press

New York

FIRST EDITION

Published simultaneously in Canada
Printed in the United States of America

First Grove Atlantic hardcover edition: May 2024

Library of Congress Cataloging-in-Publication data is available for this title.

ISBN 978-0-8021-1913-1
eISBN 978-0-8021-6290-8

Atlantic Monthly Press
An imprint of Grove Atlantic
154 West 14th Street
New York, NY 10011

Distributed by Publishers Group West

Groveatlantic.com

24 25 26 27 28   10 9 8 7 6 5 4 3 2 1

Preface

In the summer of 1995, I was living in a country at war. Where I kept my billet, in the westernmost province of Bosnia and Herzegovina, the worst atrocities had been committed two years before my arrival. Nevertheless, it was amid the blast craters and bullet holes of Mostar, a demolished city that now lay under a psycho-terror siege of random mortar launches and sporadic sniper shots, that I began to recognize "the problem of evil" as an obstacle to religious faith.

The tales of horror I heard in Mostar were moral quicksand. I kept my head above the horror by floating the surface of it in a cracked shell of professionalism, refusing either to believe or disbelieve the story of those Catholic nuns who claimed to have been captured by a unit of so-called *četniks*, gang-raped until each was pregnant, then given a choice between abortion, suicide, and bearing a Serb bastard. For me, it was enough to dip my toes in the citywide seep of sadness that lingered after the very public deaths of a young Muslim mother and her two children, blown apart by a direct missile strike as they attempted to flee down the Neretva River in a rubber raft. I could deflect everything except the expressions of the orphans on street corners. Seven and eight years old, they stood smoking cigarettes and flipping off passersby with a stony insolence that you couldn't have wiped off their faces with an assault rifle. Looking into their agate eyes, I knew it was too late for us all.

Picking a path through the gigantic pile of scorched rubble that had once been Mostar's city center, a place where two years earlier Catholic and Muslim survivors of the Serbian bombardment had fought each other with artillery at close range, I asked myself, as so many had before me, "How can a God who is all-knowing, all-powerful, and all-good abide such depravity?" And what about justice? Maybe God wasn't who I thought he was. Maybe God wasn't, period.

It didn't help my sleep that the most impressive people I met that summer made a point of telling me that the Devil, at least, was real. The first to speak these words was Mirjana Soldo, a religious visionary in Medjugorje, the Bosnian Croat "peace center" twelve miles from Mostar. There, a rapturous cult of devotion had formed around apparitions of the Virgin Mary that were already the most controversial and closely observed purported supernatural phenomena to appear on earth in at least a half century. As Mirjana urged me to recognize the Devil as an actual being who was determined to steal my soul, her pale blue eyes seemed to darken, and her expression became a discomfiting combination of pity and reproach. My sense was that she felt obliged to give me a warning she knew I wouldn't heed.

Rita Klaus was more successful in suspending my disbelief. A large, handsome, white-haired woman from Pittsburgh, Klaus was famous for her spontaneous healing from an advanced case of multiple sclerosis, the most celebrated and thoroughly documented of the many medical miracles associated with Medjugorje. Klaus had seemed to appear out of nowhere one afternoon in the village's parish office. She sat down across from me, leaned over the table, laid a hand on mine, and introduced herself with these words: "Satan exists." I felt as if I had been shot with some drug that causes a temporary paralysis. Klaus seemed to wait until the effect was complete before continuing: "The evil inside you comes from temptation. You have to make a decision, either for the good or for the bad. So the evil is inside us, as you believe, but it's also out there, and believe me, it is very real and very pervasive." Klaus then told me the story of a diabolic attack on her family that had begun when one of her daughters began to experiment with a Ouija board. The part that disturbed me most at the time, and that would haunt me later, involved a series of attacks on Klaus and her family by something that took the form of a large black dog with red eyes. "I don't want to scare you, but I think you need to hear my story," Klaus told me at one point. The emphasis she put on the word "need" troubled me.

The person I admired more than anyone I met in Medjugorje was a Franciscan priest named Slavko Barbarić, spiritual adviser to Mirjana and the other visionaries. Shortly after my meeting with Rita Klaus, Father Slavko attempted to breach my skepticism with a phenomenological report. Slavko was, among other things, an intellectual whose multiple PhDs included one in psychology. He lowered my guard by admitting straight out his own reluctance to believe in supernatural evil, then described the series of events that had changed his mind. One experience that made a deep impression involved his participation in the exorcism of a woman who was able to distinguish consecrated hosts from those that had not been consecrated. He and the other priests participating in the exorcism each had left the room on multiple occasions, Slavko recalled, only to return a few minutes later with either a wafer that had been consecrated or one that had not yet been blessed. The woman who lay on the bed never reacted once when they came into the room with an unconsecrated host, Slavko told me, but went into paroxysms of writhing and cursing whenever a consecrated host came near her. "What in her could possibly have known the difference?" Slavko asked. In reply, I simply shook my head.

I was to witness an exorcism myself only a few days later. I've attempted to deconstruct that experience many times in the years since, mainly in the hope that I would be able to put it out of my mind. Those I've spoken to about it always make reference to the "altered state" I was in at the time. I don't deny this. That night and the days leading up to it were almost unbearable in their intensity. The Youth Festival Mass in which the exorcism occurred was the most fervid and enthralling religious service I've ever experienced. The thousand or so young adults who made their way to Medjugorje from all over the world had braved warnings from the United Nations and the European Union that the situation was especially unstable at the moment and that travel to the former Yugoslavia was "strongly discouraged." The Croats were mobilizing for a final push against the Serbs, and the climax of the war was upon us. A sense that the armies of light were rallying against the forces of darkness imbued that evening's mass from the moment it began. Father Slavko was as I'd never seen him before, ferocious in his ardor, swinging an enormous gilded monstrance and the consecrated host within like a holy weapon as he stormed through the crowd. Each time Slavko turned the monstrance in a new direction, repeating the words "Body of Christ," I heard an eruption of bone-chilling noises from out of the crowd, shrieks of agony and gasps of terror, animal howls and loud, throaty curses. There were several raspy barks of "Fuck you!" The choir on the stage behind Slavko only sang louder, faces aglow with the conviction of imminent victory. As Slavko approached, his expression frightened me; the gaunt priest's reliably warm gaze was replaced by a piercing glare. He pointed the monstrance directly at me and in a booming voice shouted, "Jesus!" It was as close as I've ever come to keeling over in a dead faint. The roars of rage and cries of pain seemed to be swelling around me. A young woman standing perhaps twenty feet to my left began to produce a noise unlike any I'd ever heard, a cough so dry and deep that it sounded as if she was trying to bring up a lung. It went on and on, like an echo that did not fade but rather amplified. She bent over, then shuddered uncontrollably, a white foam issuing from her mouth in a copious stream. She dropped to the ground, kicking and writhing, and began to scream obscenities. I heard "Fuck you, Jesus," in very clear English, but also curses—or what I assumed were curses—in a variety of languages I did not recognize. The girl's voice became im-possibly deep and guttural, and the white lather continued to pour from her mouth. A crowd of people gathered around, reciting the exorcism prayer of Pope Leo XIII. At one point, the girl on the ground seemed to go still and silent, but then her screams started up again, louder than ever, gruesomely desperate. At the moment of what I could sense as a climax, she arched her back into a position that not even a world-class gymnast could have held, impossibly extended, with her weight resting entirely on her heels and the crown of her head, and let forth a hoarse, croaking expulsion of breath that must have emptied her lungs utterly. It was the smell, though, that shocked me, a ghastly stench that was like the exponential product of rotted flesh. In that moment I became utterly convinced that *something* was leaving her, that what I had just witnessed was not emotional or psychological or imaginary but *real*, whatever that meant.

I remember very little of what happened next, just blurred images of the girl being helped to her feet and led away, of Slavko finishing the mass, of the shining faces of the choir as they sang. I have no idea how I made it back to the Pansion Maja, into my room, and out onto the tiny balcony where I awoke at dawn, sprawled on the concrete floor, shivering with cold and happy in a way that was completely unfamiliar.

Two days later I was in Rome, on my way home. It was mid-August, and to escape the suffocating heat I sought the cooling mists of the Fountain of the Four Rivers on the Piazza Navona. I was leaning against the back of a bench when I noticed an elegantly dressed man walking through a sea of tourists, T-shirt vendors, and street performers that seemed to part before him. He wore a beautifully cut blue blazer with cream linen trousers, a bright yellow cravat, and sharp-toed loafers polished to a high gloss. "Quite the gent," I thought, then drew a quick breath when I saw the man's face. His aquiline features were formed into the strangest expression I'd ever seen, a sort of malevolent drollery that did not entirely mask the suffocating rage beneath it. Though all by himself, the man began to speak in a loud voice as he drew near me, in a language that was not Italian. Heart pounding, I glanced at the tourists nearby, baffled by their lack of a reaction. Not one of them seemed to have noticed this jarring oddity moving among them. It was as if, somehow, the silver-haired man and I had been isolated from the scene surrounding us. Suddenly, he let loose with a mad cackle and turned his head slightly to fix me with one eye. In that moment, I felt absolutely certain he wasn't human. I *knew* it. An unearthly calm came over me almost immediately. Why I can't say, but I reached inside my shirt to grasp the scapular medal I had taken to wearing that summer, stared back at him, and whispered, "You can't touch me." He responded with an obscene leer. I understood exactly what he said then: "I'll catch you later."

After returning home, I spoke to no one about the . . . *creature* I had encountered on the Piazza Navona. In time, the indelibility of that summer began to fade. Within a couple of years, the only thing I understood better than before was how much of memory is conviction. And by then, the practical advantages all seemed to be on the side of doubt. To claim that I had encountered a diabolical entity on the Piazza Navona made me sound either crazy or foolish—even to myself. It wasn't good for business.

I was aided immeasurably in my will to forget by the television broadcast of a "live exorcism" on a network news magazine. The contrived staging and cornball theatrics of this TV event served only to highlight the abject need for an audience that drove not only the show's producers but also the grandiose exorcist and his dim-witted subject. There wasn't enough self-awareness in the thing to raise it even to the level of farce. I thought, "What if my own state of mind is the main difference between what I witnessed in Bosnia and what I'm seeing now?" Even to allow this as a possibility undermined my recollection of that night in Medjugorje.

And because my numinous moments from the summer of 1995 were never repeated, it became easier and easier to tell myself that the extraordinary stresses and sympathies I experienced in Bosnia had induced bizarre perceptions of what were probably half-imagined shadows of a truth beyond my understanding. Or some such shit. While I didn't really believe this new version of my story, I didn't really believe the story I had come home with, either. It soon seemed both possible and preferable to shroud my memories in a haze of ambiguity.

My four-year-old son chased me out of that cloud. Gabriel got into bed next to me one morning, then whispered in my ear that something terrifying had happened to him during the night. A big black dog with red eyes, he said, came into his room and bit his baby blanket, the silk-banded square of blue flannel he had slept with since birth. My little boy was shaking as he spoke these words. When I hugged him close and tried to tell him that sometimes our dreams seem so real to us that we think they actually happened, he went quiet for a few moments, then told me plaintively that it wasn't a dream, that he knew it wasn't a dream, that it was real. When I tried again to talk about how affected a child can be by the things he imagines seeing in the night, Gabe became angry and demanded to know why I was trying to make him think he didn't know what was real and what wasn't. "The dog was real, even if it wasn't a real dog," he told me. I let it go then, though the subject continued to come up from time to time, always when my son raised it. He seemed to have a need to talk about it. I tried several other times to suggest that what he had experienced was a very vivid, powerful dream, but this inevitably infuriated him. When he was five, he saw a psychologist who told him about the night terrors that younger children often experience, and how these take place in a zone between waking and sleeping. Gabe seemed to find some comfort in this notion, but within the year he again brought up the black dog that had bit his baby blanket when he was four and insisted once more that what had happened was real, not a dream or even a night terror. I was ready for him this time, and answered with the suggestion that I might have told his mom a story I heard from a woman I met in Bosnia about a black dog with red eyes that had terrorized *her* family. He might have overheard this story when he was very young, I went on, and later somehow half-dreamed and half-imagined a similar experience. "So now you think I'm crazy?" he asked. No, no, no, I assured him: all our heads are full not only of thoughts we know about, what we call the conscious mind, but also of thoughts we don't know about, what we call the unconscious mind, and when those two mix, we can have experiences that seem completely real to us but not to anyone else. "So you're saying that it wasn't *really* real," my son accused. I didn't know *what* I was saying and shook my head in confused frustration. "It happened," Gabe told me. "I know it happened." He gave me a measuring look that I'd never seen from him before. I knew it was a big moment for us both. "You believe me, don't you, Dad?" my son asked finally. I stared into his eyes for some time before answering, "I believe you."

That was the last time we ever talked about it. It was also, for me I think, the beginning of this book.

THE DEVIL'S
BEST TRICK

PART ONE

The Author of Evil

CHAPTER ONE

---

i.

MIDNIGHT ON MARCH 6, 2015, was the Hour of the Witches in Catemaco, Mexico. The rollover into the first Friday of the month of March was the exact moment of each year, it had been explained to me, when a flood of demons poured into this remote town in the tropical jungle of Veracruz state.

I was standing just outside a circle perhaps forty feet in diameter. It had been drawn with a phosphorescent powder to intersect the points of a giant pentagram made of the same stuff, on a broad patch of packed dirt beneath a towering cliff where fires burned on the ridge. The perimeter of the circle was lit by dozens of candles that cast a dim, fluttery light on a man holding a large knife and wearing the skin and fur of an anteater as headgear. He swung around in a complete circle, displaying his blade to the entire assembly. The anteater's bared teeth rested on the man's forehead, its long tail trailing down his back. The animal's skull dangled from a cord around his neck, like a grotesque talisman. Enrique Verdon bore the title *gran brujo*, or "great witch," and was leading the Black Mass at which eight people inside the circle—*iniciados*, Verdon called them—were being bathed in the blood of sacrificed animals. One after another, the *iniciados* kneeled to pledge their souls to El Diablo, the Devil himself. As each promise to Satan was made, Verdon threw a handful of rue into the cauldron of glowing charcoal in the center of the circle, creating a whooshing flare of flame that made me cringe each time it rose up, even when I knew it was coming.

I looked across the circle at my friend Michelle Gomez, who had accompanied me to Catemaco as my translator, and could see her bug-eyed and shivering. She had been badly shaken by the sacrifice of a goat moments earlier. For me as well, it had been a horrific experience. The animal seemed to realize its fate from the moment it was led inside the circle and was surrounded by the *brujo*'s assistants, six other witches who had traveled to Catemaco from all over Mexico. They were both men and women, all dressed in what looked to me like custom-made Halloween costumes, black in most cases. The *brujo*'s number one man, though, wore a red suit, as did the high priestess, a woman whose hair had been bleached platinum blond; she carried a carved wooden staff topped by a ram's horn, festooned with assorted feathers and furs. The witch who created the most disturbing appearance called himself Joyi Ra and had used black, yellow, and red paint to turn his face into a kind of cubist mask of Nahualist symbols. Around his neck, Joyi Ra wore a necklace made of eight human finger bones.

The mustachioed witch in the red costume, which had a gold pentagram emblazoned on the back, was the first to seize the goat, but the others joined in quickly, lifting the animal by all four legs, then elevating its hindquarters. The animal's bleating, which never stopped after it was raised from the ground, became all but unbearable within moments. Anthropomorphic as it may have been, I heard a creature pleading for its life up to the moment when the two witches at the back pulled the hind legs apart until they broke at the hip with a horrific cracking sound.

Not until Michelle translated it for me later did I know that Verdon had declared to all present that "the blood from a still-beating heart is the purest form of energy," then proclaimed that the blood of the animals sacrificed during this ceremony "will be offered up to the dark powers." Holding his knife aloft and turning it in the light from the iron cauldron, the *brujo* told the assembly, "We are calling upon Satan, the prince of the earth, to appear before us." Before cutting the goat's throat, he demanded that anyone who refused to accept this animal's sacrifice should make himself known. "Randall, I wanted so badly to say something," Michelle told me afterward, "but I knew you wouldn't have wanted me to."

I winced because it was true. Michelle and I had agreed going in that we were strangers in a strange land, one where the culture was incomprehensible to us—though more to me than to her—and so needed to remain silent observers, no matter what happened. I repeated what I had heard from Antonio Zavaleta, a professor of anthropology in the University of Texas system and the closest thing to an authority on the subject of Mexican witchcraft as exists in American academia. Zavaleta, half Mexican and half Irish, told me that he had struggled for decades with what for him was still an unresolved dichotomy: "In the Mexican culture, things that would be seen by you and me as clearly defined evil aren't seen that way at all. For instance, the use of a supernatural medium to accomplish someone's death would clearly be considered evil by American standards. But here at the border [Zavaleta was living in Brownsville, Texas] it is part of everyday life. People don't see it as evil, or in terms of right or wrong. They don't understand it in those terms. It's just part of their cultural reality. If you're able to manipulate the spiritual or supernatural world, then you have a right to. This is a power you possess and you can use it if you want."

Michelle, though, knew perfectly well that a good part of my motive for wanting her to keep silent during the Black Mass was that I had no idea what speaking up might bring down upon us. "It crossed my mind that if I said something it might be me instead of the goat," she admitted. Whatever else might be said of her, Michelle was brave and resourceful, and as physically formidable as any human being four feet eleven inches tall could be. She had been described as "The World's Best Bounty Hunter" on the cover of *Wired* magazine, an acclamation that was repeated in dozens of other media outlets. She was, in her own words, "one badass bitch." Now, though, she looked like a frightened little girl lost in the dark.

When we talked later, Michelle would respond with what I took to be a slightly condescending "typical man" expression as I told her that, more than the animal sacrifices, I had been disturbed by the young girls used in the ceremonies. They were thirteen, fourteen, fifteen years old, with that combination of soft, childlike facial features and a nubile brown body that seems to be the ultimate aphrodisiac for many Latin men. They were all dressed in matching black bras and panties, barefoot, and blatantly sexualized, but all virgins, as was required, according to the *gran brujo*. These girls had carried the chickens that were the first sacrificial offerings into the circle, marching in a rotation that created a sort of bizarre human conveyor belt, achieving an effect that was simultaneously salacious and robotic. The witch in the red suit had seized the chicken delivered by the girl first in line, swinging it by the neck as he used the bird to whack a kneeling *iniciado* all about the head, neck, and shoulders. The chicken's wings flapped helplessly, feathers flying, and the middle-aged woman on her knees before the witch absorbed the blows with an expression of utter submission.

Like most of the other *iniciados*, the middle-aged woman declined to publicly declare what she had come to Catemaco to ask of El Diablo. The only two supplicants who revealed what had brought them here were a young couple from Monterrey who said they were trying to save a failing marriage. He had ruined everything with an affair, said the husband, Alejandro, and was here to "put my soul on the line to prove my commitment." His young wife, Gloria, nodded her approval, and declared that by his willingness to risk eternal damnation Alejandro had shown he was serious about winning her back. I moved closer to examine Alejandro for signs that he was just playing along with what he knew to be a farce, but I saw the young man trembling, his expression a weird fusion of fright and rapture as the blood of a sacrificed animal was smeared on his face.

The bird that the witch in red had used to whip the middle-aged woman was somehow still alive when the *brujo* Verdon stepped forward to cut off its head, then tossed that aside and let the blood spurting from the chicken's neck soak the kneeling woman's head. The girl who had delivered the creature to the witches stood by with an expression that suggested mainly how much she was enjoying the attention of the men who gaped at her.

With Michelle's assistance, I later asked a young man who had remained outside the circle, like me an observer, who these girls were, remarking that their parents must know what they were doing. "Their parents are here, watching," he told me. The involvement of these girls was *generacional*, the young man explained. "Their parents are part of this, so were their grandparents before that." "So their families literally *give* them to the *brujo*," I said. The young man arched an eyebrow, as if to emphasize what my statement implied, and said, "Exactamente."

I started to say that I had a teenage daughter of my own back home, but broke off in midsentence; I didn't want her present in this place, even in a conversation.

Two other virgins had participated in the ceremony. One was a girl in a turquoise and red costume that included an elaborate feathered headdress. Her role, Verdon had explained, was to provide a human link to the Olmec culture from which the black magic traditions that were being observed this night had been drawn. Whether the Olmecs were in fact devil worshippers, or practiced human sacrifice, for that matter, is debatable, in the opinions of many anthropologists and archeologists, but Verdon wasn't getting arguments from anyone present at his Black Mass.

The other virgin was a voluptuous young woman who looked to be a couple of years older than the girls in the black bras and panties. She wore a white gown and stood watching the sacrifices and other rituals with totemic aplomb. The virgin in white was shoulder to shoulder with the witches at the conclusion of the Black Mass, though, when they set fire to a fifteen-foot-tall pentagram and summoned El Diablo with chants I was glad I didn't understand. She followed the witches too when they led the *iniciados* to the "Black Cave," where a ten-foot-tall red devil version of Satan equipped with an enormous erect penis was waiting, surrounded by inverted crosses and assorted animal carcasses. The witches smeared the statue with the blood of the sacrificial animals, then, one by one, the *iniciados* knelt before it and whispered what they had promised to El Diablo. Verdon and all the other witches gathered around each of the *iniciados* and joined them in repeating a final blood oath warning that their souls would be forfeit if they failed to keep their end of the bargain. "If you don't fulfill your promises to Satan, he will take everything away from you," Joyi Ra told the young husband, Alejandro, as the witch wiped blood from the statue and smeared it across the *iniciado*'s forehead. "You are taking on a serious dark curse."

When I returned home, I would be asked by various people if I had felt the Devil's presence in Catemaco. The question was put to me with varying degrees of seriousness. Some posed it in a slightly mocking tone, others with earnest interest. My answer was always the same: "Yes, but not really at the Black Mass." That midnight ceremony had been spooky and unsettling. I'd certainly felt the presence of something sinister, but it didn't have a name. There was no sense of a single being behind it all, but rather an amalgamation of human and possibly inhuman wickedness, appetite, and vanity.

The Black Mass really couldn't compare in intensity to what I'd experienced just an hour or so before arriving, in the living room of a tiny woman wrapped in a purple blanket. She was the daughter of Gonzalo Aguirre, the long-dead *brujo* to whom Enrique Verdon had dedicated his Black Mass at the beginning of the ceremonies, and the man who had "put Catemaco on the map," as his granddaughter Chavela would tell Michelle and me the next day. Aguirre's teacher was the more significant and frightful figure in the Catemaco story, but it was the apprentice, Don Gonzalo, who had become the most famous black magician in Mexico (where sorcerers and shamans hold a place of importance that is incomprehensible to most Americans), the one whose spells, curses, and hexes had drawn the first of what was now a very long line of politicians, movie stars, music idols, and athletes streaming in and out of Catemaco.

The hour I spent with Don Gonzalo's daughter, Isabel Aguirre, immediately before heading to this dark ceremony had made a much deeper impression on me than the Black Mass would. By the time I left her home, I felt convinced of three truths. The first was that, as Doña Isabel had told me, there *was* a Devil. The second was that I did not want to know him. And the third was that I already did.

ii.

THE DEVIL'S APPEARANCE, like his disappearance, happened gradually.

He wasn't around in antiquity because the ancients needed no devils. Their divinities did the dirty work. Even in the Mediterranean Basin, the cradle of monotheistic religion, the Mesopotamians, Sumerians, and Egyptians had worshipped gods who were at once good and bad, angry and kind, creative and destructive. They were not so much supernatural as *supra*natural, mysterious aspects of the visible world that could be influenced with sacrifices and offerings. Their origins and their development were fraught with lust, conflict, betrayal, and redemption. They were like us, only more so, forever rebuilding what they had destroyed, and destroying what they had rebuilt.

Some ancient gods *were* more menacing than others. The Babylonian king of the wind demons, Zu, was the father of disease, the bearer of storms, and the instigator of droughts. He ushered in famine during dry seasons, and locusts during rainy seasons. Zu was certainly fearsome, with his human body and lion head, taloned feet, scorpion tail, and serpentine penis, but the Babylonians wouldn't have understood him as evil. Immorality didn't enter into it—Zu was simply Zu.

The Greeks of this same period developed a belief in an Absolute they called *moira*, a remote and impersonal force that was the fount of creation, and which had assigned to each god and to each human his or her proper function. As in Egypt, and for that matter India, the Greek gods were paradoxical manifestations of the One. In both *The Iliad* and *The Odyssey*, Homer (circa 1100–850 B.C.) draws little distinction between *theos* and *daimon*, and he portrays the characteristics of gods and demons as both good and bad. In his works, all men and all gods have destructive properties, and there is no single principle of evil, because it is part of the One.

The pre-Socratic philosophers generally placed responsibility for evil on us human beings, as much for the way we perceive things as for what we do. From the divine point of view, Heraclitus (535–475 B.C.) would explain, "all things are beautiful, good and right; men on the other hand deem some things wrong and some things right."

Like the Hindus who were writing the Upanishads during this period, Socrates (469–399 B.C.) seems to have equated evil with ignorance, insisting that wickedness and perversity resulted from a lack of *episteme*, the practical knowledge of how to seek virtue and shun vice. It was his student Plato (427–347 B.C.), though, who put forth the idea that would most influence the development of religious thought on the subject. Evil had no real existence, Plato argued, no ontology; evil was merely the lack of good, a sort of moral emptiness that arose from the imperfection of the created world. Plato portrayed the creator less as a figure of worship than as an abstract principle, the essence of *moira*. Although he wanted to assert the goodness of this remote God, Plato labored mightily to explain how the primary principle of existence had produced such an imperfect world. He offered two possibilities, one monistic, the other dualistic: either the creator himself was possessed of an erratic, imperfect element (called chaos), or chaos could be a spirit separate from the creator that brings disorder and evil into the world. With that latter suggestion, Plato might have been the first person to suggest the existence of the Devil. In the end, though, after wavering between his monistic and dualistic notions, Plato seemed to abandon any hope of absolutes and resigned himself to the idea that the world was a *meixis*, a mixture.

Epicurus (341–270 B.C.) is the first person known to have formally posed the problem of evil, and he did so in a way that has compelled theologians ever since to wrestle with the "Epicurean paradox": "Either God wants to abolish evil, and cannot; or he can, but does not want to. If he wants to, but cannot, he is impotent. If can, but does not want to, he is wicked."

The Persian sage Zoroaster (sometime before 500 B.C.) insisted upon a God who was unblemished goodness. That commitment compelled him to found the first religion to teach pure dualism, through the revelation that evil is not a manifestation of the divine at all, but proceeds from a wholly separate principle. Put simply, Zoroaster subtracted some of God's omnipotence in order to keep intact God's absolute goodness. This he did by drawing on the ancient Hindu story of a battle between the *ahuras* (elder gods) and the younger *daevas*, who triumphed and became "the gods." On the other side of the Indus, Zoroaster taught that the *ahuras* won that conflict and that one among them, Ahura Mazda, was elevated to the position of the One God, while the *daevas* became his enemies and their leader, Angra Mainyu, developed into the personification of all lies. Zoroaster, perhaps the first true theologian in the history of the human race, taught that two spiritual principles existed: Ahura Mazda, the One God, the lord of goodness and light, and Agra Mainyu, the lord of evil and darkness. These two were opposites but also twins, separate, independent principles of good and evil. Angra Mainyu, the first Devil, was to be seen as a totally alien force, never to be assimilated but only destroyed. Essentially, Zoroaster asked for what Carl Jung centuries later would argue is not humanly possible—that instead of recognizing the evil inside us and repressing it, we should deny its very existence, insist that it is outside us, and then strive for a perfection that will come only when we have separated ourselves from evil forever.

CHAPTER TWO

---

i.

MICHELLE GOMEZ WAS WITH ME in Catemaco because of a conversation that had taken place between us twenty months earlier, during June 2013, in a New Orleans hotel suite. Michelle was in Louisiana to track down a criminal who was using a half dozen "ghost selves" created on the internet to manipulate and avoid capture by the various law enforcement agencies pursuing him. She had gained control of one of her quarry's associates with a plausible threat of criminal charges. From him, she knew that the criminal she was after was living aboard a stolen Hatteras yacht hidden on one of Louisiana's bayous. We were waiting together at my hotel for the call that would tell us which bayou that might be. At one point during our hours of conversation, Michelle asserted her belief in the power and presence of supernatural evil in the world. Then she began to describe what she had experienced back in August 1988, when a young woman named Mary Reyna had showed up in Lockhart, Texas, Michelle's hometown, about twenty miles south of Austin.

I knew Michelle had won some beauty pageants as a young woman, but this was before that, she explained, back in the days when she was still a solid tomboy. Yes, she did begin competing in pageants a couple of years later, Michelle conceded, but only because she was pressured by her mother and her older sister, who were concerned that she might never grow up into the proper young woman they saw in her. During the summer of 1988, though, she still disdained anything remotely "ladylike" (a favorite term of her mom's). "I was seventeen but really young for my age," she told me. "I went everywhere on my bike, wore jeans or cutoffs and a white T-shirt with Converse tennis shoes like a uniform, always had my hair in a braided ponytail."

She had spent the first two months of summer in the daily company of a group of seven or eight other kids who were younger teens, "all boys except for me," Michelle said. They spent their days riding bikes and skateboards around town, or at the park, playing baseball and swinging on grape vines. Her large Mexican American clan was among the most prominent families in Lockhart, and they were very protective of her, Michelle explained. Her brother Mario, fourteen then, was as powerfully built as she was petite and went with her everywhere, "so no one ever messed with me."

One of the friends she hung out with that summer was Eddie Reyna, who lived in a big white house on Trinity Street that was directly behind her family's own home on Brazos. The bunch of them, and she especially, were enjoying a glorious summer, as Michelle recalled it. For her, it was a final but golden passage out of childhood. Until Eddie's cousin Mary came to town.

Eddie's mom called to invite her over to meet the family's new houseguest about halfway through August, Michelle remembered. As Mrs. Reyna described it, Mary had been sent south by her family from Childress, a town in that northern part of West Texas known as the Panhandle. The purpose was to get her away from some unspecified "troubles." Mary didn't know anyone in Lockhart, and since they were the same age, Eddie's mom hoped Michelle might show her around town and introduce her to people.

She was startled when she stepped into the Reynas' family room the next day and met Mary, Michelle remembered: "There had never been anyone who looked like her in Lockhart. She was dressed in all black clothing—even her socks and shoes were black—with long black hair that didn't look like she had brushed it in weeks and a very pale face. She wasn't an ugly person, though, far from it. She had freckles and she didn't wear any makeup, because she didn't need it; she had very nice skin and really long eyelashes. But she also had this totally blank expression. I remember she never smiled once. She didn't talk much, either."

When Mrs. Reyna called her over after a few days and asked what the two girls had talked about, "I said, 'Nothing,'" Michelle remembered. "'She's a weirdo and my mom said I can't hang out with people that only wear black clothes.'" Mrs. Reyna chuckled and said, "Try to be her friend, please, Michelle. Help her change. All she needs is one friend."

Michelle said okay, but she kept trying to avoid Mary. "But then one day the whole group of us went over to Eddie's and Mary noticed our friend Erik. She got me alone and started asking questions about him. I remember I told her, 'He's Catholic and goes to church every Sunday.' I could see she didn't like that. But she was still interested in Erik. So she started trying to join our group. Basically, she bought her way in. Somehow she always had money and she would invite us to Pizza Hut to eat and play video games. Mario and the other boys weren't going to turn that down."

Gradually, and it was difficult to say why, Michelle told me, she became intrigued by the girl in black. Although they were the same age, Mary seemed much older, and Michelle, as her senior year in high school approached, was beginning to feel embarrassed about still being such a little girl. Perhaps that was because Mary took every opportunity to suggest that she *should* be embarrassed by it.

Michelle remembered that Mary had really seemed to join their group on Halloween night.

We all got together at the field on our street and talked about scary stuff. Mary was the one with the most spooky stories and we all went home really frightened.

For some reason, after that, she started to tell me things, about where she came from and what went on there. I remember she asked me once if I had ever done anything I had to feel real guilty about. I felt like she was going to confess something, but she changed the subject. She started to talk about

Childress. She said it was "a weird town that had some weird people in it."

Just days later, Mary began to talk about dreams she was having, dreams that were making it hard for her to sleep, Michelle remembered:

They were about this group she called "the Merchants of Death." It was really creepy but it was also really fascinating. She told me about how in her dreams this group was meeting in a place they called "the Haunted House" in a town near Childress and that they kept a red bulb in the porch light that they turned on when they were meeting, on the twenty-fourth of each month, and that they always performed a "sacrifice." She said it was usually an animal, but she sort of made it sound like there were people being sacrificed, too. One time she told me the reason she had left Childress was because two boys and two girls had already been killed and she was afraid she would be killed, too. I know how crazy this sounds, but Mary had this way—she would jump from reality talk to these "dreams" and it was hard to tell the difference. It was like a series of dreams that were all connected, and she would move from one to the next, like you do when you're really dreaming. But sometimes she was talking about things that I thought maybe had really happened.

Mary spoke of one "dream" she had that the parents who owned the Haunted House had run a boy down with their car because they were afraid he was going to talk to the police about what they were involved in. "She described the whole thing in such vivid detail," Michelle recalled. "She always did. It was like I could see it happening as she talked. Listening to her was almost like going to see a really scary movie."

She never told her parents any of the things she was hearing from Mary, Michelle said. "I remember once I said something about asking for God's help, and Mary told me, 'I don't believe in God. I believe in the Devil.' I was shocked and asked why. Mary's answer was, 'Because the Devil makes things happen.' If I'd told my mom about that, I'd have never seen Mary again."

One thing she regretted, Michelle told me, was that she'd gone along when Mary convinced all the boys to join her in a Ouija board session in the attic of the Reynas' house. "The rest of us were sort of treating it like a game, but Mary was very serious," Michelle recalled. "She had talked before about someone she called 'the Thane,' who she said was the leader of this group back in Childress. And then that day when we were all together, she told us that 'the Thane' and the Devil spoke to her through the Ouija board. Some of the others were giggling, but they were all creeped out, too, I think. And then at one point Mary took her hands off that little pointer thing and I swear to you, Randall, it kept moving on its own. We were so terrified that we all ran out of the room. Everybody was screaming. These two Black kids that were part of our group, Mack and Ernie, they swore they would never go near Mary again, and they didn't. But I kept seeing her, because by then I was really curious what it was all about."

Some time that winter, right after the calendar had rolled over into 1989, she invited Mary over to her house for a sleepover, Michelle recalled. Mrs. Gomez, though, told her daughter Mary wasn't welcome unless she wore something besides black. "I actually had to loan her clothes, because she said she didn't have anything that wasn't black," Michelle said. When they got ready for bed that night, Mary said she wanted to sleep on the floor, then made up a place for herself with quilts and pillows. Moments after she lay down, though, Mary began to complain about the night-light in the hallway. "My mom had this Virgin of Guadalupe night-light," Michelle explained, "that she said warded off darkness—spiritual darkness, she meant—and Mary really didn't like it. She demanded that I turn it off, but I wouldn't, and we had a nasty fight about it. I actually told her to go home, but she wouldn't leave. And then she started talking about this one dream that she'd told me about several times before."

The scene Mary described involved the group of people who met at the house with the red porch light. Only in this "dream" they were gathered around a fire in a pasture with trees and tree stumps all around them. She could see their faces and knew who they were, Mary said, but for some reason couldn't manage to remember their names. On the sleepover, however, Mary transitioned from the description of the scene in the pasture to a story about how she was supposed to go out there to join the group. Someone was supposed to pick her up at the Hardee's restaurant at midnight to drive her out there, but never showed up, Mary said. Eventually, though, another person from the group arrived to pick her up, and told her, "Tate's dead." She knew a Tate, Mary explained, a really cute guy her age who lived in Childress. The person who picked her up said Tate had been talking about committing suicide and so "we helped him do it."

"This is still your dream, right?" Michelle asked. Mary didn't answer.

A few nights later, Mary came back to that same "dream," only this time she described seeing Tate hanging from a rope and watching as the rope broke. "They" got a stronger rope and hung him again, said Mary, who added, "We sacrificed him."

"Her description was so vivid that I felt like I could see the whole thing," Michelle recalled.

The last time she and Mary were alone was at her house, Michelle recalled. Her family were all gone. The two girls were in the kitchen and while she was looking for sodas in the cupboard, Michelle remembered, Mary said, "I've told you so much, too much, but you're too stupid to figure out what I'm telling you. Maybe I should just kill you before you put it all together." When she turned around, Michelle said, Mary was holding a knife, raised above her shoulder. "I grabbed the lid off the trash can that was right next to me, like a shield," Michelle recalled, "and I swung it at her. We danced around and I really thought she was trying to stab me. But then all of a sudden she laughed and said it was just a joke and put the knife down. But I told her to get out of my house."

She saw Mary one time after that, Michelle said, on the street in March 1989. "She told me that the Thane and the Devil had spoken to her through the Ouija board and commanded her to go back to Childress. Honestly, by then I thought, 'Good riddance.' And then Eddie told me a couple of days later that Mary was gone. I don't know why it took me until then, except that I had started to be really afraid of Mary, but I began to put things together. I started thinking that she might really have killed someone, or been part of the group that had killed someone."

Michelle, who considered herself an accomplished artist, decided to make pen-and-ink drawings of the scenes Mary had described in her "dreams": The house with the red porch light; the boy being run over with a car; the other boy hanging from the biggest tree in a windbreak planted along the border of two cotton farms. Then she took the drawings to the Lockhart Police Department.

Michelle told me she rode her bike to the police station, and she may have, but in his report dated March 23, 1989, investigator Gerald Clough wrote that the girl had arrived for her interview accompanied by her father, Rudy Gomez. Clough described Michelle in the first paragraph of his two-page report as "an intelligent, very normal eighteen-year-old girl," then noted that Michelle was "very concerned that Mary Reyna will find out she has talked to the police." He had assured the girl, Clough wrote, that "we will keep her information as confidential as possible."

Michelle told Clough the story of her association with Mary Reyna, from start to finish, then handed him the drawings she had made. What Clough saw in them he didn't say in his report, but the investigator was apparently impressed enough to send them on to the police in Childress.

Some time passed before law enforcement in Lockhart heard back that the drawings they had sent north were startlingly precise matches of locations and events that had actually taken place in and around Childress. There really had been an abandoned home in the nearby town of Kirkland that had a red porch light and was known as "the Haunted House"; it had burned to the ground only recently under circumstances that were considered "mysterious" and may have involved arson. And there had been a fifteen-year-old boy who worked as a dishwasher at a local restaurant who had been killed by a car in a hit-and-run while walking home from work one night, only a couple of blocks from the Haunted House at an intersection that was nearly identical to the one Michelle had drawn; no one had been arrested for the crime. But what had really impressed the police in Childress was the eerie exactitude of Michelle's drawing of a scene out north of town, on the steep curve in a dirt road that was known to local youth as "Boxer's Corner," the place where the corpse of seventeen-year-old Tate Rowland had been found hanging from the branch of a horse apple tree on the evening of July 26, 1988, only a couple of weeks before Mary Reyna showed up in Lockhart.

ii.

IT WAS THE JEWS who created a narrative in which both God and the Devil grew into their roles. The Yahweh of the pre-exilic Hebrew religion was not much different, really, from the ambivalent deities of the ancient monists—a blend of light and dark elements, alternately merciful and cruel. When Joshua captured the city of Hazor, the Israelites "spared nothing that drew breath, destroyed the city by fire, plundered the goods, took the cattle," then attributed all of this to the will of their God. Again and again in the early books of the Old Testament, actions and motives that in Christianity would be attributed to the Devil are ascribed to Yahweh's "shadow side" (to use Carl Jung's phrase). The notion that the Lord of Hosts was what Jung called an "antimony of opposites" is expressed most succinctly in Isaiah, where God tells the prophet, "I form the light and create darkness; I create peace and make evil; I the Lord do all these things."

Only after the moral instruction of the prophets developed into a central part of the Jewish faith did the Hebrews become uncomfortable with the idea that their God would permit—sometimes even encourage—people to sin and suffer. Their response was to extract the destructive aspect of God and give it to a malignant spirit who eventually became the Devil. But this trends toward dualism, a blasphemy for Jews. Only by denying that the Devil was evil in origin could the Hebrews allow him to exist, as an angelic being created good who fell from grace by his own free choice.

Of course, it can be reasonably argued—and is by most Christians—that the Devil was in the Bible from the beginning, in the guise of the serpent ("more subtle than any other wild creature that the Lord God had made") that leads Adam and Eve to their own fall. The serpent is a seducer and a sophist who encourages Adam and Eve to eat forbidden fruit from the tree of knowledge of good and evil, claiming that the consequence will not be nearly so severe as God has threatened, all the while knowing it will cost the couple their immortality. What's difficult to understand about the creation story, of course, is why God placed the tree of knowledge of good and evil in the Garden of Eden if he really wanted Adam and Eve to remain innocent. One also wonders why God made the serpent so subtle and malevolent. Who really, we are forced to ask, was the tempter?

We get no clear answer to this question from the Pentateuch, because God's identity seems to fluctuate in those first five books of the Old Testament. God several times refers to himself in the first-person plural in those oldest passages of the Bible, as "we," and is called the Lord of Hosts, surrounded by a heavenly council called the *bene ha-elohim*, "sons of the Lord." These "sons" at times seem more like demigods than angels. The fall of God's "sons" is chronicled in what has become perhaps the least-discussed chapter of the Book of Genesis, where the *bene ha-elohim* are first described as angels. In Genesis, and in the more detailed account from the banned Book of Enoch, the "Watcher" angels plunge from heaven because they lust after the daughters of men. The Watchers are led by one called Samyaza, who encourages them to alight on Mt. Hermon, take human wives, and teach these women the arts of magic and agriculture. Another Watcher, Azazel, teaches men to manufacture weapons and ornaments, tempting them to violence and vanity. The offspring of the Watchers' intercourse with human wives are a race of giants called *nephilim*, who turn upon mankind, destroying property and devouring human flesh. God ultimately answers the prayers of men by sending four archangels, Uriel, Raphael, Gabriel, and Michael, to slay the giants, and then to attack the Watchers themselves, casting them into "the deep valleys of the earth," where they are to remain until the Day of Judgment. A survivor of this conflict becomes (gradually) the Devil, a malignant creature alternately known as Belial, Mastema, Azzael, Satanail, and Samael, but finally as Satan.

The Old Testament has forty-six books, and angels are mentioned in thirty-one. They appear first in Genesis, when Adam and Eve are cast out of Eden and God uses cherubim and a flaming sword to bar their readmission. Most of the angels of the Old Testament appear in the guise of splendid young men who minister to human beings with adoration and rebukes, comfort and chastisement. They pray for some people but punish others. One of these angels also seems to serve at first as God's spy, then as his prosecutor, and finally as his debating partner. That angel is Satan.

Satan's first biblical appearance is in the Book of Numbers, and the scene poses a real problem for those who insist both on scriptural literalism and that the Devil fell from grace before man was created. In Numbers, when Balaam decides to go where God has warned him never to venture, he saddles his ass and sets off. "But God's anger was kindled because he went," Numbers tells us, "and the angel of the Lord took his stand in the road as his satan." By blocking Balaam, this lowercase-*s* satan, or "obstructor," is actually serving both the will of God and the interests of man. In the Book of Zechariah, Satan (uppercase now) is the angel who sits among God's heavenly counselors, playing the role of prosecuting attorney in the Lord's court. The high priest Joshua rises to his feet in the dock "before the angel of Lord, with Satan standing at his right hand to accuse him." It is in Zechariah that Satan is for the first time described as "the adversary" of mankind. Yet he still seems to be in God's service.

"Of course he's working for God. Certainly," Dr. Martin S. Jaffee, the Stroum Professor of Jewish Studies at the University of Washington in Seattle and an academic authority on the Jewish concept of the Devil, told me when I put the question to him. Dr. Jaffee seemed both irritated and amused when I pressed him to explain how the Jews could accept the idea of God—and the Devil—*evolving*. "You want God to be coherent," Jaffee said in his Long Island–bred staccato, and made it sound like an accusation. Our back-and-forth led inevitably to the Book of Job, which remains, three thousand years after it was written, the most perplexing contemplation of God's relationship to evil ever to appear in print. Satan is still in the role of accuser when he makes his appearance in Job, Jaffee noted, and keeps his place among God's court in heaven. But now he is a much more malevolent figure. When God asks Satan what he's been up to lately (as if God wouldn't know), his troubleshooting angel replies that he has been roaming the earth, seeking out sinners for punishment. "Have you considered my servant Job?" God asks. "There is none like him on earth, a blameless and upright man, who fears God and turns away from evil." Not so fast, Satan retorts. It's easy for a prosperous, healthy, happily married man like Job to remain faithful. But take what he has from him, Satan tells God, and Job "will curse you to your face." God accepts Satan's challenge (we are given no idea why) and in no time Job's family is dead and his property lost. Even as God exults in Job's faithfulness, the man himself is reduced to lying in a bed of pain, scratching himself with a broken pot, his body covered from head to foot with running sores. Three of Job's (so-called) friends show up and say that Job must have done something enormously wicked to have brought such punishment down on his head. Job defends his innocence and cries out to know why God has brought him to this. A fourth friend, Elihu, who has been listening, warns Job that he has committed a grave sin by seeking to justify himself rather than God, and declares that suffering may be decreed for the righteous as a protection against greater sin, for moral betterment and warning, or to elicit greater trust and dependence on a merciful, compassionate God in the midst of adversity.

Finally Job is granted his request for an audience with God, who speaks to him out of a whirlwind, challenging Job with questions about creation that are beyond any man's understanding. Overwhelmed, Job admits that he has no answers. But God is not ready to let him go and demands to know if Job believes he can annul God's judgment or blame the Lord to justify himself. If Job can speak thunder, adorn himself with splendor, and bring the proud low, God says, he will admit that Job can save himself. Job's final response is to humbly acknowledge God's authority over all that is. God then gives Job twice the wealth he had before, along with seven strong sons, three beautiful daughters, and a contented old age. Never, though, are we told why God felt it necessary to put Job through such torment in order to make his point to Satan.

"Job is really a critique of the Book of Deuteronomy," Dr. Jaffee asserted, "and this idea that if you follow the rules everything will be fine. Job is the Bible's recognition that things aren't fine. Job says, 'I didn't do anything wrong. Why is this happening to me?' He demands an accounting from God, and God basically answers, 'Shut up! Leave me alone. Where were you? What do you know about the mystery?' The whole point is that God's mystery can't be rationally explained in terms of good and evil. There is suffering and we can't know the reason. We just have to trust that there must be one. And that's probably the normative view of the Jewish tradition."

As Yahweh morphed into Jehovah, Jaffee agreed, God was no longer described as a mix of good and bad but was characterized as wholly good. The bad now belonged to someone else, an angel whose pride had gone before his fall from heaven. How this happened is described most eloquently in the Book of Isaiah, where a new name is given to the Devil—Lucifer (which in ancient times was a name for the planet Venus):

> *How you have fallen from heaven, bright morning star,*
> *felled to the earth, sprawling helpless across the nations!*
> *You thought in your own mind,*
> *I will scale the heavens;*
> *I will set my throne high above the stars of God,*
> *I will sit on the mountain where the gods meet*
> *In the far recesses of the north.*
> *I will rise above the cloud banks*

and make myself like the Most High.
Yet you shall be brought down to Sheol (hell),
To the depths of the abyss.

"That passage from Isaiah is pretty vague," Professor Jaffee pointed out. "Most Jews would say, 'Who knows what it means?' Okay, it was interpreted as being Satan during the Second Temple period, and I guess that's what you're talking about. But you gotta remember that this stuff dies out in later Judaism."

Jaffee had to admit that neither he nor any other academic authority could say with certainty why the Second Temple period (516 B.C.–A.D. 70) produced such an intense focus on Satan. It could have resulted from the repression of the Roman Empire, Jaffee speculated, or from Jews discovering Zoroastrianism. Perhaps it was a product of the Dead Sea community, where the Essenes focused their faith on the battle between cosmic good and cosmic evil. Jesus was born, lived, and died on the cross during the late Second Temple period, and assorted scholars have attempted to connect him to the Essenes ever since the discovery of the first Dead Sea Scrolls in 1947. Similarities between the teachings of Jesus and those of the Essenes' "Teacher of Righteousness" are undeniable, especially in the conception of sin, the idea that this world is a testing ground in the universal battle between good and evil.

In the books of the Old Testament written after the description of Lucifer's "fall" in Isaiah, virtually every terrible thing done to men was attributed not to God but to the Devil, a supernatural being who takes on the attributes of characters from Hebrew demonology and folklore: dwelling in a dark underworld where sexual and other abuses are not only condoned but actively encouraged, and with the features of a goat, a toad, a serpent, and a dragon. Still, this Jewish Devil remained very vague. The four references to "the Devil" in English editions of the Old Testament have been translated twice from the Hebrew word *sair*, which literally means "goat" or "hairy one," and twice from the Hebrew word *shed*, which means "spoiler" or "destroyer." All four of these Devil citations have to do with forms of idol worship that are contrary to God's commandments, and it is difficult to conceive that they refer to the fallen angel of the New Testament. Those passages from the Old Testament that might indicate the Lucifer figure from the Book of Ezekiel all have been translated from the Hebrew *ha-satan* ("the satan," lowercase *s*) and do not describe a being who possesses anything remotely like the maleficent import of the New Testament's Satan. The worst that *ha-satan* does is try to provoke disobedience of or rebellion against the Lord. And even then *ha-satan's* principal function seems to be testing men and women in what might be service to God.

"The idea of God sending tests to people is very well understood in Judaism, and regarded as central," Dr. Jaffee pointed out in that clipped, impatient-sounding voice of his. "The idea is, 'How do you withstand tests?' Why does God test people? Well, there's the idea that God tests those who he loves for the pleasure of seeing them withstand temptation. It's this very masochistic belief that is embedded in Judaism."

Jews never really got comfortable, Jaffee agreed, with what the great religious historian Jeffrey Burton Russell calls "the combination of explicit monotheism and implicit dualism" produced by the existence of their Devil. Rabbis continued to teach (and still do) that the battle between light and dark was fought within the souls of human beings, where the *yetzer tov*, or good inclination, and the *yetzer ra*, or bad inclination, dueled perpetually, creating a tension that could never be fully eased, only tipped to one side or the other.

When I told Jaffee that I pictured the *yetzer tov* and *yetzer ra* as being like the dueling good and bad angels I saw on the shoulders of a cartoon character many years earlier, the professor snorted. "The root meaning of *yetzer* is 'desire,'" Jaffee said. "*Yetzer* can be used to mean 'spirit,' but it usually refers more to motive. The *yetzer tov* is more like a conscience than an angelic spirit. It's rooted in one's creaturehood. Judaism assumes that human beings are caught in this dynamic of wanting to be good and wanting to be bad at the same time. Satan really doesn't figure into it, at least in the rabbinic tradition."

Ha-satan might have developed into a personification of wickedness but was never the original instigator of evil—not its first cause. As Professor Jaffee pointed out, Judaism did not really *need* a capital-*D* Demon to support its theology.

After my first conversation with Professor Jaffee, I began to explore the problem of evil as it had been framed outside Judeo-Christian theology. It fascinated me briefly that while Buddhism generally rejects any concept of a personal God, that religion's cosmology is filled with various demons that are led by a figure who is very nearly equivalent to the Judeo-Christian Satan. This is Mara, whose name can mean "death" or "thirst," and whose daughters are Desire, Unrest, and Pleasure. The story of Gautama's enlightenment includes a personal struggle against Mara that is remarkably like the Gospel passages that describe Jesus being tempted by Satan in the desert. The endurance of Mara in art and legend might say something about the ubiquity of human belief in a supernatural source of evil, I thought at one point, before learning that the Buddhist devil is generally understood as a *symbol* of the causes of suffering that inhabit the human mind.

I was committed to a consideration of the Devil not as a symbol but as an actuality, I told Martin Jaffee during my second conversation with the professor. Jaffee seemed bemused, but then, as if it followed, made the observation that the idea of evil as a cosmic force had only really become "significant" in Judaism when the Kabbalah emerged during the Middle Ages. "The mainstream idea in Judaism is not to mess with Kabbalah at all, but if you do, you better be rooted in the Talmud so that you can resist the temptations that will come. Kabbalah is regarded as dangerous knowledge."

"Dangerous how?" I asked.

"Certain forms of Kabbalah are predicated on the idea that human beings can help God overcome evil, including in himself," Jaffee replied. "It confronts the idea of God being evil, and of God having a sexual component within him. It's very troubling to most Jews."

Within "the mainstream," Jaffee said a moment later, "the figure of evil that Jews are much more concerned with these days isn't the Devil but Amalak." I'd never heard of Amalak. "It's an evil presence in the world that is embodied in certain people, who are always enemies of the Jews," Jaffee said. "Amalak is a historical concept of evil that is concretized either in a cosmic tendency toward evil or in historical individuals, Hitler being one. When you talk about anti-Semitism or anti-Israel feeling, you don't talk about the Devil, you talk about Amalak."

"So Amalak must be significant in terms of how Israelis talk about the threat posed by Islamic terrorism," I said.

Jaffee hesitated, and did not sound pleased to be answering such a question, but he did, sort of: "The president of Iran [then Mahmoud Ahmadinejad] is Amalak. All agree on that."

This second conversation with Jaffee triggered an interest in the Muslim concept of the Devil, and eventually led me to a man who might be considered Jaffee's Islamic counterpart, a professor at DePaul University in Chicago named Khaled Keshk. When I asked Keshk to describe the Muslim Devil in the most basic way possible, the professor's first sentence outlined the essential similarity and the key difference between the theodicy of his religion and the Judeo-Christian tradition: "In Islam, the Devil, Iblis, is seen as the first disobedient being to God, and his disobedience is that he refuses to bow down to God after God created Adam."

"So the Muslim Devil wasn't refusing to bow down to God, per se?" I asked.

"No. His rebellion was actually a form of speciesism. In the Quran he says to God, 'I am made out of fire and men are made out of earth, and fire is better than earth.'"

All of this is described in Surah VII 7–13 as part of Muhammad's direct revelation from God. "Then go down hence!" Allah tells Iblis. "It is not for thee to show pride here, so go forth! Lo, thou are of these degraded."

"But the Devil is not the source of evil," Professor Keshk hastened to add. "That's man. What Satan and his progeny do is that they persuade or try to seduce men into evil. They whisper in mankind's ear."

I already knew that the Muslim Devil is not a fallen angel, but hearing it explained had me struggling to take the whole idea seriously. "The Satan in Islam is the head of the angels," Keshk told me, "but he is another sort of creature, called a jinn." In Islam, angels have no free will, Keshk explained: "They cannot fall. They cannot but worship God. Jinns, though, can choose, and some of them choose to follow Iblis. They can also repent and be saved. Jinns too can marry and have offspring. Iblis has offspring, all jinn."

At one point Keshk mentioned that "the Arab word for 'crazy' means 'possessed by a jinn.'" I asked if that meant there were exorcisms in Islam. "Most certainly. If you go to Egypt or Morocco or Nigeria, there are all kinds of such ceremonies. They aren't formalized the way they are in Catholicism, but they all involve reciting verses from the Quran. There are no 'exorcists' per se in Islam, but there are scholars known for their piety and good sense who are called upon to perform exorcisms. These people almost always have a reputation for miraculous feats around them and are considered holy men. Basically, they pray over a possessed person just as Catholic priests do." The same word that Muslims use for preaching, *da'wah*, is also the word they use for exorcism.

The Sunni–Shia split in Islam had created an intensely bifurcated approach to both the Devil and to evil, Keshk told me. "The main question in Islam early on was how to deal with evil and with sinners," the professor said.

"Just as among the early Christians," I pointed out.

"Similar," Keshk said, "but not the same. What the early Muslims had to decide was whether a sinner should be driven out of Islam, cut off, or even killed, or should the sinner be reprimanded but given a chance to redeem himself and return to Islam. The Shias went the first way, and the Sunnis went the second. Sunnis will accept Shias as fellow Muslims, but Shias do not accept Sunnis. If a Sunni comes to their house and eats off a plate, for the Shia that plate is defiled. Shias have always felt that what opposes them or their leaders is from evil. And this has been transferred to the United States, the Great Satan."

"And to Israel, of course," I said.

"Yes," Keshk replied in a terse tone that suggested our conversation would remain on friendlier terms if we dropped the subject of Israel.

After hanging up, though, I began to imagine that I might frame the story of the Devil as a sort of Amalak-versus-Iblis battle for Jerusalem. The evil ones of Judaism and Islam, though, simply didn't have the centrality that the Devil did in the other major monotheistic religion. Only for Christians has the Devil been absolutely essential from the very beginning.

CHAPTER THREE

i.

CHILDRESS, TEXAS, sits in the southern section of what topographers call the Rolling Red Plains, the vast tallgrass prairie that stretches from northwest Texas through Oklahoma and into Kansas and Missouri. The town is about a hundred miles southeast of Amarillo, which has the nearest major airport. Reporters who flocked to Childress in 1991 and 1992 would describe the landscape as "featureless," but this wasn't entirely accurate. The land is flat and sparsely vegetated, true, and only thinly shaded by lonely stands of mesquite, acacia, and cottonwood, spectral trees, more gray than green. Coated with the dust that shimmers in the West Texas heat, they create a vague blur of motion when one looks at them from a distance.

What *does* grow abundantly on the rangelands surrounding Childress are grasses. Buffalograss, burrograss, bahiagrass, barnyardgrass, broomsedge, black grama, blue grama, bush muhly, and bluestem—the *B* varieties alone tempt one to wild excesses of alliteration. Those grasses fed huge herds of buffalo until well into the nineteenth century and drew cattle ranchers after the buffalo had been hunted to near extinction. The 20,000-acre Ox Ranch was the main commercial enterprise of the region back in 1876, when Childress County and the City of Childress were created, named for George Campbell Childress, who had authored the Texas Declaration of Independence. Conditions changed dramatically in the late nineteenth century, though, when the Fort Worth and Denver City Railroad built a line that ran through the middle of town. For decades afterward, railroad shops were the city's main employers and Childress was a bustling town, but then the construction of the Interstate Highway System, which began in 1956, sent both the epoch of railroading and the town of Childress into decline. Childress did at least get its own highway running through town, US 287, the principal route north to Oklahoma or west to New Mexico. The highway became Childress's Main Street, lined with restaurants and motels that catered to truckers and tourists passing through to other destinations, and allowed the town to announce itself as "the Gateway to the Panhandle." Not until the Texas state prison system opened its Roach Unit east of Childress in 1991, though, were there a significant number of jobs available that paid better than minimum wage.

There was no prison in July 1988. Cotton farming was the main industry left in the Childress area at that time, and most people among the town's population of 5,800 struggled to pay the mortgage even on houses that cost, on average, less than $30,000.

In that environment, Tate Rowland looked to be one of the more privileged kids in town. His daddy, Jimmie Rowland, operated heavy equipment for the Burlington Northern Railroad, a job that permitted him to provide well for his family, and *very* well for Tate, the apple of Jimmie's eye.

"Spoiled rotten," Tate's stepmother, Brenda Rowland, called the boy, but the way she said it made him sound like a sweet sort of spoiled. "He was a good-hearted kid," Brenda said, "but Jimmie had given him too much stuff, to make up for what else he was afraid Tate wasn't getting."

Jimmie had won full custody of Tate after a divorce from his second wife, when Tate was twelve. "They were as close as they could be, given how much time Jimmie spent away from home," Brenda said. Jimmie's job with Burlington Northern required him to be gone from Childress during the week, traveling to towns all over West Texas. "Jimmie would drive home to spend Wednesday nights if he was within a hundred miles," Brenda said. "And he was home on weekends." During the other days of the week, though, Tate's daddy counted

on the boy's aunt and older sister to watch out for him, along with
Brenda, whom he began dating when Tate was thirteen. Jimmie was a
devoted parent when he was home, and to say he supported Tate's incipient career as a motorcycle racer was an understatement. "Jimmie
bought him two new motorcycles every year," said Brenda. "I thought
it was ridiculous." She took some pride herself, though, Brenda admitted, in the more than three hundred trophies Tate had won racing dirt
bikes, and in his number two ranking in the Texas Junior Division.

Tate was a popular kid, everyone would agree when he was gone.
Even the people who called him "rowdy" or "sassy" said it with affection. "Fun-loving" and "fearless" were more common descriptions of
the sandy-haired boy. The girls had liked his trim, compact build,
bright blue eyes, and impertinent smile. The boys grinned when they
talked about how Tate would fight anybody who challenged him, even
though he lost 90 percent of the time. He'd established a minor local
legend when, on a dare, he jumped his motorcycle over a pickup truck
front to back, with a bunch of girls all standing in the bed.

The image of Tate that people recalled most often, though, was
of him not on the back of his bike but rather at the wheel of that sweet,
souped-up 1980 Ford pickup with the high-dollar stereo Jimmie
bought him for his sixteenth birthday. Tate had zoomed up and down
the Drag, the mile-long stretch of US 287 where kids trying to save
gas gathered in the parking lots of My-T-Burger or the United Supermarket to watch the hot rodders speed from stoplight to stoplight, night after night that summer. He couldn't remember Tate ever
losing a race, said his friend Finney Trone, whose 1979 Camaro Tate
had beaten again and again.

It was hard to describe how forlorn Tate had been after he
wrecked that blue truck, Trone said: "It was like he lost a part of
himself."

When people pictured Tate in his pickup, though, it was more
often chasing than racing, and the one he was after always seemed to
be Karen Hackler. Karen was the tiny blond daughter of a prosperous cotton farmer, a spritely young woman who never seemed to tire
of being called "cute as a button." She and Tate had become an item

during his sophomore year in high school, and it had been tempestuous from the start. Tate's friend Ty Copeland would describe the two of them as being "always in their cars, chasing each other up and down the Drag, jealous or mad at each other about something." The one thing that both their families agreed upon was that the relationship had no future, owing mainly to the difference in their ages. Tate was not quite sixteen and Karen was closing in on her twenty-first birthday when they first got together. Karen's family told people she was refusing to grow up, and Tate's family said the boy was in the sexual thrall of an older, more experienced woman.

Karen seemed to recognize after a year or so that it couldn't last. According to her family, she tried to break up with Tate more than once, but he wouldn't let her go. He stole her pocketbook and her jewelry, they said, and did childish things like drive up in front of the house, then squeal away, spraying gravel against the front door.

Jimmie Rowland warned his son that he was in "way over your head," but Tate didn't want to let it go. The boy had never been in any real trouble before, but now he was acting out in ways that had the potential for some serious problems with the law. One day in November 1987, Tate was arrested two separate times, first for riding in a stolen car, then later for siphoning gasoline from the same vehicle. He was charged with burglary, but given his age and testimony that he had been trying to impress some older boys, a grand jury reduced the charge to a class B misdemeanor and the district attorney's office didn't file on even that count. Two months later, though, in January 1988, Karen had Tate charged with assault for choking her in a parking lot on the Drag. A month after that, Tate and Karen's brother Kevin got into a fracas in the driveway of the Hackler family home. Tate told the cops that Kevin hit and kicked his dad's truck. Kevin said Tate had responded by trying to run him over with it. The Rowlands claimed that Kevin had been "harassing" and "bullying" Tate for months. The Hacklers said Kevin was simply trying to protect his sister and his family's property. Local authorities laid the entire Rowland-Hackler matter in front of a grand jury, which heard the case in March 1988 and decided, after seeing Tate and Karen hugging in the hallway during a break, "that if they don't care, we don't care either," as District Attorney David McCoy explained it.

Immediately after the grand jury returned its "no bill," the Rowlands decided that Tate would move to Louisiana to live with his older sister Sherrie while he completed his junior year in Vermilion Parish. He finished with four A's, three B's, two C's, and a D—the last in the health education class he rarely attended.

When Tate returned to Childress in June he was confronted by the reality of two separate marriages that had taken place in his absence. One was only a slight surprise: Jimmie Rowland had married his girlfriend, Brenda, after four years of dating. There were a lot of jokes about the old man robbing the cradle. Jimmie was a slightly grizzled forty-seven-year-old who had been married twice before, while Brenda was a still very attractive thirty. She already had two young children of her own from her first marriage, though, and appreciated Jimmie's willingness to raise them like his own. Few people begrudged Jimmie Rowland his young bride. There was a feeling that the man had suffered enough. Two of his four children by his second marriage had died when they were still little ones, an infant son in a crib death and a four-year-old daughter in an automobile accident. Even Tate and his married older sister Teri Trosper seemed happy for Jimmie and fond of Brenda.

The second marriage, though, was a shock to Tate: while he was going to high school in Louisiana, Karen Hackler had up and married Phillip Klapper. Her family was happy about it. Phillip was not five years younger than Karen, but rather two years older. Plus he wanted to be a farmer.

How hard Tate took the news would be a matter of some dispute. Everyone agreed that he had been incredulous at first, refusing to believe Karen had actually married, and that right after he got back to Childress he tried to convince her she had made a mistake and to meet him for a date. Jimmie and Brenda, and most of Tate's closest friends, all said that he seemed to bounce back within a week or two and was flashing the same mischievous smile that had been his trademark for years. Tate was drinking beer almost every night, but hell, they all did, his friends said; in Childress there were very few guys over the age of fourteen who didn't drink beer on hot summer nights. Just one friend, Clifton Hodges, said later that Tate had "showed some depression over Karen when he would have a beer or two," and that he had once remarked he wanted to have the George Jones song "He Stopped Lovin' Her Today" played at his funeral. Tate's other friends, though, remembered him as looking forward to finishing high school and talking about joining the Air Force after graduation. They said Tate seemed a lot sadder about having to drive Brenda's old Ford Thunderbird instead of his blue pickup truck than he did about Karen Hackler being married to Phillip Klapper.

The only thing that truly struck most of Tate's friends as odd that summer was all the time he was spending in the company of Chad Johnston. Chad, not quite fifteen, was new to Childress, having moved to town less than a year earlier, when his family opened a donut shop downtown. Not to be mean about it, some of Tate's other friends said, but Chad wasn't much liked. "A quiet, unpopular kid," he would be described in a *Texas Monthly* article published several years later, and the description fit, most of the other teens in town said. They all understood why Chad would want to hang around Tate, who was well liked by everyone and always seemed to be stirring up excitement. Why Tate would want to spend time with the dour Chad, though—that was a mystery. "Tate had girls chasing him and guys wanting to party with him," one friend observed. "I don't think anybody was wanting to party with Chad."

Be that as it may, Tate would spend most of the last day of his life, Tuesday, July 26, 1988, in Chad's company. They hung around the house mostly, recalled Brenda Rowland, who was in and out all day. That was fairly unusual for Tate, who "liked to be out doin' somethin' most of the time." Tate didn't seem unhappy, let alone depressed, though, Brenda recalled. She remembered that at one point he came out into the backyard, where she and his sister Teri were sorting items for a big garage sale they had planned for the weekend, and promised to help them move the stuff and set up on the day of the sale. Tate was coaching the woman's softball team she was playing on that summer, Brenda recalled, and assured her he'd be there for their seven-thirty practice that evening. She didn't see Chad, who stayed inside, though she spotted the younger boy as he and Tate were leaving the house around four o'clock that afternoon, Brenda remembered, "and Tate seemed fine."

Several of Tate's friends remembered seeing him for the last time at around five that afternoon on the Drag. One of Tate's closest friends, Bobby Reynolds, recalled that they met in the parking lot of the United Supermarket right about then and made plans to meet up after softball practice and split a half case of beer. Then Tate got into the driver's seat of that old brown Thunderbird and drove off with Chad sitting in the passenger seat next to him, Bobby recalled.

About an hour later, at right around six o'clock, Brenda Rowland was in the kitchen of the red brick house on Avenue I that Jimmie had owned for years, "standin' at the stove, cookin' dinner." Jimmie had made a surprise visit home—"he was hardly ever there on a Tuesday," Brenda recalled—and she was frying him up some chicken. Suddenly the front door burst open and Chad Johnston came running into the living room. Brenda was still at the stove when she heard the boy tell her husband, "Jim Earl, Tate's dead."

"I turned around and said to him, 'Don't be kiddin' around about nothin' like that,'" Brenda recalled. "And he said, 'No, he is.' We said, 'Where?' My little girls were six and eight and I turned off the stove and told them, 'Wait right here.'"

She and Jimmie and Chad all piled into Jimmie's truck and drove out 7th Street, past the high school toward the cotton farms on the northern edge of town, Brenda recalled. "Jimmie and I were still thinkin' car wreck, or somethin' like that." She realized at some point that they were headed toward Boxer's Corner, Brenda recalled. It was on the curve of a rutted dirt road where adjoining farms were divided by trees planted as windbreaks. The place had gotten its name because it was where the high school boys staged their fistfights. Before they were even close enough to park, Brenda remembered, they saw Tate, hanging by a rope slung over the thickest branch of a sagging old horse apple tree, his lifeless body slowly twisting counterclockwise, the toes of his sneakers just inches from the ground.

What she remembered was a blur from that point forward, Brenda said. "I panicked. I wasn't much help. I just stood there screamin'." She thought maybe her failure of support in that moment was part of why she later became so determined afterward to get justice for Tate, Brenda said. She couldn't even recall how exactly Jimmie had cut his own son down out of that tree, but she did remember seeing her husband "tryin' CPR and beatin' on Tate's chest."

Nothing worked. Tate was gone.

IT SEEMED THE ONLY PEOPLE in Childress who believed Tate Rowland's hanging had been a suicide were the ones in a position to make a ruling on the matter.

Sheriff's deputy David Morris was the first called to the scene. Morris was just twenty-three at the time, freshly appointed to the position of senior deputy by Sheriff Claude Lane, who himself had been elected to his position without any background in law enforcement. Lane was a big man, though, six feet four inches and more than 300 pounds, with a loud voice and a confident manner.

"We have a saying around these parts: 'Right off the tractor,'" observed Reece Bowen, who was the junior deputy, despite being fifteen years older than Morris. "That was Claude Lane. He was literally a farmer who ran for sheriff. He had no training, had been through no academies, nothing. That was the old-school sheriff—right off the tractor."

According to Bowen, Sheriff Lane made it clear from the start that he had no intention of investigating Tate Rowland's death as anything other than a suicide. "And David Morris, who wasn't smart or experienced enough to know that it stunk, and who owed his job to Lane, was going to do what the sheriff wanted him to do," said Bowen.

On the surface, there appeared to be every good reason for Morris to go along with what the sheriff expected of him. Tate Rowland's was that rare suicide where there was an eyewitness, and that witness, Chad Johnston, had told an entirely plausible story.

He had gone over to Tate's house that day right around noon, Chad said. The two of them watched a movie on the VCR, then Tate made a phone call to Karen Hackler Klapper that lasted about thirty minutes. Tate called her back soon after the first call ended and spoke to Karen for another fifteen minutes, Chad said. It was about three o'clock then. Tate began to sharpen a knife, Chad said, and "was talking about life not being worth living. He was telling me not to get involved with a girl because they do you wrong. I took the knife away from him." Tate then suggested they go find somebody who would buy them beer so he could get drunk "for the last time." They left the house in Tate's car, and Tate got a young woman named Lisa (Chad claimed not to know her last name) to buy them a twelve-pack of Coors Light bottles. Right after that they drove out North Ross Road to Boxer's Corner. They'd been there drinking for about forty-five minutes when Tate said he wanted to go back to the house. That was when Tate must have gotten the rope and put it in the trunk of his car, Chad said, but he didn't see that, "because I had went inside the house." They drove back out to Boxer's Corner, Chad said, where Tate began to talk about his funeral—"who he wanted there," mostly. "I asked him if he wanted Karen there," Chad told Deputy Morris, "and he said if she wanted to come." According to Chad, he at some point "walked around the corner" to throw a beer bottle away and "use the bathroom." Morris took that to mean that Chad had stepped out of sight to urinate in the bushes. "It took me about three minutes," Chad said, "and when I came back Tate was hanging from the tree by his neck. When I got to him he was dead. I didn't have anything to cut him down with, so I got in Tate's car, which was parked under the tree limb," and drove to the Rowland place, where he told Jim Earl and Brenda that Tate was dead. He rode back out to Boxer's Corner with the two of them, Chad said, where he helped Jimmie cut Tate down and take the rope off his neck. Jimmie sent him in his truck to fetch an ambulance, and he rode back to the scene with the paramedics, who pronounced Tate dead and drove his body to Childress General Hospital. He then picked up Jimmie's truck and drove it back out to Boxer's Corner, where Jimmie still was, then drove Tate's daddy home, Chad said.

Reece Bowen would say he "never believed the suicide story" and thought David Morris, deep down, doubted it also. Bowen gave three main reasons. First, and for him actually mainly, Bowen said, was that Tate "just wasn't the kind of kid who would kill himself." He'd had some dealings with the boy in a professional capacity, Bowen explained, and while "he was a real wild kid," he also seemed a basically happy one. "He was an outgoing, real popular kid whose main interests seemed to be hot-roddin', raisin' hell, and chasin' girls. And he had lots of girls chasin' him back. Him goin' out there one afternoon and hangin' himself, it just didn't make any sense."

He was also bothered, Bowen said, by "the cold personality of the kid who was with him, Chad. He was just so matter-of-fact when he described how Tate had hung himself. No feelin' to him at all. Most people would show more emotion if they told you it was raining outside."

Okay, those were subjective reasons, matters of personal opinion, Bowen conceded. But there was one very good forensic reason not to believe it was a suicide. At the hospital, David Morris had done at least one thing right: he'd had Tate's body photographed. And when the photos were developed, you could see real clearly that there were two distinct sets of rope marks on Tate's throat, one above the Adam's apple and one below. Everybody in law enforcement knew that when a person was hung, the rope slid up above the Adam's apple and left just that one mark, Bowen noted. "So how did that other rope mark, the one below the Adam's apple get there? It made you think, 'Maybe he was hung twice.' Or maybe he was strangled with that rope, then hung when he was already dead, and the whole thing had been staged to look like a suicide."

The separate rope marks were not even mentioned in the inquest held the following morning at the Childress County Courthouse. Neither were the obvious omissions in Chad Johnston's sworn statement— his failure to say anything about how the rope got slung over the branch of the horse apple tree, when and where the knots in it were tied, or how it came to be placed around the throat of Tate Rowland. "It wasn't a regular rope, it was like a water ski rope," Brenda Rowland recalled. "And it wasn't tied in a noose, it was just tied in knots, like thirteen or fifteen knots. I mean, there was no way you could tie that rope around your neck and loop it around a tree. I thought it was strange, but we were in such shock that we weren't askin' questions that maybe we should have asked." Based entirely on Johnston's interview, both a county judge and a justice of the peace signed off on the ruling that Tate's death had been a suicide.

Neither his family nor his friends believed it. Some of Tate's friends, in fact, were seething with suspicion of Chad Johnston. A boy who had never been liked in Childress was now despised, and it got a lot worse after word spread of the visit Chad had made to the Rowland home two days after Tate's death. "He come to me and Jimmie and said, 'Tate wants this color of coffin. He wants this song played at his funeral. He wants me to have his car and he wants me to have his bank account.' And Jimmie told that boy exactly, 'You get the hell out of our house! You ain't gettin' nothin'!'"

Chad's family, heretofore considered merely odd, now became unsavory in the eyes of many. Brenda Rowland considered it "very strange" that Chad's mother had signed the guest book at Tate's funeral not with her name but as "Chad's mother." The spread of rumors about Chad, his mother, and his stepfather only escalated when, less than a month after Tate's death, the family closed its donut shop and moved out of Childress.

A weird atmosphere had surrounded Tate's funeral service at the Calvary Baptist Church. A young man in the front row began to rock on the bench where he was seated, repeating the word "suicide" over and over. All sorts of stories spread about a woman dressed in black with a veil covering her face who "mysteriously" slipped into the back row of the church during the service, until Brenda Rowland told people it was an old friend of hers. That gave people brief pause about listening to rumors, but then just a few days after the funeral the Childress Police Department got a tip from a local high school student and sent a car out to Boxer's Corner. There, just a couple of hundred yards from what was now called "the hanging tree," the officer who had responded to the call found a cow skull lodged in the branches of a smaller tree; below it was a stack of logs surrounding a pile of rocks—"an altar," the officer described it in his report.

How soon and how quickly the story that Tate had been the sacrificial victim of a satanic cult active in the Childress area permeated the town would be said later to have been a matter of days, or of weeks, or of months, depending upon how close to the original source one was. A different Childress police officer from the one who had found the cow skull reported that while out on patrol one night in August he had seen a "figure" standing by Tate Rowland's grave, and said that when he returned later he found spittle all over Tate's gravestone. Other reports received by the Childress Police Department during the last weeks of summer included one about a cross that had been seen burning over Tate's grave and another about a schoolteacher's dog that had been stolen and ritually sacrificed.

By the time school started in September, *Texas Monthly* would report, "every high school student seemed to have heard that Tate was a member of a cult and had been killed by fellow cult members because he would not bring them a blond-haired, blue-eyed child to be sacrificed." The child was to be either one of Brenda's two daughters (both blondes) or one of Tate's older sister Teri Trosper's four blond daughters. The story got more than a little traction when Teri Trosper told the family that Tate had warned her to keep her daughters indoors. "To make this even thicker," District Attorney David McCoy would tell *Texas Monthly*, "about the same time as these rumors started, we had strangers in cars showing up at the grade school parking lot, trying to pick up little kids."

The high school continued to be the main hotbed of rumors in Childress, and it was widely believed among the student body that some of their fellow students were members of the satanic cult that had infected the town and was responsible for Tate Rowland's death. It was the first time in as long as anyone in Childress could remember that the football team was not the main topic of conversation on campus or in town. High school football was embraced as a secular religion in Childress in a way that was exceptional even by Texas standards. Reece Bowen would say he knew any number of parents who had stayed in town even when they had to work two minimum-wage jobs to get by just so they could boast that their sons were members of the Bobcats team. The success of its football squad was the main thing that most of Texas knew about Childress—its wins during the playoffs the only times the town's name was mentioned in the pages of the Dallas or Houston newspapers—and the leading source of civic pride. "For anything to be more important to people here than the next football game—that just doesn't happen in this town," Bowen would say. But in the fall of 1988 it *was* happening. A star lineman on the football team, in fact, was the one who organized the "investigation" of a widely reported rumor that the cult was planning to dig up Tate Rowland's body on Halloween night. The cult "needed a pinky bone," as he understood it, the hulking 240-pounder would explain later, for some sort of ceremony they were planning.

A group of approximately fifteen kids had assembled at the cemetery on Halloween night, he said. They parked their cars by the storage shed near the entrance, then all climbed into the bed of his pickup truck before he drove it slowly toward Tate's grave. As they approached, the football player said, they heard "sounds" like singing or chanting from the area where they knew Tate's grave was. Someone asked, "Is that music?" he remembered, and he stopped his truck so they all could listen. "Then all of a sudden some headlights turned on right where Tate's grave was supposed to be. We all started going crazy, and I whipped the truck around as fast as I could." As he roared back through the gates at the cemetery entrance, someone noticed the pentagrams that had been drawn on the cemetery shed, "which started everyone screaming again." And the headlights following them kept coming closer. Several kids jumped out of the back of the pickup while it was still moving and ran to their cars, then sped off in separate directions. He kept driving toward downtown Childress with most of the kids still in the back of his truck, the football player said, and the headlights followed him all the way to the Childress County Courthouse before the vehicle finally turned away. He and the others sat for some time in stunned silence, the football player said, then he finally turned his truck around and headed back to the cemetery, so that those who had left their cars could retrieve them. When they arrived at the shed, they saw that a large pentagram had been painted on the door and that dozens of lit candles were burning all around their cars.

He was one of the few who returned to the cemetery the next day, the football player said. They walked in a small group to Tate's burial plot. Beer cans were scattered all around the perimeter and someone had overturned the headstone. The group of them were so terrified that they agreed to say nothing to anyone about what they had found, the football player said, but a few whispered the story anyway, and eventually it got back to the police, who came to interview them, one by one. "We knew something was happening," Reece Bowen would recall. "But we didn't know what it was, exactly. And so people kind of believed what they wanted to believe."

ii.

THE EARLY CHRISTIAN CHURCH was encumbered not just by the various accounts of the origin and role of the Devil it inherited from the Old Testament, but even more by the New Testament's insistence that the primary purpose of Jesus's incarnation, Passion, and resurrection was to break the power of Satan over humankind. Christian theology from the first made Satan an absolutely central character in the story of salvation—made him, in fact, Jesus's primary adversary, the enemy whom Christ came to conquer in the name of God.

The four Gospels have made it difficult—if not impossible—for Christianity to discard the Devil without nullifying any belief in Jesus beyond that of moral philosopher. And as countless evangelical ministers have pointed out, "teacher" is not the principal title given to Jesus in the New Testament—"Savior" is. The very name Jesus means "God saves." One doesn't have to read the Gospels very closely to realize that if the Devil doesn't exist, then Christianity has been founded on a falsehood.

In Mark, both the earliest and the shortest of the Gospel narratives, there are thirteen references to either a personified Satan or a casting out of demons. Mark describes four exorcisms by Jesus, and there are also four references to the ability of Christ's disciples to perform exorcisms themselves. Mark introduces "the devil" early in his narrative, then goes on to portray Jesus's ministry as a struggle to his last breath between God's spirit and the demons who belong to Satan's "kingdom." Immediately after describing Jesus's encounter with John the Baptist in the Jordan River, Mark explains that God's spirit "drove him into the wilderness, and he was in the wilderness forty days being tempted by Satan, and was with the animals, and the angels ministered to him." Mark's Gospel moves directly from Jesus's battle with Satan in the desert to his first public appearance at the synagogue in Capernaum, where Christ is confronted by a man in the possession of an "evil spirit" that challenges both his power and his purpose: "What have you to do with us, Jesus of Nazareth? Have you come to destroy us?" Jesus "rebuked [the evil spirit]," Mark writes, "saying, 'Be silent, and come out of him!' And the unclean spirit, convulsing him and crying with a loud voice, came out of him, and they were all amazed."

The later Gospels of Matthew and Luke make Jesus's struggle with Satan the spine of their narratives, creating a drama in three acts of Christ's confrontations with the Devil, each more intense than the one preceding it. Luke writes that after Jesus repulsed Satan in the wilderness, the Devil withdrew "until an opportune time," then "entered into Judas Iscariot" to bring about Jesus's death. John's Gospel is in its entirety the story of a cosmic conflict between God's light and the darkness of the Devil, between Jesus and his followers and those from "the world" that is ruled by Satan. What is different about John, the last of the four Gospels, is that Satan never appears as a character but is behind the scenes as a dark force acting through the human beings who attempt to thwart Jesus's mission. Near the end of his Gospel, though, John states very clearly that the entire purpose of Jesus's life and death was to overcome the power of Satan: "The light shines in the darkness, and the darkness has not overcome it."

The other books of the New Testament repeat again and again the idea that Jesus came to break the hold of Satan, that is, the Devil, over mankind. All of the apostles, we are told, had been instructed by their master to do two things: spread the Good News and use the power of Christ to heal the sick and drive out the demons of the possessed. In Acts, Peter tells the household of Cornelius, the first gentiles to enter the Christian community, "how God anointed Jesus of Nazareth with the Holy Spirit and power, and how he went around doing good and healing all who were under the power of the devil, because God was with him." Corinthians II calls Satan "the ruler of this world." The follower of Paul who wrote the Letter to the Ephesians (after Paul himself was beheaded by order of a Roman magistrate) warns Christians that they are not contending merely with human evil: "Our contest is not against flesh and blood, but against powers, against principalities, against the world rulers of this present darkness, against the spiritual forces of evil in heavenly places." And, of course, the Book of Revelation describes the climax of life on earth (and thus of salvation history) as a final battle between the armies of Satan and those faithful to Christ, a battle that ends when the Devil is thrown into the "lake of fire," where he will suffer for all eternity.

The books of the New Testament scarcely answered every question that was raised by and about the importance of Satan. The first subject to be settled was whether the Devil was an independent principle or a creature of God. The church fathers swiftly decided that the Devil was a fallen angel, but this raised still more questions. Was God in any way responsible for the evil actions of this angel he had created? Did God command the Devil to obstruct humanity, or merely tolerate his obstructions? Christianity's insistence that the Devil was subordinate to God but also locked in a cosmic struggle with Him would create what Jeffrey Burton Russell calls "the weakest seam in Christian theology," because it simultaneously divided God and asserted God's essential unity and totality. Unbelievers recognized that weakness from the very first and have been attacking it ever since. Even among the faithful of the first and second centuries, the fight over who the Devil was and what the Devil meant would become the fundamental dispute in the formation of the Christian Church.

What the New Testament most firmly established was the Devil's ubiquity. He is mentioned throughout the Christian books of the Bible, twenty-two times in Mark alone, seventeen in Matthew, fifteen in Luke, and eleven in John. The Devil also appears in Acts, Romans, Corinthians I and II, Ephesians, Thessalonians I and II, Timothy I and II, Hebrews, James, Peter I, John I, Jude, and, of course, Revelation. Nowhere, however, does the New Testament discuss the evil one's origin. The beliefs that the Devil was a fallen angel, the head of a demonic host, and the principle of evil all were inherited from the Old Testament. The Gospels make no mention of original sin, so of course there is no discussion of the Devil's inducement. Even Paul's letters make only two direct references to original sin (both in Romans), first declaring that sin and death entered the world through Adam's fall, then stating that the serpent of Genesis was Satan. This latter assertion of course raised further questions about how and when Satan became the Devil. Further adding to the confusion were one passage in the Gospels in which Peter is called "Satan" for tempting Jesus to avoid his crucifixion and another in which Judas is described as a servant of Satan for helping bring the crucifixion about. First- and second-century Christians debated whether Satan's fall had resulted from a defect in his nature (which tended to directly implicate God) or from his own exercise of free will. Did this fall take place before humanity was created, or when Adam and Eve were in the Garden of Eden? Did it directly involve Christ? And what was the Devil's fundamental sin—pride, envy, or lust? If envy, was it envy of God or envy of humans?

Every assertion about Satan's role and meaning raised new questions. The essence of early Christian teaching was that the Devil had been increasing his power over the world since before the creation of man, until his power was almost complete, but then God sent Christ to break that power, and to replace the old eon with the new kingdom of God. Why then, some naturally asked, does evil continue to exist? The only answer the church fathers could come up with was that Christ's Passion, culminating in his sacrifice on the cross, was the first and most important battle of a long war, a war that would not end until the Second Coming. In the time remaining, God permits Satan to test the faith of each man or woman who would be saved. Explaining *why* God permits this has made pretzels of the greatest minds in Christendom's long history.

St. Ignatius, the bishop of Antioch who was the most influential Christian voice at the end of the first century, insisted that confronting and overcoming the temptations of the Devil was the central mission of each human life. In his letters (many written as he was being transported to Rome at the behest of the emperor Trajan to be eaten by lions in the Colosseum), Ignatius warned his fellow Christians that the Devil pits himself against each person individually, and he pleaded with friends to support him in his own battle with Satan, who was trying to break his faith and persuade him to avoid martyrdom.

Perhaps nothing so illustrates the importance of the problem of evil in the development of Christianity as the fact that the struggle with it gave rise to the first, greatest, and most enduring heresy in Church history, Gnosticism. Offended by what they saw as obvious contradictions in the belief system that eventually became orthodox Christianity, the Gnostics insisted there must be some better explanation of both Christ's incarnation and the Devil's continuing power to deceive men. Their solution was to radically separate God not only from the existence of evil but also from the creation of the material world. Responsibility for both of these abominations was given to a pair of inferior spiritual beings. The world, those first Gnostics taught, had been created by the Demiurge, a spirit of primeval cruelty (identified with the Old Testament's Yahweh by a number of sects). The Demiurge's agent of wickedness was the Cosmocrator, a bestial but clever being who directed the demons in their attacks on the faithful. The main idea that united the various Gnostic sects was their belief that the world is completely evil and cannot be redeemed. The Docetists carried this to the extreme of arguing that matter was so corrupt that Christ could not have had a real physical body, that what people saw was an illusion, and that he did not suffer and die on the cross, because he was never a real living man in the first place. The Elkesaites argued that Christ and the Devil were the good and bad brothers of the great Lord God. The most eloquent early Gnostic writer, the Syrian Marcion (A.D. 85–160), contended that there were two gods, the first being the *conditor malorum* (author of evils) revealed in the Old Testament, and the second a loving and merciful God who had been largely hidden from men until the advent of Christ. Some Gnostic teachers created incredibly complex systems of understanding intended to separate God from evil. The Egyptian Valentine (who died in either A.D. 269 or 270) described the emanation from God of twenty-eight eons (eight higher and twenty lower) to explain the vast distance of God from the evil of the world. In the end, though, even Valentine could not avoid the assumption that God must permit the ignorance and evil that result from all these emanations.

What may be most interesting about Gnosticism from a twenty-first-century perspective is how many of its underlying beliefs were shared by the orthodox Christians of their day: the existence of a spiritual entity called Satan who was responsible for the depredations of the world, the association of the material universe with Satan ("the god of this world"), and the ceaseless struggle of Satan to corrupt mankind and thwart the will of God. The main difference was that orthodox Christians were determined to moderate their dualism: the Devil, they insisted, was clearly inferior to the Lord, a spirit created good but corrupted by his misuse of free will.

Justin Martyr (A.D. 100–160), the first apologetic church father, produced the initial discussion of the problem of evil in theological terms. Born in Samaria, where he received a Greek education and adopted Platonism, Justin came to Rome around A.D. 140 to pursue philosophy. His conversion to Christianity began when he went to the Colosseum one day and watched the followers of Jesus being led into the amphitheater to be torn apart by wild animals. Astounded by the "serene courage" with which these Christians faced their horrific deaths, Justin became convinced that he was witnessing a miracle, and wondered at the power they drew upon. When he discovered that the Christians' incredible calm was the result of their belief that by dying as martyrs they were hastening God's victory over the forces of evil, Justin decided to be baptized himself as a Christian. Almost at once he understood that the "gods" he had been raised to worship, Apollo, Aphrodite, and the others, were really *daimones*, that is, servants of Satan. In almost the same moment came Justin's realization that the moral relativism which passed for sophistication among the Romans was an affront to God. "The worst evil of all," he would write, in a sentence that resonates to this day, "is to say that neither good nor evil is anything in itself, but that they are only matters of human opinion." In his great works, *First Apology* and *Second Apology*, written between 152 and 160, he produced, among other things, the most detailed diabology in Christendom. Justin's was a universe filled with angels and evil spirits that he divided into three categories: the Devil, other fallen angels, and demons. The chief ploy of these evil spirits, Justin contended, was to persuade people that they were gods, which made paganism the most evil system of worship ever created. Justin warned that Gnostic leaders like Marcion and Menander were under the influence of demons, and asserted that the miracles attributed to Menander were really worked by evil spirits.

Irenaeus (A.D. 140–202), the bishop of Lyon who founded the church in Gaul, did more to consolidate Christian doctrine (and, in the process, to stifle internal dissent) than any other church father. Irenaeus was adamant in his rejection of the Gnostic belief that the world was the product of an evil demiurge. The world had been created by the Logos (the Word of the Lord), Irenaeus insisted, and the Devil was a creature forever subordinate to God. The Devil had fallen from grace because he wanted to be adored like his creator, Irenaeus preached, and envied human beings even more. Irenaeus also developed the first complete theology of original sin, explaining that God had wanted to keep Adam and Eve near him in the Garden of Eden, but that Satan, recognizing human weakness, had entered the Garden to tempt them. When Adam and Eve freely chose their sin, and thus their fall, they passed on this responsibility to all of humanity, making us slaves of Satan until God, in his mercy, sent his Son to save us. The force with which Irenaeus made this argument is evident in its endurance.

The great Alexandrian theologians Clement (A.D. 150–215) and Origen (A.D. 185–254) were asking questions that have remained the themes of novels and dramas to this day. Why, these Egyptian Christians wanted to know, do some people sin while others do not? Even more aggravating, why do the good seem to suffer every bit as much as the bad? Can such seeming injustices be made right by the mercy of God? Clement was unique for his time in his insistence that the Devil existed both as an objective reality and as a metaphor for evil in the human soul. His ontological system, "the great chain of being," produced a spectrum of good and evil, rather than a simple dichotomy. Clement was stymied, though, by where to draw the line at which those who are saved are separated from those who cannot be saved. He ventured right to the brink of universalism, suggesting that in time even Satan might be redeemed, because the limitless nature of God's mercy seemed to call for the ultimate salvation of all intelligent beings. Clement took his thinking on this question to the verge of Hinduism, then drew back, fearful of invalidating Christ's crucifixion and resurrection.

Origen was Christianity's most inventive diabologist, describing in detail the cosmic conflict of higher intelligences (he did not like to call them angels), some good, some corrupt, in which human society was the main battlefield. Much of his theology was laid out in debates with the pagan philosopher Celsus, who contended that the Christian idea of a Devil was not only absurd but also blasphemous, since there was no possibility that the will of God could be impeded. Origen replied that "no one will be able to know the origin of evils who has not grasped the truth about the so-called Devil and his angels, and who he was [before] he became" the Devil. In his elaboration of *privatio boni*—the privation theory, or the theory that evil is merely the absence of good, first put forth by Plato—Origen argued that the whole purpose of the world was to teach us to love God, and that any action not aimed at the love of God was without purpose and therefore without being. Since the Devil was given over almost entirely to evil, he was almost totally nonbeing. That left Origen with the problem of explaining how a being that in essence did not exist could also be the most powerful source of harm in the cosmos. Origen's life ended miserably: After castrating himself as an ultimate expression of his disdain for the material world, he was branded a heretic and chased out of Alexandria. During the persecutions under the Roman emperor Gaius Messius Quintus Decius, Origen was tortured, pilloried, and bound hand and foot to the block for days on end without renouncing his faith, and died of his injuries. Origen had been enormously influential as a writer and preacher, but only one of his great accomplishments has endured to this day: his success was in convincing not only his contemporaries but also generation upon generation of theologians who followed that the Devil's envy was of God and not man, that it was the product of his pride, and that his fall had come before the creation of Adam and Eve. Like Clement, though, Origen was in the main separated from orthodox Christianity by his insistence upon apocatastasis, the idea that all things return to God, and that even Satan might be saved eventually. The bishops of their day would not have it: the Devil must be damned eternally.

HOW DIFFERENTLY history might read if Origen had been chosen over Irenaeus as the authoritative voice in deciding second-century Christian doctrine. A belief that forgiveness was universal would have fundamentally altered the Western world's relationships with sin, evil, and redemption. People might still have feared the Devil, but they also would have pitied him. And prayed for him.

The course of human events likely would have been no less strongly impacted if, in the fourth century, the Church had chosen Pelagius over Augustine. The rise of Augustine (354–430) as the preeminent theologian of the early Church was prefigured by another North African, Lactantius (250–325), the foremost Christian theologian of the third century. Lactantius was the first to explain evil as a logical necessity, writing, "Good cannot be understood without evil, nor evil without good." It was actually desirable that evil exists, Lactantius contended, because a world without evil would be a world without freedom. That elegant argument has held sway with countless theologians since, and it is at the core of the most sophisticated modern attempts to explain the existence of evil.

Augustine, though, couldn't leave it at that. For him, the problem of evil was subordinate to the problem of freedom. He addressed these related subjects, evil and freedom, with an enormous body of work that was at once magisterial and confounding. In his work *On the Free Choice of Will*, Augustine began by asking whether God was the cause of evil. He answered by asserting his belief in "the vast power of the Devil," but then immediately insisted that God allowed evil powers to rule the world *under his control*, creating a cosmos in which each person must struggle against the demons within his or her own soul. So who was ultimately responsible, God or the Devil? The Devil, of course, Augustine said. Satan's free-will choice was what had introduced evil into existence, just as Adam's free-will choice had introduced evil into human experience. God had merely made these choices possible. This argument might not have been so difficult to grasp if Augustine had not gone on to say that evil doesn't actually exist. Drawing on the Platonic concept of evil as the absence of good, Augustine defined evil even more specifically as a kind of disordered or misdirected love, an adoration of things that are less than perfect (the flesh of a beautiful woman is the example that Augustine's life and work first bring to mind). "Defection from that which supremely is, to that which has less being—this is to begin to have an evil will," Augustine wrote. That perhaps explained Augustine's alliance with those who insisted upon celibacy for priests, but it said nothing about what might be the essential cause of such "defection." Seeking to answer that question, Augustine explained, was like trying "to see darkness, or hear silence." In other words, he didn't know.

Augustine would not resign himself to incomprehension, however. On the contrary, his determination to solve the problem of evil (and to simultaneously settle the question of free will) would consume his life and define the doctrine of the Christian Church. In his rejection of the Gnostic faith he embraced as a young man, Augustine had insisted upon free will. Yet as a Christian, he took a position that made free will into little more than a limited mechanism for "defection" from God. A human being could choose to sin, Augustine maintained, but could not choose to be saved. Only those to whom God granted the mysterious blessing of "grace" could draw near to the Lord and achieve salvation, Augustine decided. This meant that only human beings (by succumbing to the Devil) could be held responsible for sin, while God received sole credit for virtue. Furthermore, since the damned and the saved were known to God (and therefore written into the book of life) from the first moment of creation, Augustine's theology was undeniably deterministic. And yet he continued to maintain that free will existed. But what was free will good for, some asked, if a person could not choose the path of salvation? Other, even more perplexing questions were raised by Augustine's contention that the evil in the world resulted entirely from the free will choice to sin. For example, if a man's sin results from a mental defect, one might ask, then how can God not be the ultimate cause of that sin, since God created the man with that defect? And if a man's sin results from a failure of his will, then again, how can this not be the responsibility of the God who made the man what he is? And what does it matter if a man sins, anyway? If those God has chosen are destined to be saved, while those God has not chosen are destined to be damned, doesn't it seem clear that neither vice nor virtue will make any difference to the outcome?

These questions profoundly troubled Pelagius (350–425). The Celtic monk, who had established himself in Rome as a much-admired Bible teacher, recoiled against the fatalism implied by Augustine's strict subordination of human free will to God's omniscience. This made men into mere automatons, Pelagius contended, and the world they inhabited into little more than a puppet show in which judgment had been passed on each individual before birth. The smug churchmen who accepted the doctrines of unconditional election and irresistible grace preached by Augustine especially infuriated Pelagius, who saw their moral laxity as the result of a theology that told them they were destined for Heaven, no matter what sins they committed in the short term. To those who had been led to believe that many among them were damned, no matter how virtuously they attempted to live,

Pelagius taught that each person had power over his or her own fate, and that those who followed the example of Christ would be saved. This naturally attracted a following. It also threatened the Church. If people could achieve salvation simply by being good, then what role was left for the clergy? It did not help Pelagius's standing among Rome's priests that the Church was at that time waging a war on the Donatist heresy—the claim that the efficacy of the sacraments depended upon the moral character of the clergy who administered them. Though Pelagius never assumed that position, his teachings implied a support for the Donatists, in the eyes of Augustine and others. But it was Pelagius's denial of original sin that sealed his fate. Free will could not truly exist, Pelagius reasoned, unless each of us was born with a clean slate upon which we mark our fate by the choices we make. Just like Adam before the fall, each infant is born in a state of innocence, Pelagius preached; Adam's sins were his and his alone, and even before the advent of Christ there were men who had achieved sanctity. Augustine, aghast, swiftly became the point man in the persecution of this preacher, whom he himself described as "a saintly man." Augustine produced four letters that specifically targeted Pelagianism, forcefully affirming the existence of original sin, the need for infant baptism, the impossibility of a sinless life without Christ, and the necessity of Christ's grace to achieve salvation. Pelagius answered with letters in which he accused Augustine of allowing the Manichean fatalism of his youth to infect Christianity, and in particular of making more of the Devil than the Devil deserved, essentially elevating the author of evil to the position of God's equal.

In 418, as the bishop of Hippo, Augustine called the Council of Carthage, at which he laid out the nine canons of Christianity that Pelagianism denied, thereby persuading Pope Zosimus to declare Pelagius a heretic and banish him from Rome. Interestingly, the ninth of those canons, that children who die without baptism are excluded from both the Kingdom of Heaven and eternal life, has since been abandoned by the Roman Catholic Church and throughout most of Christendom. That slight vindication came too late for Pelagius, though, who died in disgrace, shunned by virtually all Christians.

Augustine himself lived long enough to see the rise of what would become known as "semi-Pelagianism." This apparent attempt at compromise accepted original sin and affirmed that salvation came only through the saving grace of Christ. But the semi-Pelagians taught that man was born sick, rather than dead, in sin, and that each person had the freedom to choose or refuse God. Augustine rejected semi-Pelagianism no less forcefully than he had the original heresy. Allowing for even the most minute free-will choice in the separation of the saved from the damned, Augustine insisted, amounted to the same thing as Pelagianism—infringement on the grace of God.

Augustine's theodicy became Christian doctrine in most important regards. It was Augustine who cemented the belief that the primary cause of the Devil's fall was pride, because Satan refused to be indebted to God for anything, demanding to be the source of his own glory. Out of that pride sprang the envy Satan felt when the human race was created, Augustine had argued triumphantly, and this of course had led to original sin, and the introduction of suffering and death into human experience. With his insistence that a true Christian was compelled to find a just God even in "the agonies of tiny babies," Augustine lodged the problem of evil in the core of Christianity. And it was Augustine who swept away the last remnants of a pre-Christian monism that perceived good and evil as twin aspects of God, ensuring that the Devil would remain an indispensable figure in the dogma of the Church. In the end, Augustine left the Church with a trinity of related explanations for the existence of evil. The first explanation was that evil exists because God tolerates it as necessary for the greater good. The second explanation was that evil exists because the Devil wills it to be and promotes its spread among the human race. The third explanation was that evil exists because some human beings freely choose it.

CHAPTER FOUR

i.

OF COURSE THE STORIES circulating through Childress were getting back to her and the rest of Tate's family, Brenda Rowland said, and of course they listened to them. "I always suspected somethin', you know," she explained. "I knew the stories couldn't all be true, but I felt like there was truth in them. I mean, Tate killin' himself just didn't make no sense to none of us. He had everything goin' for him. There was no problems at home and he sure didn't have to worry about money, because his daddy gave him everything he wanted. He had the same friends he'd had for years. He had all kinds of girls from all ages chasin' after him. He was in love with Karen, but he never seemed that distraught about losin' her to me. He was movin' on."

It was several months before Jimmie would let her clean out Tate's room, Brenda recalled, something she was impatient to do "because I thought I might find some kind of clue to what had happened. But I couldn't find a thing."

Pretty much everyone in town had heard the story of a satanic cult being involved in Tate's death by the time she went to the sheriff's office "to ask 'em, 'So what are we gonna do?'" Brenda recalled. "And Sheriff Lane, he just always sort of brushed me under the carpet and out the door."

Lane's deputy Reece Bowen offered a pretty small reason for the sheriff's refusal to open an investigation: "Back in those times, there was people in positions that really didn't know what to do. A person like Claude Lane, what they'll do is just say, 'Nah, there's nothin' to investigate.' Rather than go to the Texas Rangers or somethin' like that. Because they're afraid they'll make themselves look like they don't know what they're doin'. That's my opinion."

Despite Sheriff Lane's lack of interest in reopening the Tate Rowland case, though, his department continued to collect evidence that suggested there was something to this whole devil cult story that was spreading through town. One incident the deputies didn't mention to Brenda Rowland came out of the Cottle County Jail in Paducah, about thirty miles south of Childress, a town where Tate and some of the other boys from the Panhandle used to drive occasionally to drink beer and flirt with girls from families with oil money. It seemed Tate had been arrested on a drunk-and-disorderly charge at a dance in downtown Paducah on July 9, 1988, just a little more than two weeks before his death. Trooper Carl Holloway of the Texas Department of Public Safety had answered a call from the dance about a young man who was "causing problems" that evening, and when he arrived he found a wobbly-legged Tate on the edge of the dance floor, "intoxicated and belligerent." After Trooper Holloway dropped the boy off at the county jail, the deputy who booked him into lockup, Beatrice Perkins, said she had been shaken by her encounter with Tate. "I remember he kind of acted weird, hypertensive, excited," Deputy Perkins recalled. "I remember he said he was with the Devil. He was talking about this bunch of satanists he was with. The reason it stuck in my mind is that we never had anyone talk about that before. I remember that word ["satanists"] standing out."

Cottle County sheriff Frank Taylor said he heard basically the same story from other deputies who were working at the jail that night—a bunch of talk from the young guy in lockup about the Devil and some satanists he was involved with.

Justice of the peace Jewel Gibbs, on the other hand, said she was impressed by how well-mannered young Mr. Rowland had been in her dealings with him. Tate had phoned her personally the week after he was arrested and "was real nice and extremely polite," Gibbs remembered. He explained that traveling to Paducah would be a real hardship for him, so she agreed to let him off with a $50 fine and $13.50 in court costs. Tate had paid in two installments, she remembered, but for some reason only sent in $63.00, which left him fifty cents short, so she reduced his fine by a half dollar, on account of "he was so nice on the phone."

Then during the early morning hours of November 6, 1988, a week exactly after the Halloween incident at the cemetery in Texas, a man phoned the Childress Police Department to say that someone was in the process of stealing his maroon two-door 1977 Chevrolet from outside his residence on Southeast 3rd Street. Two patrol cars were dispatched. On their way to the location, they spotted a car matching the description of the stolen vehicle speeding east on Avenue A, then watched it slide off the road and crash into the support cable of a utility pole. When the officers arrived at the vehicle, they found a youngster named Ray Wilks (still three days from his sixteenth birthday) alone in the front seat. The Wilks family was well known to law enforcement in Childress and much of the rest of the Panhandle. "A bunch of outlaws," District Attorney McCoy called them. Father Frank Wilks and his two youngest sons had been convicted of four felonies between them, and calls to the Wilks house on Southeast 2nd St. were at least a weekly occurrence for police in Childress. As they approached the stolen vehicle, Ray Wilks lay face down on the seat, the two officers reported, placed his hands under his torso, and informed them he intended to kill them both. The two officers nevertheless managed to get the suspect out of the vehicle and into handcuffs without suffering or inflicting any injuries and transported him to police headquarters to be "evaluated" by a juvenile probation officer. Shortly after the "heavy metal" and swastika tattoos on the boy's forearms were noted, "the suspect became violent acting, and he attempted physical attack upon officers," read the offense report. "Suspect attempted furtive movement in attempt to take Officer Murphy's weapon. Suspect was further restrained by use of leg irons and a restraining belt." After the probation officer arranged for Wilks to be held at a juvenile facility in Potter County, she suggested that she take the boy by the Childress County Hospital first for a medical evaluation. Two police officers accompanied the probation officer and her young charge to the hospital "for safety factors," according to the Offense Report. While en route "the suspect did make terroristic threats to kill his father and mother if released to their custody, and he further stated that he was a member of a cult (Satanistic) group locally, and he made the statement that he and several other persons locally had been involved in a cult sacrifice (killing) of an individual in Childress County in July, 1988, of subject identified as Tate Rowland."

THE DEVIL WAS AFOOT in Childress. That much was certain. Whether Satan's work was most evident in the death of Tate Rowland or in the stories spread about those suspected of involvement, though, remained to be determined.

As the year rolled over into 1989, no one was the object of more suspicion than the former Karen Hackler. It was said that she kept witchcraft books and a Ouija board in her bedroom. She was called the cult's "queen bee," and any number of people reported hearing that she had seduced young Tate Rowland into the cult. When high school kids saw her on the Drag, they would hold up two fingers to form a cross, as if warding her off. Brenda Hackler said Karen fled down an aisle when they encountered each other while grocery shopping and that when they walked by each other in town Karen refused to look her in the eye. "I thought I had known Karen pretty well," Brenda said, "but all of a sudden I wasn't sure I knew who she was at all."

Chad Johnston, of course, remained the subject of much discussion. Within weeks Brenda had heard that Chad's family were central members of "the cult," and that the boy had been raised among devil worshippers. As the weeks passed, though, many other names were added to the list of those said to be involved. "There were so many rumors about so many people in town that were supposedly members of this cult," she recalled. "And the thing was, just about every one of them moved out of town. It could have been coincidental, but the ones whose names were brought up, within a short period of time, anywhere from two weeks to less than a year after Tate died, there was none of these people livin' in Childress. So then you started hearin' that they had decided to move the cult someplace else, because they knew they were bein' watched here."

Local law enforcement continued to collect evidence of satanic activity in the area. The Childress Police Department and the sheriff's department had kept a lid on the report that Michelle Gomez had made about Mary Reyna nearly 400 miles to the south in Lockhart. Word got out, though, about what sheriff's deputies had found when they ran a search warrant on a ramshackle old house on the south side of town. "The owner had a contract with the government to house disabled people, older retarded folks," Reece Bowen recalled. "We had received reports that he was abusing them sexually and in various other ways. And when we went in with the search warrant we discovered evidence of the occult in the fella's bedroom." Most disturbing to him, Bowen said, was a cache of art in which the pornographic and the satanic were blended. One was of what appeared to be a man with a demonic goat head having sex with a woman. Another had the state of Texas drawn inside a pentagram. "And then we also found a black cloak and a pointed hat, and this wand with a goat head on it," Bowen recalled.

Right around the same time, in June 1989, eleven months after Tate Rowland's death, Dallas's *D* magazine published an article about reports of crimes committed by avowed satanic worshippers in small cities all across North Texas. There was an account of a murder in Midlothian, where seventeen-year-old Richard Goeglein Jr., assisted by two other teenagers, had killed an undercover police officer with a bullet to the head. The crime had garnered national attention, including a lengthy article in the *New York Times*, which focused almost entirely on the fact that the twenty-one-year-old victim had been posing as a high school student to ferret out drug buys at Midlothian High School. The *Times* article did include a brief reference near the end to rumors that Goeglein and other students had "dabbled in Satanism and the occult." As *D*'s writer gleefully demonstrated, the *Times* reporter would have discovered how much substance there was to those rumors if he had bothered to interview the police officers involved in the case. Goeglein had been quite open—even boastful—about the fact that he was a practicing satanist, the cops who interrogated him said. He had been regaling fellow students, *D* reported, with stories of the "devil-worshipping rituals in which he had participated." While he was questioned about the murder by Midlothian investigators, Goeglein, a young man whose shoulder-length black hair contrasted strikingly with his "piercing blue eyes," had "nervously reached into his pocket" and withdrawn a black plastic heart, which he kissed repeatedly. The silver-dollar-sized amulet was "Terry Heart," Goeglein had explained to the police officers in the room with him, a medium he used to communicate with the spirit of a girl who had died of a drug overdose. It was "Terry" who had convinced him he should kill the narc, Goeglein said.

The *D* article also described several other murders with satanic undertones, including one in a Dallas suburb where a teenage girl had committed suicide in a cemetery near her home, leaving behind a diary in which she offered her life to the Devil. Friends at school said they understood that the girl had been part of a group of satanists who had conducted the "ritualistic death lottery" in which the girl was chosen as their sacrifice to the Prince of Darkness. A case in another Dallas suburb, Greenville, was also described. In this one, a sixteen-year-old girl who had been abducted out of a movie theater was found dead, buried in a shallow grave. The twenty-year-old eventually charged with and convicted of the crime, *D* magazine noted, had tattoos of the number 666 and the biblical "mark of the beast" on his forehead. In his bedroom, police had discovered a large library of occult literature, including Anton LaVey's *Satanic Bible*, the magazine reported, along with black candles and a ceremonial black robe—exactly like the one found in the home for mentally disabled adults in their own town, people in Childress said as they passed the *D* article around among them.

"This is a very serious thing that is going on," Dallas psychiatrist Gary Malone had told the magazine. "It presents a very real danger that wasn't there just five or six years ago." The buyer for Taylor's, the largest chain of bookstores in Dallas, was quoted as saying *The Satanic Bible* had been "a very good seller" in recent years, and that most of the buyers were teenagers. A police sergeant from the Dallas suburb of DeSoto told the magazine, "I've sat in my office talking to a twelve-year-old girl who has told me stories that are all but unbelievable. I've got a daughter just about the same age. I'm still buying her Barbie dolls. And here is a child telling me about drinking the blood of some animal that she saw killed."

Readers of the *D* article in Childress were particularly attentive to a list of "warning signs" of involvement in a satanic cult among teenagers that had been prepared by a professor of religious studies at the University of Denver, with assistance from the Cult Awareness Network in Chicago. Among these were "an obsession with movies, videos, books and records that have themes of violence, rape, death and demonism," along with "interest in Satanic symbols—pentagrams, inverted crosses, demons and werewolves."

A conviction among many in Childress that there was widespread satanic activity happening right under their noses was frighteningly affirmed by a killing spree in neighboring Carson County on July 13 (a Friday), 1990. A handsome teenager from the town of Panhandle whose main reputation before this was as a ladies' man had murdered two people and attempted to murder a third shortly after recording a videotape in which he looked directly into the camera and said: "My name is Kenneth Glenn Milner. I'm nineteen, and this is my confession of what will probably happen within a few days—probably on Friday the thirteenth. I've got a lot of talent, a great family . . . many girlfriends who are very beautiful. It's not enough. I want more. I guess the one thing that I do have, which is kind of the downside, is the desire to kill." The videotape jumped ahead three days to a shot of the West Texas plains, the blades of a windmill turning slowly in the background next to a barn, its moving blades casting eerie shadows among a nearby stand of cottonwood trees. The camera moved inside the barn and, as the sounds of chirping birds faded, closed in on the prone figure of a seventeen-year-old boy named Frankie Garcia, who lay face down in a spreading pool of blood. "Now I know all of you probably think . . . I'm a deranged lunatic," Milner told the camera.

"I am not an insane person who goes around babbling to himself. I'm someone who is different. I'm not at all like everybody else . . . I want to make people see what I'm capable of. I want people to know my name, the name I go by—Damion. It fits me more than anything, the dark side of me."

When he was arrested the next day, July 14, Milner told the Texas Ranger who interviewed him that it had all begun when he was given a copy of the *Necronomicon*, a book of instructions for demonic spells and astral projections. He wouldn't say who had given it to him.

"People were scared, but even though Panhandle is nearby, it's not Childress," Reece Bowen recalled.

But then on Memorial Day in 1991, Tate Rowland's sister Teri Trosper was found dead in the Wilks house, Bowen said, "and that really stirred everything up."

ii.

CHRISTIAN DIABOLOGY in the Middle Ages was dominated by a pair of titanic figures, Gregory the Great and Thomas Aquinas. Both belief and unbelief in the Devil, though, were driven by a churning confluence of social, political, theological, and intellectual currents that would shape themselves into what has become the most notorious development in the history of the Church, which we remember today as the Inquisition.

Gregory (540–604) became pope at the age of fifty, serving for the next fifteen years not only as the head of the Church but also as its foremost theologian. He was a sort of one-man Lateran Council,* consolidating a Christian orthodoxy that could be described as three parts Augustine to one part Origen. Gregory cemented medieval thought on the subject of the Devil, declaring that Satan was the first being God made, a cherub (highest of all angels) who could have remained at the pinnacle of creation had he not chosen to sin. Gregory's

---

* Lateran Councils were the synods (high clerical gatherings) in which the Catholic Church defined its ecumenism, or universal standards.

affirmation of *privatio boni* made dogma of the assertion that evil has no real existence and is in fact nonbeing. Gregory also fixed in Christian doctrine the belief that the Devil fell at the beginning of the world (rather than after the creation of Adam and Eve) and that pride and envy of God (not resentment of humankind) were what caused Satan's fall. Gregory offered an elaborate description of Satan's methodology in his outline of the four stages of sin: the Devil (1) initiates the process of corruption by placing "suggestions" in our minds, then (2) observes with satisfaction that these unclean thoughts have produced a pleasurable response, delighting as he (3) watches a human being give in to his or her desires, and finally (4) chortles in triumph at the rationalizations by which we permit ourselves to commit the forbidden act. Nothing pleases Satan more, Gregory warned, than our fascination with external reality, because the Devil knows only too well that we are closest to God when we focus on our internal reality.

Gregory's most important contribution to Christian thought may have been his assertion of epektasis, or constant progress. It was a concept that marked a final break for the Church from the Platonic philosophy that stability is perfection, while change always increases imperfection. To the contrary, Gregory's doctrine of epektasis held that human beings were *called upon* to change, to advance steadily in both virtue and godliness. While God himself always had been and always would be perfect and unchanging, Gregory acknowledged, the human race must move ever forward in its pursuit of such perfection. Gregory went so far as to offer an implicit reconsideration of Origen's banned belief in ultimate universal salvation, insisting that prayers should be offered for even those who had been great sinners. The Devil was still humanity's great adversary, but Satan's power did not seem so overwhelming in a world where people need not simply ward him off by holding fast to faith but could actually triumph over evil by active progress toward God.

Gregory's greatness notwithstanding, the unsettled question of predestination would dominate Christian thought for more than 500 years after his death. The issue would be bitterly fought in the centuries-long battle between "realists" and "nominalists." The realists (behind their great champion, John Duns Scotus) insisted that the Devil was an actual being and argued strongly for the sort of predestination that Augustine had favored. The hero of the semi-Pelagian nominalists was William of Ockham (1287–1347), who employed Ockham's razor (the simplest explanation consonant with the evidence is usually the best) to cut the realists' theories to ribbons. William advocated powerfully for free will, even daring to propose that the "Devil" was no more than an abstraction—only a word. This battle for the soul of the Church achieved a dramatic climax in the twelfth-century contest between Bernard of Clairvaux and the scholastic monk Abélard. The life of Abélard (b. 1079) has been used to illustrate so many themes that it is difficult to remember that his most important role in Church history was as advocate for a sort of modified, middle-ground nominalism that came to be known as conceptualism, in which words such as "Devil" were both abstractions and realities, albeit realities that existed only in the mind. After routing in argument both of the two great French teachers of the day, William of Champeaux and Anselm of Laon, Abélard billed himself as the world's only undefeated philosopher. His conceit was the tragic flaw that in Church histories (as opposed to romantic fictions) made him susceptible to satanic invidiousness. While holding the chair at the cathedral school of Notre-Dame de Paris, Abélard seduced the brilliant and beautiful young student Héloïse, making her pregnant. The two later married but were separated by Notre Dame's canon, Fulbert, who sent Héloïse to a convent and had Abélard castrated. After retreating to the abbey at Saint-Denis, Abélard emerged once more as a philosopher and theologian, publishing his lectures in the book *Summi boni*, and in his late fifties he was lecturing again at Mount St. Genevieve, where he was confronted by Bernard of Clairvaux. Bernard (1090–1153), the champion of "immediate faith" who is today best remembered for asserting the Virgin Mary as intercessor between man and God, and for helping to establish the Knights Templar, was deeply offended by Abélard's exaltation of rationalism and denounced him to the pope. A council was called at Sens in 1141 to consider the matter. Abélard asked for a public debate and agreed to let Bernard speak first. All we know of what happened next is that Bernard made his case with such clarity and force that Abélard could offer no reply and was condemned. When the pope confirmed the judgment at Sens, Abélard retired to Cluny, where he died two years later.

The battle between realism and nominalism was not finished, however. Apart from the fact that William of Ockham and Duns Scotus (1266–1308) carried it into the fourteenth century, this contest was central to the study of Thomas Aquinas, the theologian who was arguably the greatest thinker in the history of Christianity. Aquinas (1225–1274) was a moderate realist who contrasted his position to the radical Aristotelianism that was rampant in universities under the rubric of "Averroism." While serving as regent master at the University of Paris, Thomas wrote a series of works that attacked Averroism as incompatible with Christian doctrine. The most forceful of his many arguments in this regard was rooted in Aquinas's rejection of the Averroists' beginningless universe. It is remarkable how closely his thirteenth-century rebuttal of what twentieth-century astronomers would call the "steady state universe" parallels the development of the big bang theory. And this was just one instance among many in which Aquinas's philosophical or theological arguments conformed to scientific breakthroughs that were hundreds of years in the future. Aquinas's description of how angels moved instantaneously from one place to another without passing through time or space stunned Niels Bohr, the father of quantum physics, who marveled that a theologian who died in the year 1274 had articulated a core principle of modern nuclear physics nearly seven hundred years before it was discovered by science. The pioneer of neurodynamics, Walter Freeman, has acknowledged drawing on the work of Aquinas in his remodeling of intentionality, the capacity of the mind to direct itself toward the objects of awareness. Authors as diverse as James Joyce and Umberto Eco have explored (and extolled) Aquinas's ideas about the relationship between generalities and particulars.

The depth and subtlety of his thinking made Aquinas capable of arguing persuasively that angels were both entirely immaterial (bodiless spirits possessed of both intelligence and free will) and entirely capable of manifesting visibly and audibly to one or more people at any given time. This was rooted in Aquinas's belief that the universal always makes itself known through the observation of particulars and is given meaning by the operation of an intellect bestowed by God.

He took the same approach in considering the problem of evil. Aquinas began by agreeing with Plato's description of God as perfectly realized and perfectly good, and also with Plato's argument that all things can exist only *in* God. This meant, Aquinas concluded, that only good actually exists and that people or events are evil exactly to the degree that they lack existence. And yet Aquinas frankly acknowledged that evil does *appear* to exist in the world, and that this is the strongest argument that can be made against the existence of God. He answered first with his five rational proofs for the existence of God but was left then with the problem of reconciling his intelligent designer to the presence of evil. Since no principle other than God could exist, there could be no independent cause of evil, Thomas reasoned. And evil, because it is nothing in itself, must have its origin in what actually exists—the goodness of God. Ergo, the Devil must be a being created good by God who perverted himself by abusing the only reality that exists outside God's control, the moral choices of creatures with free will.

But . . . angels as Aquinas conceived them could never choose moral evil. So how to explain Satan? Angels must possess the capacity to choose *supernatural evil*, Aquinas reasoned, and Satan must have been the first among them to do so, rejecting the ultimate good produced by God's grace to try to obtain a selfish satisfaction. What the Devil chose then, Aquinas explained, was not *equality to* God, but rather *independence from* God—separation. Though he couldn't have imagined it at the time, Aquinas had produced a description of the Devil that prepared the ground for the image of Satan as a freedom fighter seeking liberation from a despotic God that emerged among the Romantics and Decadents of the eighteenth and nineteenth centuries, and was crucial in the development of what modern historians call the Enlightenment.

And yet Aquinas was also giving Satan a sort of theological demotion, insisting that the sinner himself, rather than the Devil or his demons, was the essential cause of sin. Aquinas actively sought to dispute the notion that Satan was the originator of evil (and even questioned whether the Devil was necessary). The Devil was not a principle of evil, Thomas argued, but merely the leader who rallied its forces.

Only in the very last months of his life did Aquinas begin to doubt that reason and logic were the primary paths to God. Something occurred during his celebration of the Mass of St. Nicholas on December 6, 1273, that caused Aquinas to cease the dictation of his latest work and to describe what he had previously composed as nothing more than "straw." He took to his bed, retreating into silence and meditation. Whether he altered his positions on the existence of evil and the role of the Devil is not known. In February 1274, Aquinas was summoned by Pope Gregory X to the Second Council of Lyons. While en route, riding a donkey along the Appian Way, Aquinas struck his head on the branch of a fallen tree and was seriously injured. He attempted to convalesce at a nearby Cistercian abbey but died on March 7.

It was perhaps fitting that the greatest proponent of rationality in Church history disappeared from the face of the earth in almost the same moment when Christendom was beginning its descent into a particularly destructive phase of irrationality. What we know today as the Inquisition had already begun by the time Aquinas completed his masterwork, *Summa theologiae*. It had begun, really, more than a century earlier, in the year 1184, with the publication of a papal bull (official letter) by Innocent VIII, titled "Summis desiderantes affectibus," that condemned the Cathar heresy growing in southern France.

The Cathari formed the ranks of the last major Gnostic movement, a final attempt to promote the Devil from fallen angel to god of darkness. Rex Mundi, they called him, "king of the world." Incorporating major elements from the Manichaean and Bogomil heresies that had preceded them, the Cathari also revived central tenets of the movements that had attempted to subvert the orthodoxies of first- and second-century Christianity.

The Persian sage Mani, born two hundred years after Jesus, had generated a powerful Gnostic sect that flourished in the third and fourth centuries (Augustine was a Manichaean for nine years) and sustained the heresy until nearly the Middle Ages. Born into an aristocratic family of southern Babylonia, Mani at the age of twelve began reporting visions in which an angel of God had told him he would be the last prophet of a new and ultimate revelation. The visions ended when Mani turned twenty-four and journeyed east as a Christian missionary. Enormously influenced by his encounters with Buddhism while living in India, Mani returned to Persia and proclaimed himself the final link in a chain of prophets that included Zoroaster, Buddha, and Jesus, whose partial revelations were subsumed, he announced, by his own teachings. Under the protection of the Persian emperor, Mani preached throughout the Middle East and sent missionaries to the Roman Empire. He was regarded at first as posing far less threat to Christianity than to Zoroastrianism, whose priests managed to have him put to death as a heretic around the year 275. His teachings resonated most deeply, though, among the Gnostic sects centered on Rome. Like them, Mani taught that existence was divided into contending realms of good and evil, Light and Darkness, and that each had its own ruler. What we know as the human condition, Mani taught, had resulted from a primal catastrophe created when the Lord of Darkness (the one Christians knew as Satan) had invaded the realm of Light, thereby creating the material world and pitting the forces of good and evil in a perpetual struggle that eventually produced (as its ultimate battleground) the human race. The human body was material and therefore evil, Mani taught, while the human soul was a fragment of the divine light that must be redeemed and released from the prison of earthly existence.

Manichaeanism had died out in Western Europe by the beginning of the Middle Ages, but it lingered on in Eastern Europe and began a breathtaking expansion in the Balkans during the last years of the tenth century, guided by a previously obscure Bulgarian Orthodox priest who called himself Bogomil (Dear to God). The one great God, Bogomil preached, had sired two sons. The eldest, Satanael, had rebelled against his father and attempted to usurp God's role as creator, but was capable only of fashioning grotesque replicas of his father's work. Instead of heaven, Satanael produced earth; rather than angels, men. Satanael could not make his creatures live, though, according to Bogomil, until he stole a flame of divine fire and hid a tiny spark inside each human heart. God had responded by sending his second son, Christ, down from Heaven to assume a phantom body and break Satanael's power over the human race.

Both the Roman Catholic and Greek Orthodox Churches had persecuted the followers of Bogomil relentlessly for the next two and a half centuries. The Council of Constantinople decreed that all the heretics must be burned alive. Rome, on the other hand, insisted upon an attempt to "reconvert" the followers of Bogomil, killing only those who refused salvation. The urgency of this mission increased dramatically when the Gnostic revival spread into Western Europe, moving from the Balkans into Italy, then into the Swiss Alps, and finally into southern France, where those known as Cathari (also called the Albigenses) became the hub of a heresy that threatened the authority of the Roman Catholic Church like nothing else in nearly a thousand years. As had been the case with each of the Gnostic movements that preceded it, Catharism was fueled in part by disgust with the corruption and indulgence of the Catholic clergy. The Cathari recognized no priests, instead dividing themselves into two general categories: the *credentes* (believers), who included the vast majority of the sect's members, and the *perfecti* (perfects), who never numbered more than a few thousand, and observed a code of self-denial that was remarkably stringent. *Credentes* became *perfecti* through a ritual of baptism with the Holy Spirit that involved the laying on of hands, and they were required to immediately surrender all worldly goods to the larger community, to vest themselves in a simple, corded black or blue robe, and to serve as mendicant monks who devoted their lives to prayer, preaching, and charitable work. Even the *credentes* were expected to refrain from eating meat or dairy products, from killing, and from swearing oaths. They were also discouraged from procreation, which would only serve to increase Rex Mundi's kingdom of evil. One must renounce anything connected to the "principle of power" embodied by the Dark Lord, the Cathari taught, so as to achieve union with the "principle of love." Escape from the realm of materiality into the realm of pure spirit, where the God of Light dwelled, was the ultimate goal of all Cathari.

Their repudiation of the visible world required the Cathari to reject the Christian symbol of the cross. Like the Docetists ten centuries earlier, they insisted that Jesus's earthly body had been but an illusion, and that therefore his crucifixion and resurrection were illusions also. The Cathari likewise rejected the concepts of salvation and damnation, embracing instead a belief in reincarnation that had been imported from the East. Little by little, each spark of the divine was being drawn out of its corrupt earthly shell into an inevitable communion with the God of Light who had produced it.

Innocent VIII found all this no less abhorrent than had his predecessors. The rejection of Christ's sacrifice was an attack on the salvation theology at the heart of orthodox faith. The separation of God from creation and the elevation of Satan to virtual parity with the Lord together constituted a ghastly deformation of Jesus's ministry. While the Cathari regarded the Gospel of John as a sacred text, they were indifferent to the rest of the New Testament, and they scorned the Old Testament entirely, insisting that the Jehovah of Jewish scripture was none other than Rex Mundi himself. Errors as grievous as these, Innocent announced, must be corrected.

The pope sent his legate Pierre de Castelnau to meet with Count Raymond VI of Toulouse, ruler of the Languedoc, where the Cathar heresy had taken deepest root, in January 1208. After a fierce face-to-face argument, Castelnau excommunicated Raymond; the legate was murdered (reportedly by a knight in Raymond's service) while returning to Rome a short time later. Innocent VIII immediately called for a Crusade and enhanced the effect by producing a decree that allowed for the confiscation of lands owned by the Cathari and their supporters.

Charged with devil worship, human sacrifice, cannibalism, and incest, among other iniquities, the Cathari were slaughtered by the thousands. During an early battle, Arnaud, the abbot-knight leading the Crusade, was asked by his men whom among the heretics should be put to the sword. He answered with a line that is still echoed seven centuries later: "Kill them all. God will know his own." The Cathari movement suffered its final defeat in March 1244, at Montségur, in the foothills of the Pyrenees, where more than two hundred heretic priests were massacred.

The last serious Gnostic threat to orthodox Christianity was ended and the theological argument settled: the Devil was an angel created by God who had fallen by his own act of volition, separated forever from the Kingdom of Heaven and determined to take as many human souls as possible with him.

THE WITCH HUNTS that scourged Europe during the fifteenth, sixteenth, and seventeenth centuries were more complex in both origin and development than is popularly understood. Two events, eight years apart, were the principal propulsive forces of what turned into a continental frenzy. The first came in 1478, when Ferdinand and Isabella of Aragon, the future sponsors of Christopher Columbus, initiated the Spanish Inquisition. The main intention of the Spanish monarchs was to undercut the power of the Iberian Peninsula's large Muslim and Jewish populations. The Catholic Church, in the person of Pope Sixtus IV, actually opposed the Inquisition, vehemently at first. Sixtus was forced to acquiesce, though, when Ferdinand threatened to withdraw his armies from Italy, which was at the time being invaded by the Turks. The pope then attempted to confine the Inquisition to Castile, but again yielded in the face of pressure from Ferdinand, though he did continue to complain that the whole thing was a cynical ploy by the Spanish king to confiscate the property of wealthy Jews.

Like some modern historians, Ferdinand's apologists would point out that the institutional Church was not without responsibility for the persecutions of the Inquisition. The Spanish throne cited the papal bull written by Innocent VIII to launch the twelfth-century Crusade against the Cathari. In preparing his letter, Innocent had drawn upon chapter 15 of the Book of Acts, in which the first Christians had convened a council in Jerusalem to rebuke the "Judaizers," who were arguing that only Jews should be allowed to become Christians. Three hundred years later, Innocent's letter was used by a pair of German priests named Heinrich Kramer and Jacob Sprenger as the preface to their 1486 tome *Malleus maleficarum* (Hammer of the witches), a volume that served only briefly as the handbook of the Spanish Inquisition but was the operating manual of the witch hunts that spread all across the European continent in the two centuries that followed.

The publication of *Malleus* was the second and perhaps even more significant event that drove the witch scare. Two years earlier, Kramer had attempted to organize a prosecution of witches in Tyrol that failed miserably; he was banished from the diocese and dismissed by the local bishop as "a senile old man." *Malleus* was his response. The book was divided into three parts. In Part One, Kramer and his co-author asserted the existence of a Devil with the power to accomplish enormous evil. Witchcraft, the two priests wrote, was the product of human wickedness, permitted by God but encouraged by Satan. The Devil was most able to corrupt humans through their sexuality, according to Kramer and Sprenger, and that was why most witches were women: "All witchcraft comes from carnal lust, which in women is insatiable." Libidinous women became witches and obtained their powers, according to *Malleus*, by having sexual intercourse with the Devil. Part Two of the book explained how witches were recruited and described their diabolical practices, which included infanticide and cannibalism, as well as how spells and curses could be removed and how the godly might protect themselves. Part Three was a step-by-step guide to the interrogation, charging, and prosecution of witches.

The Church actually condemned *Malleus* only three years after its initial publication, and by 1538 even the Spanish Inquisition was warning its members not to believe everything they read in the volume. That did little to stop the spread of the book all across the continent in virtually every European language. The enormous influence of *Malleus* owed in large degree to Johannes Gutenberg's recent invention of the printing press. The book was the first international

bestseller after the Bible, reprinted a total of twenty-nine times between 1487 and 1669.

The appeal of *Malleus* was not simply to the imagination. White
and black magic were widely practiced in the Europe of those times,
as they still are today in most of the rest of the world. The Roman
Empire had long disdained and suppressed magic, but beginning in
the thirteenth century, the Renaissance revived a widespread fascination with the various "sympathies" that existed in earth, water, air, and
fire, and how they might be manipulated. Two of the three most
important practitioners and proponents of "natural magic" were the
fifteenth-century Italians Marsilio Ficino and Giovanni Pico della
Mirandola, who drew upon the work of Plato to argue that man was
not damned by original sin but rather born with access to "won-
drous" powers through the application of the rational mind to the
natural world. The Hermetic/Kabbalist magic these two advocated
had considerable influence on the likes of Leonardo and Michelan-
gelo, among many others. Ficino and Pico were not anti-Christian—
far from it. They argued that exploring the secrets of nature would
inspire wonder at the works of God. That line of thought was picked
up by the German alchemist Agrippa (1486–1535), who nevertheless
was persecuted as a heretic. Agrippa's book *Occulta philosophia libri tres*
did more than anything else to stimulate interest in and the practice
of magic in England, where he received much of the blame for the
swerve into necromancy and demonology by more than a few educated persons.

In Spain, the Inquisition was still driven by mainly political motives. Ferdinand saw dire threat in the tens of thousands of resident
conversos, Muslims and Jews who had publicly converted to Catholicism but continued to practice their original faiths in private. After it
was demonstrated that a number of practicing Jews had become
priests, and in a few cases bishops, popular support for the Inquisition grew. In the ten years after Tomas de Torquemada was appointed
by the king to head the Inquisition, more than 13,000 *conversos* had
been tried. How many were executed (somewhere between 1,000
and 9,000) is still debated, but what is not in dispute is the manner in

which the convicted *conversos* died: they were burned at the stake, alive if they refused to repent, after death by strangulation if they confessed to their deception. While the Spanish Inquisition would last nearly 350 years, its climax came early—in March 1492, when Ferdinand issued an edict declaring that all unconverted Jews must leave Spain no later than the last day of July, two weeks before Columbus set sail for the New World.

By the end of that century, the concerns of the Inquisition had grown increasingly theological, and nothing was more critical to Church leaders in Spain than preserving belief in the Devil as an actual being who was capable of great harm, especially if aided by earthly allies. It was for this reason that the Inquisition began to target the followers of Erasmus (1366–1436), the Dutch priest and scholar who had become the hero of an incipient humanist movement because of his insistence that judgments should be based on rationality and empiricism rather than articles of faith. The Church was particularly unhappy that Erasmus and his followers maintained that the Devil and his demons were metaphors for the evil tendencies of human beings.

Martin Luther (1483–1546) and his allies in the Reformist movement were even less sympathetic to Erasmus's views than the Church in Rome was. Luther insisted absolutely on a Devil who was at once God's servant and his enemy. God permitted the Devil to subject believers to tests and trials, said Luther, because doubt, despair, and desolation served to strengthen the faith of those who held fast. Those most advanced in faith were the ones Satan attacked most relentlessly, wrote Luther, who described in detail the ways in which the Devil had attempted to distract him from God's work: pelting the roof with nuts and rolling casks down a stairwell during his stay at Wartburg Castle; appearing at Coburg in the forms of first a serpent and then a star, grunting audibly like a pig and disputing with him like a scholastic. Luther's belief in witchcraft and possession was such that he personally exorcised a student named Johann Schlaginhaufen. The Reformist leader's most famous hymn, "A Mighty Fortress Is Our God," was notable for these lines:

> *The old, evil enemy*
> *Is determined to get us.*
> *He makes his cruel plans*
> *With great might and cruel cunning.*

As Jeffrey Burton Russell has observed, belief in the Devil and his "immediate and terrible powers was revived throughout society to an extent unsurpassed even at the time of the desert fathers." Across Northern Europe there was popular consensus on the scenario of a witch coven's operation: On a Thursday or Saturday night, groups that were mostly women gathered in a "synagogue" to commune with Satan. Those who lived far away were said to rub their bodies with a magical ointment that let them fly in the shape of animals, or on a broomstick. Neophytes who wished to enter the coven were required to bring the body of a murdered child to the meeting. They also had to renounce Christianity and soil either a crucifix or a Eucharistic host with their urine or their feces. After their initiation, the entire group enacted a gruesome parody of the Last Supper, dining on the flesh of murdered children who had been "sacrificed" to Satan, then celebrated with a sexual orgy that encouraged practices such as incest and pederasty. Some were said to have intercourse with the Devil himself.

In towns and villages all across the continent, to be publicly charged with witchcraft was a sentence of certain death, and many accusers were motivated by grudges, envy, or economic opportunism. Confessions were extracted by the use of hot pincers or thumbscrews.

Witch hunting achieved its apogee during the 1640s in England's East Anglia region, where one Matthew Hopkins declared himself "witchfinder general" and led dozens of "searches" in which he claimed to be able to identify witches by inspecting their bodies. Hopkins, the son of a popular Puritan vicar, claimed that he began his career as a witch hunter in 1644, when he heard assorted women in the town of Manningtree discussing their meetings with the Devil. On the basis of accusations made by Hopkins and his associate John Stearne, twenty-three women were accused of witchcraft and tried at Chelmsford; four died in prison, and nineteen were executed by hanging.

Hopkins soon was traveling throughout the region, accompanied by a group of woman assistants who specialized in "pricking," which involved the use of pins, needles, and bodkins to determine whether an accused person bled when his or (usually) her skin was punctured; if she did not, this was considered conclusive evidence that she was a witch. Professional "witchfinders" such as those who traveled with Hopkins earned a considerable living, which perhaps explains the subsequent discovery of hollow wooden handles and retractable points from the toolkits of various "finders," as well as specially designed needles some carried, with one end sharp and the other blunt. Hopkins also used sleep deprivation and what he called the "swimming test" to prove that accused women were witches. The latter involved tying the accused to a chair and throwing her in the water; if she floated, she was a witch. Historians believe that Hopkins and his associates were responsible for the deaths of about 300 women between 1644 and 1646, more than half of all those executed for witchcraft in England between the early fifteenth and late eighteenth centuries.

Hopkins's book *The Discovery of Witches* was published in 1647, the same year the "witchfinder general" retired from his duties, under pressure from John Gaule, a cleric whose sermons not only criticized Hopkins's methods but sought to suppress witch-hunting by others as well. *The Discovery of Witches* crossed the Atlantic Ocean, however, and served as a handbook for those who directed the New England witch trials that came to a climax in Salem, Massachusetts, during 1692–1693, leading to 19 executions and 150 imprisonments.

The great witch scare was already petering out in Europe. The three women executed at Exeter in 1682 were the last to die in England for witchcraft. Joseph Addison's 1711 article for *The Spectator* excoriated the irrationality and injustice of treating elderly and feeble-minded women as witches, and one year later, when Jane Wenham was convicted of witchcraft, the authorities intervened to pardon her and set her free. How far the pendulum had swung back from the extreme reached by Matthew Hopkins in the middle of the previous century was evidenced by the Act of 1735, which specified that those who claimed to be witches should be convicted of fraud, since they could not possibly possess supernatural powers granted by Satan. The rationalism and empiricism advocated by Erasmus were ascendant, just as fear of Satan and his cohort began to wither away.

As Russell has observed, "The phenomenon that did the most to advance belief in the Devil for several centuries was largely responsible for its decline from the eighteenth century onward."

Much as the stalwarts of modernity might want to believe they had vanquished Satan, though, the problem of evil was not going away.

CHAPTER FIVE

i.

NO ONE WAS SURE how much Tate's death had to do with it, but his sister Teri had gone way off the rails in the two years after his hanging. "She was twenty-six years old, had four young kids," Brenda Rowland explained. "Her husband was workin' out of town and she got to slippin' around and drinkin' and druggin'. It wasn't cocaine or meth or none of that stuff. She got to poppin' pills and she got messed up with the wrong crowd."

There was no crowd in Childress more wrong than the one that formed around the Wilks boys and the Bradford brothers. "The Wilks were a bunch of poor redneck scumbags, whatever you want to call 'em," said Reece Bowen. "They were trash, to use that term. The Bradford boys, though, they were seriously bad. Ricky was trouble enough, believe me. He had already been to prison for aggravated assault. But his brother Larry was the worst. He was one bad dude. We'd probably arrest him two or three times a month, usually for some kind of assault. Beatin' up his girlfriend, mostly. But we would never go out there for him unless there was at least three of us, because we knew it would be a fight. He was sent away to prison again, though, in '90 or '91, so it was Ricky that Teri Trosper took up with."

Her friends and family could not make out entirely what was going on, because Teri kept telling them it was all part of investigating her brother's death. "She never believed Tate took his own life," her friend Lisa Barber would say. "Right up to her death, she never accepted it. She was hell-bent on finding out who killed him." Recalled Brenda Rowland, "She told Jimmie and I one day, 'If anything happens to me, you all look at Ricky Bradford. 'Cause I'm gettin' close on Tate's death.' This was less than thirty days before she died."

Ricky's best friend was Darwin Wilks, the older brother of Ray Wilks, the boy who had told the police he was part of a group that had sacrificed Tate Rowland. The Wilks family home, a scrofulous shack in southwest Childress, the poorest part of town, was the informal headquarters of the Bradford-Wilks gang and the place where they did their partying. Locally, it was known as "the Devil's Den" because those words had been painted—and then painted over—on the back wall of the house, neighbors said. Frank Wilks, Darwin and Ray's father, insisted this was a misunderstanding. Ray was trying to get the attention of a local girl he hankered after and used a paintbrush to write "I love Lettie" on the back of the house, his father told *Texas Monthly*: "I said, 'Ray, get that shit off the wall.' So he painted over it, and now everyone thinks it says, 'I Love the Devil.'"

While just about everyone in Childress was convinced that there was, or at least had been, a satanic cult active in the community, a lot of people had a difficult time picturing the Wilkses and the Bradfords—a bunch of beer-swilling, pill-popping badasses—as part of it. And Frank Wilks was quick to point out that both his boys had ironclad alibis for the day and night of Tate Rowland's hanging: Darwin was in the Childress County Jail and Ray was in the Amarillo Youth Detention Center.

Teri, though, insisted that the Wilkses and Bradfords knew something about Tate's death and that she was going to get it out of them. To her family, it looked as if she thought sleeping with a devil was her way to the truth.

Teri was part of a good-sized crowd that gathered to drink and drug and fornicate at the Wilks house on the night of May 30, 1991. Ricky Bradford would tell the city police that Teri, who had been drinking heavily, went to bed with him, then at one point got up, staggered around the living room, collapsed, and was helped back to bed. At about nine-thirty the next morning, Bradford said, "I just touched her, and she was cold and stiff. I didn't even look at her. I just got up. And I informed everybody that I thought she was dead." Ricky's tone and expression as he told them this, one cop said, was "flat as a fencepost."

To Reece Bowen's mind, Teri's death was "suspicious from day one," but the Childress Police Department had jurisdiction over the case and the chief there, Billy Don Hinton, seemed to be another Claude Lane: "Chief Hinton goes over there and just sort of stomps through the house, is told some story about how she drowned on her own vomit, and says, 'Uh-huh,' and that's that," Bowen remembered.

When he was questioned in court by District Attorney McCoy a year later, Hinton stunned the dead woman's family with his answers. Had he become suspicious when he observed the splotches of blood on the pillow and sheets near Teri Trosper's mouth? "Not particularly," the former police chief replied. What about the small pool of blood near Teri's vagina? asked McCoy. Had that indicated to him that her death might be a homicide? "No, sir," answered Hinton, who explained that someone on the scene had told him that Teri was "in her period."

"Everyone in the house told you it was not a murder and you believed them?" McCoy asked.

"Yes, sir," Hinton replied.

"It's hard to believe everything that was just passed over," Bowen recalled. "For instance, there was blood on the car parked at the house, blood on the car door. But Bradford and Wilks told some story about a fight and Hinton accepted it. One of his officers had scraped the blood off the car, but Hinton didn't want to have it tested. The officers themselves knew there was somethin' wrong. One of 'em came to me at the sheriff's department just a little bit later and told me, 'Man, that was a crime scene.'"

When Dr. Ralph Erdmann, the state pathologist who had been assigned to perform the autopsy on Teri Trosper, concurred with Hinton's conclusion that the young woman had indeed suffocated on her own vomit, though, the matter seemed settled. A blood test had showed that Teri's blood alcohol level was .23, almost three times the legal standard of intoxication.

Very soon after, though, "dominos began to fall in Childress," as Reese Bowen recalled it, and nothing seemed settled anymore.

The biggest thud came when Claude Lane hit the ground. Lane's tumble began on a summer day in 1990 when the sheriff's department took a call from a farmer who said he had rolled up on a couple of people walking along a country road carrying trash bags. The pair of them had panicked, dropped the bags, and run until they were picked up by a car with two other men in it, the farmer said. When he looked inside one of the bags, he believed he'd seen marijuana.

Deputy Bowen was on duty and drove out there. Within a few hours, Bowen and a local game warden had discovered a boxcar next to a barn that was filled with hundreds of cut marijuana plants hanging from the ceiling, dozens of drying racks, and a table covered with one-pound bags of pot that were ready for sale. Shortly after that, they apprehended a father and son who were transporting the marijuana packing boxes in the bed of their pickup truck.

Because of the size of the operation, the Drug Enforcement Administration was called in, and its agents worked alongside Sheriff Lane for a time, until their investigation led them to the conclusion that the man who had been growing the marijuana was the sheriff himself. Bowen hustled over to the courthouse in downtown Childress, where he learned that Sheriff Lane had been arrested. Bowen and a second deputy were on the courthouse steps when the feds walked the sheriff out of the building in handcuffs. "He just looked at us and said, 'It ain't true, boys,'" Bown recalled.

The town's movers and shakers wanted to believe him. In January 1991, not long after the federal charges against Lane were filed, the Childress Coffee Slurpers Club, which included every important business owner in town, gave the sheriff its vote of confidence. By June, though, Lane had been removed from office, and on September 4, 1991, he was sentenced to thirty-seven months in federal prison after being convicted not only of running the marijuana growing operation but also of stealing $9,600 from the sheriff's department, as well as filching much of the marijuana that had been booked into evidence by Deputy Bowen.

Bowen was appointed to complete Claude Lane's term as Childress County sheriff on June 18, 1991, less than three weeks after Teri Trosper's death. "My second day on the job," Bowen recalled, "Tate Rowland's stepmom, Brenda, walks into my office and says she thinks Teri's death is connected to Tate."

Bowen had been bothered for three years by the failure to investigate Tate Rowland's hanging, and the recent death of the boy's sister troubled him further. It seemed as if there had to be some connection. Any number of people said Teri had told them that shortly before his death Tate had warned her to keep her children indoors, because "the cult" was going to sacrifice one of them in a satanic ritual. And nearly as many said Teri claimed to be investigating Tate's hanging because she knew it was no suicide. "There were just too many things wrong, too many questions," Bowen said. Shortly after the Fourth of July he asked District Attorney McCoy to go to court to arrange the exhumation of Tate Roland's remains. On July 29, 1991, McCoy filed a motion to disinter before Judge Dottie Bettis, who approved it that day.

What was left of Tate Rowland's body came out of the ground the following morning. "And after that, so many things happened, one right after another, that the whole town was turned upside down," Bowen remembered.

THE SAME DAY she signed the order to disinter, County Judge Dottie S. Bettis also put her signature on a document labeled "Authority to Perform an Autopsy." The events themselves, though, were something of a letdown. "Tate was buried in a wooden casket that was put in a concrete vault," Reece Bowen recalled. "But they didn't seal the vault when they put the lid on, so his casket had rotted out and his body was in real bad shape."

The only new fact the autopsy on Tate Rowland's remains produced was that the boy had traces of Elavil in what was left of his vital organs. "I knew nothin' about Elavil," Brenda Rowland said, "so I went to the pharmacy to ask about it. And they told me it was a tranquilizer, and if you're not used to it, it will relax you into a semiconscious state. You'll be awake, but you won't be able to function." District Attorney McCoy would call Elavil "the kind of drug that you would take and then lay down and go to sleep" and suggested that the drug, as *Texas Monthly* put it, "could have been the very thing a cult would use to sedate someone and then kill them."

Those who knew Tate best were adamant that he did not use drugs of any kind. In fact, he would walk away if somebody so much as lit up a joint, his friends claimed. "So we just assumed somebody slipped it into his beer," Brenda said.

The forensic pathologist who performed the autopsy, Dr. Sparks Veasey, was able to confirm that there were two separate rope burns on Tate's neck. To him this suggested the possibility—and perhaps the likelihood—that the boy had been choked to death first, then hung, Veasey stated. The decomposition of Tate's remains, however, was too advanced to draw a definitive conclusion, the doctor added.

The sheriff department's new chief deputy, Kevin Overstreet, examined the photos of Tate's body that had been taken on the evening of his death at the hospital and pointed out that both bruises on the boy's neck were straight-line marks. "Usually in a hanging, there's an inverted 'V' bruise on the neck," Overstreet explained, "caused by the pressure of the body as it pulls down the rope." Dr. Veasey agreed that this was more evidence of the possibility that Tate was already dead by the time he was hung from the horse apple tree out at Boxer's Corner, but still not enough to issue a ruling that the boy's death had been a homicide. He did believe, though, that the death should be the subject of a criminal investigation, Veasey said.

Veasey added one startling detail from his autopsy of Teri Trosper: like her brother Tate, she had died with Elavil in her system.

Sheriff Bowen assigned Overstreet to investigate both Tate's death and the death of his sister Teri as possible murders. The new chief deputy was distressed by how poorly what might have been a crime scene was handled back in 1988. "If there were tire tracks or footprints, none of that stuff was looked at," he said. "The rope hadn't been saved. There was no autopsy, no forensic examination of any kind, really. The only thing they had was the photographs of Tate's body. When I realized how many things that should have been done had not been done, I got discouraged."

Overstreet was of a different stripe than anything Childress law enforcement had seen previously. It wasn't just the quality of his haircut and the shine on his boots. Overstreet was well-spoken in a way no law officer in town ever had been. He'd attended college and had taken training classes with state agencies. He talked forensic examinations and toxicology reports. Brenda Rowland was not the only woman who said he was the best-looking man in town. "A dark-haired Alan Jackson," she described Overstreet, which was no small compliment coming from a woman who had decorated the walls of her living room with portraits of the blond country music star.

Reese Bowen would decide eventually that Overstreet was "full of himself," but even the new sheriff seemed pretty impressed by his new chief deputy at the beginning. Bowen himself was a solid man. "A redheaded, straight-backed Childress area native," Skip Hollandsworth would describe him in *Texas Monthly*. And the new sheriff was no dummy, either; he had been the one and only law officer in town to openly question the rulings that Tate Rowland's death had been a suicide and that Teri Trosper's death had been accidental. But Bowen seemed a little outshone by his new hire and "more or less stepped aside," as Brenda Rowland put it, to let Overstreet take over the investigations into the deaths of Tate and Teri.

Bowen couldn't disagree when Overstreet bemoaned the shoddy work the sheriff's department had done back in July 1988 when Tate was found hung out at Boxer's Corner. For a while it looked as if Overstreet might just say the case had been too badly botched to press forward with it. Then Overstreet read the interviews that had been conducted with Michelle Gomez in March 1989 and looked at the drawings the girl had made. "The interview and the drawings were both remarkable," he recalled. "This girl, Michelle, knew a whole lot about Childress, when she'd never ever been there. It was a very detailed picture she'd drawn to illustrate Tate's death and the details were right. There was the high grass and the dirt road and the shadow of a figure hanging from the biggest branch of the tree."

Overstreet arranged a trip to Lockhart to meet with Michelle Gomez and came away impressed. "Her story was consistent," he remembered. "She seemed truly afraid of Mary and of the people Mary was involved with."

Nobody had said anything to him about the "satanic cult connection" until he spoke to Michelle, Overstreet said. When he got back to Childress, Overstreet read the various reports of "cult sites" that had been investigated. "It was obvious there had been something going on, but the problem was it had all pretty much shut down by then. The people who were accused of being involved were all gone, which struck me as strange. It just seemed a little too convenient that they would leave Childress right after this whole thing started coming out into the open. But there wasn't much we could do about things that had been going on two years earlier."

Overstreet did decide that he needed to reinterview Chad Johnston and arranged to meet with the boy at his new home in a town two hundred miles away. The main point was to confront Chad with the evidence that Tate had been choked with the rope before he was hung by it. Chad responded by changing his story. Shortly after they arrived at Boxer's Corner, Chad said, Tate had made a failed attempt to hang himself. "I can't even kill myself," Chad quoted Tate as saying after the rope broke. Then he and Tate drove back to Childress for another rope, which Tate then used to hang himself a second time—successfully. Chad again had a plausible explanation for why he had lied about the circumstances of Tate's death back in July 1988: he was afraid people would think he was responsible, the boy told Overstreet, especially if he admitted that he had actually watched Tate hang himself.

Chad would eventually change his story two more times, but it only took this once for Overstreet to become convinced that the boy—young man now, really, Chad being almost nineteen when the chief deputy first spoke to him—needed to take a polygraph examination. He arranged for Chad to take the lie detector test three separate times in 1991 and 1992, Overstreet recalled, and young Johnston canceled every time. "Very frustrating," remembered Overstreet, who did obtain one tantalizing piece of information about Chad: back in 1988 the boy had had a prescription for Elavil.

"The family leavin' town, the boy changin' his story, the prescription, it all made you wonder," recalled Reese Bowen. "But his mother became real hostile. I knew his stepdad, who was raised near me up in Chester, but the mother, she said, 'Ain't nobody talkin' to Chad anymore about the Rowland boy.' So that pretty much put a stop to things."

Overstreet, though, had by then heard the stories about Teri telling people she was investigating Tate's death and that before he died Tate had told her to keep her little girls indoors, because "the cult" was looking to use them in a sacrifice ceremony. "The sheriff and I both thought there must be some connection between Teri's death and Tate's," Overstreet remembered.

Late in the autumn of 1991, Bowen and Overstreet prevailed upon District Attorney McCoy to convene a grand jury to look into both deaths. And in early December the grand jury submitted a request that Teri's body should be disinterred so that a second autopsy could be conducted. "And man, when that happened, things really got crazy," Reese Bowen said.

ii.

THE BRIDGE ACROSS the chasm that would open between the absolutist philosophies of Augustine and Aquinas and the scientific rationalism of the philosophes who proclaimed the Enlightenment was built during the seventeenth and eighteenth centuries by a succession of European geniuses. They were a Frenchman, a German, and a Dutch Jew who made metaphysics and mathematics into mirror methods of comprehension, and in the process forever blurred the distinction between theology and philosophy.

First among them, at least in chronological order, was "the father of modern philosophy," René Descartes (1596–1650). The crux of

Descartes's approach was his insistence that the material universe remained completely separate from the spiritual world. In Cartesian cosmology, God was a "blind watchmaker" who existed entirely apart from what he had brought into being, enabling the universe to function mechanically, but granting complete freedom to both the creatures in it and to himself, leaving the original act of creation as the sole connection between this world and the one beyond.

It was a system of thought that left no need for a Devil, but Descartes continued to consider himself a devout Catholic who believed in the revelation of scripture, and so he essayed to construct a rational analysis of evil. The result was what has become known among theologians as the free-will defense: error (and thus sin) is the fault of humans, not God, because humans insist upon extending their will beyond their knowledge. It might be argued that God could have given us knowledge that would prevent errors, Descartes conceded, but in truth God could not have created a perfect cosmos without creating something identical to himself, since anything not identical to God is by definition imperfect. And what God wanted for humans was a cosmos of plentitude where we could experience ourselves fully and make choices that determined the outcomes of our lives.

Descartes never addressed the question of the Devil's existence or nature directly but did offer the hypothesis in *Meditations on First Philosophy* of an "evil demon" who is "as clever and deceitful as he is powerful, who has directed his entire effort to misleading me." Whether Descartes was suggesting the Gnostic dualism of a good God counterbalanced by an evil deity or was proposing that God himself was a deceiver can be and has been debated. A number of contemporaries believed the latter and accused him of heresy.

Be that as it may, Descartes had more influence on theology—and on history—as an advocate of rationalism, particularly when he was perceived as the antecedent to Gottfried Wilhelm Leibniz (1646–1716). Leibniz is remembered best for his optimistic assertion that the admittedly imperfect world in which we live is the best possible one God could have created, the only world that actualizes every possibility. His most enduring work, though, was a volume with a title that has become the standard theological term for study of the problem of evil: *Theodicy*. Striving to answer the question of how a God who was all-powerful, all-wise, and all-good could have permitted evil into the world, Leibniz answered that while God's wisdom and power are boundless, the limited understanding of human beings, combined with the free will God has granted them, predisposes us to false beliefs and bad decisions. The moral sins and physical evils suffered by humans are not inflicted on us arbitrarily, Leibniz insisted, but rather exist as a necessary consequence of the metaphysical evil, or imperfection, required to maintain our material reality, separate from God. It is through our errors and our pain, Leibniz contended, that each individual exercises his or her free will, and is offered the opportunity to identify and correct errors, then aspire to true good.

In *Theodicy*, Leibniz refers to the Devil only briefly, but seems to be describing an actual being, one who is clearly subordinate to God: "God is infinite, and the devil is limited; the good may and does go to infinity, while evil has bounds."

Baruch Spinoza (1632–1677), though born fourteen years before Leibniz, was not recognized as a titan of modern philosophy until much later. His formulations have proven more influential in the long term, however, echoing through the intellectual elites of the nineteenth and twentieth centuries. Spinoza's public break with his synagogue as a young man not only made him into Amsterdam's first well-known secular Jew but also initiated what would become the most forcefully reasoned rejection of a personal God ever to appear in print. The abstract and indifferent deity Spinoza proclaimed was indistinguishable from nature; in fact, God and nature were simply two different words for the same reality, in Spinoza's view, aspects of the metaphysical "substance" that is the underlying essence of all that exists. Spinoza asserted that free will was illusory, that all occurrences take place as a matter of necessity, and that the only actual choice humans have is to accept that they can never say no to what happens in their lives, that only saying yes gives them the possibility of either understanding or happiness. Such a deterministic universe clearly does not require a Devil, and Spinoza did not believe that one existed, even as an abstract principle. Spinoza argued what Justin Martyr had declared centuries earlier to be the greatest of sins, the belief that good and evil were relative concepts that possess no intrinsic meaning but merely describe what is useful and what is not useful to human beings in any particular situation. Spinoza's God was the creator of what Albert Einstein called "orderly harmony," not a source of moral judgment; this God had no interest in the fates or actions of human beings, and therefore needed no Devil to tempt them.

The ideas of Descartes, Leibniz, and Spinoza, combined with a spreading shock at the excesses of the witch scare, contributed to the mounting skepticism among the intellectual elites about the existence of angels, good or bad. The Protestants, meanwhile, were taking an increasingly dim view of the Catholic concern with evil spirits; the Puritan John Hall decried exorcism as "foul superstition and gross magic," while the Anglicans abolished the office of exorcist in 1550. Dutch pastor Balthasar Bekker dealt a devastating blow to belief in Satan among the Reformed churches, contending in his hugely influential 1691 book *The Enchanted World* that all beliefs about the Devil and his demons derived either from paganism, from Gnostic-influenced interpretations of scripture, or from the perverted traditions of Catholicism. Even Isaac Newton, who in his earlier writings had addressed Satan as an actual being, began describing the Devil as a "symbol" for "the spirit of error."

By the end of the seventeenth century, the most significant contemplations of the Devil as an actual being were literary. The story of Faust and his bargain with Satan has been as influential as any in the history of Western culture. The tale made its first appearance in print in Johan Spiess's *Historia von D. Johann Fausten*, published in 1587, but had been around for a thousand years. The Faust story was actually based on a historical figure, Theophilus of Adana, a sixth-century Turkish cleric who purportedly had obtained his position as a bishop by signing a contract with Satan. Spiess's version was the template for all subsequent renderings, however. It told the story of an individualist who sold his soul to obtain knowledge by his own efforts, rather than through grace. Spiess's Faust summons the Devil by arriving at a crossroads in the middle of the night, scratching magical figures into the dirt, then invoking Beelzebub. An evil spirit that identifies itself as Mephistopheles appears to him as a dragon, a fiery globe, and finally as a Franciscan monk who invites Faust to enter into a great hierarchy, with Lucifer at the top. Faust writes a pact with Mephistopheles in blood, denies Christ, and promises to be an enemy of Christians. In exchange he is given twenty-four years of absolute freedom, at the end of which he must pay the devil his due. After a brief tour of hell, Faust's thirst for knowledge and power degenerates into mere lust. He journeys to Rome to feast at the palace of the pope, dallying among the drunkards and whores who pack the place. Faust travels then to Constantinople, where he poses as the Prophet Muhammad in order to gain access to a sultan's seraglio, and later summons Helen of Troy for a sexual tryst. Finally, as the end of his twenty-four-year-long orgy approaches, Faust gathers his colleagues and students, tells them what he has done, and warns them against the wiles of the Devil. In the night, the others hear screams, then find the mutilated body of Faust thrown upon a dung heap.

The power of the Faust tale and the sway that belief in a literal Devil continues to hold in Western culture is demonstrated by the fact that during the next 400 years the story was retold by a succession of authors, composers, and playwrights who include Christopher Marlowe, Johann Wolfgang van Goethe, Wolfgang Amadeus Mozart, and George Bernard Shaw. The most significant characterization of the Devil himself, though, was John Milton's in *Paradise Lost*. The epic blank-verse poem was published in 1667 and confronted readers with a Satan who was a mock-heroic parody of God, a creature whose ugliness, stench, and incestuous relationship with his daughter Sin have remained the hallmarks of infernal characters ever since. Milton (1608–1674), who was deeply religious, calls Satan an archangel and charts his course from an original fall that took place before the creation of the material universe, at the moment he realized that it was God's intention to place Christ above the angels. From "obdurate pride," Milton's Satan descends to a motive of envy and, finally, revenge. His first act of evil is to persuade one-third of the angels to rebel against God, "Our Enemy," and then withdrawing with them to the north of heaven, where he erects his own throne and denounces the exaltation of Christ, "the Son," as an insult to the dignity of angels. Satan suggests to the other angels that, since they cannot remember the moment of creation, they might not be created at all but rather "self-begot, self-rais'd." The war in heaven that follows is a stalemate between armies led by Satan and those led by the archangel Michael, until God sends his Son to cast the rebels down into hell. Satan is astonished that God not only declines to destroy them all but actually leaves them with the power to tempt and degrade humankind. In the final section of *Paradise Lost*, God explains himself with a free-will defense of how he created both angels and humans. "I made him just and right," God says of man, "Sufficient to have stood, though free to fall." He speaks in virtually the same way about his angels: "Freely they stood who stood, and fell who fell." Satan replies by inducing the fall of Adam and Eve in the Garden of Eden and later takes on personally the task of tempting Christ in the desert.

Milton's depiction of Satan is so powerful that it has superseded all others in the three and a half centuries since its publication. Milton himself, though, would have been startled to learn that the great English poets who were born only a little more than a hundred years after his death would seize upon his Satan as an inspirational figure, a heroic protagonist who had been the original rebel with a cause. First, though, Satan, like God, would have to survive the Enlightenment.

"THE ENLIGHTENMENT" was a self-flattering term invented by the French philosophes who made up the ranks of the first to proclaim themselves enlightened. While the philosophes wrote and spoke extensively about throwing off the yokes of ignorance and tyranny, placing their faith in empiricism and scientific discovery, and inventing a new social order, at bottom they were anti-Christian. Their great leader, François-Marie Arouet, better known by his pen name Voltaire (1694–1778), was the first among them to publicly denounce Christianity as a failure, both intellectually incorrect and socially destructive. The rejection of religious dogma, Voltaire insisted, was not the road to hell but the path to liberation. After Voltaire, whatever divisions or differences developed among them, the philosophes were united on one front—their enmity toward Christianity.

In the aftermath of the Inquisition and the witch scare, the traditional doctrines of faith were viewed with growing suspicion by the intellectual elites of Western Europe, and no religious tenets were more suspect than those involving belief in the Devil. Even within the Roman Catholic Church, there was a powerful movement to adopt Descartes's division of the cosmos into a world of spirit and a world of nature. Many if not most Jesuits were contending that grace and revelation were a superimposition upon the natural world, salutary but not really necessary to life on earth. For these clerics, "scientific explanations removed the why of the world and replaced it with the how," as Jeffrey Burton Russell has pointed out. Thus, "as icing on the cake, rather than the cake itself, religion could eventually be done away with." The Jesuits paved the way for the hostility of the Enlightenment to Christianity, Russell would argue, and also allowed the philosophes to claim they were the advocates of a "true Christianity" that emphasized Jesus as an ethical teacher rather than the Messiah, and in which the essential goodness of the world and the perfectibility of humanity became the new foundations of faith.

Among this first wave of secular progressives arose a new belief system known as Deism, which held that while God exists, he reveals himself only in nature, and that scripture, tradition, miracles, and revelation all could be discarded, replaced by a conviction that we worship God best by living constructive moral lives.

Some of those who resisted the deconstruction of Christianity answered with fideism, which adopted the belief of medieval nominalists that God's truths are beyond the scope of human reason. Voltaire himself recognized that the "democratic mysticism" of fideism was the strongest retort that Christians could make to Deism, but Voltaire also recognized that in its rejection of traditional theology (especially as regards the existence of the Devil) fideism would eventually dovetail nicely with his own movement.

Other Christians adopted what would become the core of main-line Protestant faith, optimism, a religious philosophy drawn largely from Leibniz. Voltaire lampooned both optimism and Leibniz in his novel *Candide* through the character of Dr. Pangloss, whose repeated assertions that this was "the best of all possible worlds" in the face of increasingly overwhelming evidence to the contrary provided the book's belly laughs. Alexander Pope (1688–1744) espoused optimism more eloquently in his rejections of such doctrines as original sin, salvation, and damnation, asserting in the alternative that the beauty and harmony of the universe demonstrated its essential goodness. "One truth is clear," Pope declared. "Whatever is, is right."

Voltaire traded in optimism for Deism and in the process embraced the concept of a God who was indifferent to human suffering. He derided the idea that evil was the product of some fallen angel and recoiled from Christian belief in the Devil as a grotesque superstition. Only as he approached the end of his life did it seem to occur to Voltaire that rejecting the concepts of absolute good and absolute evil would result in a moral relativism that was even more destructive to social order than Christian dogma.

The competition between optimism, Deism, and fideism was eclipsed by the advent of David Hume (1711–1776). The radical skepticism of the Scottish philosopher produced the most devastating attack on traditional Christian theology that has ever appeared in print, an attack that remains to this day the basis of intellectual atheism. Much of Richard Dawkins is warmed-over and watered-down Hume.

Like Thomas Aquinas, only in reverse, Hume made five main points. The first was that human beings can know nothing about God, including whether God in fact exists, because our knowledge is empirical. There are no innate ideas, Hume declared, only those we discover by trial and error, hypothesis and testing. Hume's second point was that the origin of religion lies entirely in human hopes and fears, projected onto external objects. The third point was that religion, as a human invention, has evolved naturally from animism to polytheism to monotheism. The fourth point was that miracles (including the incarnation and the resurrection) are impossible, because they violate the laws of nature, "established by firm and unalterable experience." Finally, Hume focused on the problem of evil, finding in it an especially effective line of attack on Christianity: Christians cannot reconcile the existence of God with the existence of evil without conceding either that God is not all-powerful or that God is not good in any way that human beings can comprehend. That assertion (made by Epicurus two thousand years earlier) launched Hume into his most powerful attack on religious faith, in which he pointed out that it was intellectually illegitimate to argue from an imperfect effect (the cosmos) to a perfect cause (God), and then to use the perfect cause to explain the existence of a cosmos already observed to be imperfect. Nature does not, Hume pointed out, demonstrate the wonders of God, but on the contrary leads to the conclusion that God does not exist.

The German Lutheran philosopher Immanuel Kant (1724–1804) provided consolation to Deists, optimists, and fideists alike, conceding Hume's argument that humans are incapable of absolute knowledge, yet at the same time insisting it was both possible and desirable to transcend skepticism. Kant focused on the problem of evil even more intently than Hume and scandalized fellow philosophes with his assertion that observation strongly suggests that human nature is not basically good. Evil is a universal reality, Kant contended, one that will never be eradicated by education or any other plan of social improvement. The reason for this, Kant went on, is that evil is an absolute that exists beyond the scope of the human mind and can never be explained or justified. For Kant, the Devil existed as a transcendent a priori concept; whether the Devil is also a "person" was for him irrelevant. It was necessary to accept the existence of the Devil, Kant argued, as a symbol of the radical evil that transcends the sinfulness of human nature. Such evil was not merely the absence of good, Kant wrote, but a force that lives within each human being. Evil was not a zero but rather a minus that does its best to cancel out the plus that is God. It was actually the problem of evil that made him religious, Kant stated. Without evil, the universe might be seen as a perfectly functioning mechanism, but the existence of evil was a flaw so radical that no naturalistic observation could suffice to explain it.

Kant, however, was abstruse. The more lucid and concise arguments of Hume won a far greater number of adherents, including Denis Diderot (1713–1784), successor to Voltaire as champion of the Enlightenment, who proclaimed atheism as the movement's banner. Diderot bluntly dismissed the notion of an active spirit in nature and insisted that things were simply what they were. For him and those who joined him, the universe was material, infinite, and eternal, formed by chance. These men insisted that human intelligence was a random anomaly that had arisen out of mechanistic sources utterly indifferent to moral "values." Good and evil were not transcendent absolutes, Diderot and his cohorts insisted, but mere constructs, labels that were convenient to social relationships and existed nowhere but in the human mind.

CHAPTER SIX

i.

TERI TROSPER'S BODY came out of the ground in much better shape than her brother's had. "Her vault was sealed," Reese Bowen recalled, "so she looked like she'd just been buried the day before." That was a problem for Dr. Ralph Erdmann.

It was Erdmann who had performed the autopsy on Teri Trosper on the first day of June 1991. He was the best-known pathologist in West Texas, one who had testified at hundreds of criminal trials, including some of the highest-profile murder cases in state history. Erdmann had long been known as a friend to law enforcement. "Old-timers will tell you that Erdmann, before he started an autopsy, he'd ask 'em, 'What are you tryin' to prove?'" Reese Bowen said. "And then he'd do the autopsy, and it would back up what they wanted to prove."

No one realized just how extreme the shortcuts Erdmann was taking had become, though, until the day Teri Trosper was exhumed. Erdmann was one of two doctors who had been assigned to perform the "second autopsy." The other, Sparks Veasey, was a stickler for getting things right. "Veasey saw right away that all her organs were in place," Bowen remembered. "They hadn't been removed, which Erdmann had claimed in his autopsy he had done. His report had the weight of her brain, but her head hadn't been cut. It was obvious he hadn't really done an autopsy. Veasey looked at Erdmann and Erdmann looked at Veasey, and I think Erdmann knew in that moment he was over."

In his own autopsy report, Veasey detailed the false claims in Erdmann's original one. Two major incisions are made in autopsies, Veasey would later explain in court. One is a Y-shaped cut extending across the chest from shoulder to shoulder, then continuing in a straight line down the center of the abdomen to the pubis, so that the internal organs can be removed one by one. There was a Y-shaped cut on the corpse of Teri Trosper, Veasey noted, but none of the young woman's organs had been removed. The other major incision in an autopsy was made at the top of the skull, Veasey went on, cutting down through the scalp to the bone of the skull, so that the scalp can be pulled down over the front of the face, the front quadrant of the skull cut away, and the brain removed. There was no such cut at the top of Teri Trosper's skull.

"That was when the snowball formed," Bowen remembered, "and it just kept rollin'." Indeed it did. By the spring of 1992, the best-known journalist in Texas, Molly Ivins, had written a column that was being printed all over the country: "Good grief, they're digging up bodies all over the Panhandle," it began. "Turns out the man who has been performing autopsies for 40 Panhandle counties for most of the past 20 years has been exceedingly, ah, careless at best. He's being indicted all over the place, motions for retrial are being filed, prosecutors are re-examining old convictions, hundreds of cases are at stake and lawsuits are flying. It's a giant, collective 'Oops!'"

Recalled Bowen: "All of a sudden, our grand jury was the biggest news these parts had seen in—well, ever, really." It was also big news when Dr. Erdmann pleaded no contest to seven felonies and lost his medical license.

On December 29, 1991, the *Amarillo Globe-News* ran a banner headline across the front page of its year-end "roundup" edition that read, "Childress Stories Top '91 Headlines." An increasingly frightened and at times frenzied atmosphere enveloped the town. A television crew from Amarillo interviewed a local man who told them he had seen cult members dancing around bonfires on the banks of the Red

River. People circulated a handout from the Texas Department of Public Safety that had been intended for law officers only, listing thirty ways an investigator might determine if a person had been murdered as part of an occult ritual. District Attorney McCoy claimed publicly that he had been receiving death threats from people who warned him to shut the grand jury down, and breathlessly told *Texas Monthly*, "This is the stuff movies are made of."

The people in Childress had not even a vague apprehension that they were living through the last days of what the American media would before long be calling "the satanic panic." There would be arguments among pundits and arbiters about when it had begun, but the consensus was that the whole thing started in 1980, when a book called *Michelle Remembers* was published. Cowritten by Canadian psychiatrist Lawrence Pazder and his former patient and eventual wife Michelle Smith, *Michelle Remembers* had introduced the subjects of satanic ritual abuse and suppressed memory to the American public. The book is essentially the story of a girl introduced by her mother into "the Church of Satan," an institution that, according to Smith and Pazder, predates Christianity and has no connection to Anton LaVey's San Francisco–based Church of Satan. *Michelle Remembers* describes a five- and six-year-old girl who, during the years 1954 and 1955, was caged, tortured, sexually abused, compelled to witness a number of murders, and forced to participate in rituals in which she was rubbed with the blood and body parts of murdered babies and adults. The horror culminates in an eighty-one-day ritual in 1955 in which the Devil himself was summoned, and which, according to Smith, she survived only through the intervention of the Virgin Mary and the archangel Michael, who removed not only her physical scars but also her memories of what had happened to her, at least "until the time was right."

That time apparently was when, as a young woman, Smith began therapy with Pazder, a doctor who boasted impressive credentials, including membership in Canada's Royal College of Physicians and Surgeons. The combination of Pazder's resume and Smith's shocking story proved irresistible to the media in the United States, where *Michelle Remembers* was introduced with lengthy articles in *People* and the *National Enquirer*, leading to an eventual appearance on *The Oprah Winfrey Show*. The book was a sensation and a sensational success, despite an exposé in *Maclean's* magazine shortly after its publication. The author of the article, Paul Grescoe, interviewed Smith's father, who not only claimed he could refute every one of the allegations in the book but also vehemently defended Smith's mother, who was described by one of Smith's childhood friends as a kind and delightful woman.

Questions about Smith's book were at once subsumed and swept aside in 1983, though, when the McMartin preschool case exploded in the Los Angeles media. I was writing a column for the *Herald-Examiner* at the time, and although I stayed away from the McMartin case, an awareness of it was unavoidable. I recall that the story emerged in a way that made the early revelations appear quite convincing. The mother of a young student enrolled at the preschool had gone to the police with the story that when she questioned her son about his difficult bowel movements the boy told her he was being sodomized by McMartin teacher Raymond Buckey. Apparently the woman, Judy Johnson, had also told the police her son was being abused by her estranged husband, though I don't remember that being reported initially. Based on what she said she was being told by her son, Johnson's accusations became stranger and stranger: she told police her son said school administrator Peggy McMartin had "drilled a child under the arms" and that Ray Buckey "flew in the air." That wasn't reported initially, either. Buckey was arrested and questioned by police, but the district attorney's office declined to prosecute.

The Los Angeles Police Department followed up with a form letter sent to parents of children at the school that read:

> This Department is conducting a criminal investigation involving child molestation. Ray Buckey, an employee of Virginia McMartin's Pre-School, was arrested September 7, 1983 by this Department. The following procedure is obviously an unpleasant one, but to protect the rights of your children as well as the rights of the accused, this inquiry is necessary for a complete investigation. . . . Please question your child to see if he

or she has been a witness to any crime or if he or she has been a victim. Our investigation indicates that possible criminal acts include: oral sex, fondling of genitals, buttock or chest area, and sodomy, possibly committed under the pretense of 'taking the child's temperature.' Also, photos may have been taken of children without their clothing. Any information from your child regarding having ever observed Ray Buckey leave the classroom alone with a child during any nap period, or if they have ever observed Ray Buckey tie up a child, is important. Please complete the enclosed information form and return it to this Department in the enclosed stamped return envelope as soon as possible.

The response to this letter was, not surprisingly, panic among the parents. Hundreds of them contacted the LAPD, but many complained about the blunt approach police investigators took to questioning their children. The Los Angeles district attorney's office referred the parents to the Children's Center, a private therapy center that had been in business for eighty-six years and was widely respected. There, mostly in interviews with a social worker named Kee MacFarlane, the children poured out a series of extraordinary—and extraordinarily disturbing—stories. These were leaked to the public through a single reporter at the local ABC affiliate. He delivered scoop after scoop that shocked the local viewing public: stories of sex with animals, of orgies in a car wash, of a system of tunnels and hidden chambers under the school where children were taken to be sexually assaulted. Several children had described a "Naked Movie Star" game in which they were apparently photographed in the nude. What was not reported, at least for a very long time, was that MacFarlane had obtained descriptions of what had been done to them from the children by using an anatomically correct doll and what were ultimately judged to be extremely leading questions. Nor was it widely known that the ABC reporter and MacFarlane were romantically involved. Some of the more bizarre stories that MacFarlane had obtained from the children did gradually filter out into public, and these tales, such as one about children being flushed down toilets to secret rooms where they were sexually violated, then cleaned up and returned to their unsuspecting parents, gave people pause. But the overwhelming sense that surrounded the case between 1983 and 1985 was that the McMartin Preschool had been a house of horrors where a cabal of child molesters had committed unspeakable acts against the innocent.

At the same time the McMartin case was unfolding, and to a significant degree because of what was being reported about it, a belief in what would become known as satanic ritual abuse (or "SRA") spread through the mental health industry. All over the country "F.B.I. agents, police officers, lawyers and social workers gathered to share what they could," as the *New York Times* described it, "and shared their findings at conferences and seminars. They handed out satanic calendars, traded pamphlets about symbols like the 'cross of Nero' and the 'horned hand,' and copied lists of supposed occult organizations." These organizations were allegedly headed by a highly organized but extremely secretive group of wealthy and powerful individuals who arranged for children to be either abducted or bred to serve as human sacrifices, or to work in pornography and prostitution. At the same time, it was said, satanic cults were being formed in small towns all over the United States (towns like Childress, Texas) for the express purpose of conquering America through the corruption of its young in what had once been God-fearing communities.

The satanic panic (a phrase coined by sociologist Jeffrey Victor, drawing on the "moral panic" theories of Stanley Cohen) reached what now seems to have been both its apogee and its nadir in October 1987, when NBC broadcast a special hosted by Geraldo Rivera that was titled *Devil Worship: Exposing Satan's Underground.* The show began with Geraldo speaking directly into the camera: "Satanic cults! Every hour, every day, their ranks are growing. Estimates are there are over one million satanists in this country. The majority of them are linked in a highly organized, very secret network. From small towns to large cities, they've attracted police and FBI attention to their satanist ritual child abuse, child pornography, and grisly satanic murder. The odds are this is happening in your town."

While Kee MacFarlane was testifying before Congress, social worker Carol Darling was insisting to a grand jury that the satanic conspiracy included high government officials, and her police officer husband, Brad Darling, was addressing conferences about a satanic apparatus that dated to antiquity. Psychiatrist Roland Summit organized many such conferences and suggested that skeptics were part of the conspiracy. Michelle Smith and Lawrence Pazder met with the parents of McMartin Preschool students and helped them form what became the group Believe the Children, which became, among other things, a sort of clearinghouse for those who reported "recovered memories" of satanic ritual abuse.

The media was already cooling to the subject, in part because of the backlash against the Rivera documentary, but also because both the claims in *Michelle Remembers* and the case against the McMartin defendants were being picked apart by debunkers. London's *Mail on Sunday* published a lengthy article in which Smith's father enumerated the false statements he said had been made in his daughter's book and revealed that he had filed a notice of intent to sue that had prevented the book from being made into a film. The *Mail*'s reporters interviewed former neighbors of Smith who dismissed the book as "crazy" and "the hysterical ravings of an uncontrolled imagination." This was followed by a book in which the authors reported that they could find no newspaper record of the car crash described in *Michelle Remembers*, in spite of the fact that the local newspaper at the time reported all vehicle accidents. Interviews with former neighbors, teachers, and friends revealed that there was no evidence of Smith being absent from school for lengthy periods of time, which made the supposed eighty-one-day nonstop ceremony she described highly unlikely to have happened.

The slow collapse of the McMartin prosecution, though, was what most deflated the satanic panic. By the time of the Rivera special in 1987, those who followed the McMartin case had heard stories of children witnessing the mutilation of a corpse and the slow slaughter of a horse, of devil worshippers drinking blood and sacrificing a baby in a church. They had also, however, heard a newly elected Los

Angeles County district attorney in 1986 describe the evidence in the case as "incredibly weak," then announce that he was dropping charges against five of the seven defendants, including the preschool's founder, Virginia McMartin. The charges against the remaining defendants, Raymond Buckey and his mother, Peggy McMartin Buckey, would result in the longest criminal trial in US history. In the course of it, jurors would learn that despite an extensive investigation by the FBI and Interpol, none of the pornographic films that were supposedly the main purpose of the McMartin molestations had ever been located, and extensive archeological excavations had produced no evidence of tunnels or underground chambers beneath the preschool. Jurors also learned that Judy Johnson, the mother who had made the initial accusations in the case, had been diagnosed with mental illness (prosecutors said it had developed later, as a result of the stress and guilt she felt about allowing her child to attend a preschool where he was abused). The evidence was not entirely exculpatory, however. Doctors said that all of the eighteen children who had testified in the case showed medical evidence of sexual abuse. In 1990, Raymond Buckey and his mother were acquitted on all counts. Eleven of the thirteen jurors who spoke to the media afterward told reporters they believed Ray Buckey had molested children but that there had not been the proof beyond a reasonable doubt required to convict him on criminal charges.

During the years between the deaths of Tate Rowland and Teri Trosper, there was still a deeply held belief across much of America that satanic cults had taken root in the country's small towns, and this conviction was particularly powerful in Texas. The Dallas-based Cult Awareness Council had become perhaps the most active and influential anti-satanic organization in the United States. The Fort Worth Police Department had joined with the Texas Department of Public Safety and two dozen other law enforcement agencies in the state to form a secret task force meant to investigate reported occult activities. The city of Amarillo, just slightly more than a hundred miles from Childress, had assigned a pair of detectives to a national network of police investigators to investigate satanic crimes; the two regularly held one-hour seminars all over the US Southwest in which they displayed photographs of altars found in drainage tunnels where satanic graffiti covered the walls, of various grave desecrations, and of a house in Amarillo that had been vandalized by a satanic group that called itself "the Opposition."

In Childress, 450 people attended a presentation by "occult expert" Garvin McCarrell (the youth minister at Amarillo's Trinity Fellowship Church) in which he told those present about his meeting with a girl who had been raised by satanists. This young woman was eighteen years old, but looked forty, McCarrell told those present, and described to him rituals in which she had been made to drink a cocktail of drugs, blood, and urine before being sexually used and abused by a succession of adults. Later she had been prostituted to finance the group, the girl said, and at the same time had prepared to serve as a human sacrifice; a bone from her foot was removed for use in the ceremony. She had come to him only because she knew the moment when her life would be taken was coming soon and she wanted out, McCarrell told his audience. He made the girl promise that she would stay in touch with him, the minister went on, but six weeks later she had left town to meet up with the satanists in Albuquerque and he hadn't heard from her in more than a year.

Brenda Rowland was among those in McCarrell's audience. "He told us that these cult members could be anybody," she remembered, "from a upstanding lawyer to a doctor to all kinda people involved. It didn't have to be lowlife scum or nothin' like that. I had the heebie-jeebies sittin' there and listenin' to that. Man, if it hadn't gone on in a church, I wouldn't have been able to sit through it. It was that scary. I mean, I still had little girls at home."

The overheated atmosphere did not cool when, in March 1992, almost three years exactly after Michelle Gomez's drawings had been sent north from Lockhart, Ricky Bradford was arrested for the murder of Teri Trosper.

"SUICIDE OR MURDER? That's the Question," read the front-page headline on the September 30, 1991, edition of the *Childress*

Index. Actually, it was one of only several questions before the grand jurors who convened that morning, two months to the day after the exhumation of Tate Rowland's body. According to the *Index* article, the grand jury had been formed in response to the discovery of Elavil in the tissues of Tate's remains, along with evidence that photos of his body taken on the night of his death showed two separate rope burns, "which are not consistent with suicide."

It had taken the grand jurors only one week, though, to decide that their inquiry into the death of young Tate should be expanded to include the death of his sister Teri, after her body was disinterred on October 9. Their probe also should attempt to determine if a "satanic cult" had been involved in the deaths of either or both siblings, the jury had agreed.

Journalists flocked to Childress, a town so small that the movie theater was open only on Friday and Saturday nights. Television cameras were on the scene when Teri Trosper's casket was lifted from the ground, but, given that the grand jury was meeting in secret, reporters could only turn to the town's teenagers as their primary sources. *Texas Monthly* cataloged the stories the kids in town were telling: there was one about a boy eating pages from the Bible and foaming at the mouth, another about a lamb with its heart cut out that had been found near a cotton gin, and yet another about a local man who had proved he commanded the powers of Satan by pointing at a cat and commanding it to die. The cult was meeting at a mobile home factory, one report stated; no, it was a dry cleaning store where they gathered, said another.

Much was made in the media of the town's "association" with the 1974 horror film *Texas Chainsaw Massacre*. That connection consisted of little more than a line of dialogue from the movie in which a man pretending to help a terrified girl says, "There's no local phone here. We'll have to drive over to Childress." Somehow, though, the story became that the killer was *from* Childress. Lisa Littlejohn became a magnet for visiting reporters after she told one of them about the time when she was in the eighth grade and she and a bunch of other girls had watched *The Texas Chainsaw Massacre* during a slumber party at a house across from the cemetery. After the movie, they decided to take a walk through the graveyard, just to keep the creepy mood alive, and out of nowhere Tate Rowland and another boy appeared, both dressed in big old overalls and carrying chainsaws. "They chased us through the cemetery, all the way back home," Littlejohn remembered. The girl had told the tale to illustrate what "a joker" Tate was, but it took on an increasingly ominous ring as it was repeated in article after article.

Local teenagers led a camera crew to a spot on the shore of the Red River where they had found a pile of stones they believed were an altar, with what appeared to be some "burnt remains" of a sacrificed animal nearby. The *Amarillo Globe-News* ran a big article on its front page under the headline "Those Who Knew Childress Teen Don't Believe He Killed Himself." Brenda Rowland was quoted in the article saying, "I just know it wasn't a suicide. Somebody else was involved."

Brenda made no secret of her frustration at being unable to learn who was sitting on the grand jury and what they were hearing. Most of what she knew came from District Attorney McCoy, a man the reporters filling up the rooms at local motels had found to be the ideal sort of public official: one who enjoyed their attentions and liked to talk. Under a headline reading "Woman Was Smothered, Autopsy Shows," McCoy was quoted as saying, "It looks to me like [Teri] could have been held down by someone" while another person smothered her. After he described to another reporter the testimony of the teenagers who had gone to the cemetery to check out Tate's grave on the previous Halloween night, McCoy exclaimed, "It's getting more bizarre by the minute. But some of the loose ends seem to be coming together . . . It's strange, too many things just sort of fit together, but don't quite."

The district attorney seemed to especially enjoy talking about what he described as the "threats" being made against him. "Someone called up on the phone and said, 'If I were you, I would look out for my life,'" McCoy told one reporter, adding that he refused to be intimidated.

Most in town took an increasingly dim view of McCoy after he appeared on the Halloween edition of *The Maury Povich Show*. "He went on there and talked Tate down," Brenda Rowland remembered. "Said Tate was a smartass who always picked a fight but never won one. What sixteen-, seventeen-year-old boy isn't a smartass? This became a glory thing for McCoy. I didn't trust him."

Still, just about all she or anyone else in town knew about what was happening in the grand jury room was what the district attorney told reporters. Under a headline reading "As Indictment Nears Anxiety Is Mounting" in the October 29, 1991, edition of the *Index*, McCoy had described the testimony of Chad Johnston as of "little help." The boy had been "cocky" on the witness stand, McCoy told the *Index*, which reported that "the witness, who has given authorities at least four versions of what happened, on Monday claimed the rope used in hanging Rowland was already in the tree when he left Rowland to get a beer in the trunk of the car. The youth, now 18, said Rowland had hanged himself when he returned."

"A stocky Chad Johnston arrived, repeated his third hanging story and stuck to his claim that Tate's death was a suicide," another paper reported. "According to McCoy, 'Chad's testimony was that Tate thought Karen was messing with his mind and that Tate got sick of it. And Tate thought he could make her feel sorry.'" But the young man now had no explanation at all for the second rope mark on Tate's neck, McCoy had added.

Johnston had so far offered three different descriptions of what he knew about how Tate had hung himself, McCoy told a writer from *Accent West*, a magazine published in Amarillo. "One, he said Tate jumped from the bumper of the car. Second, he said Tate slid off the car. Third, he said he went to throw a beer can away and came back and found Tate hanging."

Kevin Overstreet also spoke to the *Accent West* writer, and his description of the "inconsistencies" in the stories Chad had told him didn't seem to exactly jibe with McCoy's. The first time he described the hanging, Overstreet said, Chad had claimed he watched Tate hang himself. "I still thought he was playing around until I saw the look on his face," the chief deputy described Chad as saying. "He had stopped smiling and laughing." But when he interviewed young Johnston a second time, Chad had said he was not looking when Tate hanged himself, according to Overstreet, and didn't know what was going on until he returned from "taking a leak" and "saw Tate hanging from a tree." Chad also had offered a new explanation for the two sets of rope marks on Tate's neck, Overstreet added: "He said Tate started jacking around with the rope by swinging around the tree with it." Everyone she talked to found it highly suspicious that Chad had told "seven or eight versions of what happened and wouldn't take a lie detector test," according to Brenda Rowland. She and most everyone else were confused by the testimony of a cotton farmer who said that while out plowing his field that afternoon, he had seen two boys come out to the "hanging tree," then leave—together.

Reporters, if no one else, enjoyed the "mounting anxiety" outside the jury room. Brenda Rowland and Tate's aunt, his biological mother's sister Brenda Stokes, got into an argument that turned into a shoving match and had to be separated. The "Battling Brendas" made good copy for reporters. So did the arrival of the Hackler family. Karen's daddy, James Ray Hackler, showed up wearing a big white cowboy hat and "thrust a briefcase" into the face of an Amarillo photographer just outside the entrance to the courthouse. Karen herself would say only she had testified that she knew nothing about a cult and that the whole family was there to clear their names. He and his family had been "the victims of lies," James Ray declared.

There were civic-minded folk in Childress who tried to get reporters to write about the football team or the local girl who had just recently finished as first runner-up in the Teenage Miss America pageant, but even to them it became clear that the deaths of Tate Rowland and his sister Teri were all the town could offer that was of interest to the media.

Through McCoy, word was leaking out that the grand jury seemed to be focusing more and more of its attention on the death of Teri Trosper and that the Wilks family was being implicated by the testimony of numerous witnesses. The Wilkses soon were receiving more attention from their neighbors than any of them had ever imagined possible. A line of teenagers in cars and trucks drove by the "Devil House" nightly after it was reported that, according to the testimony of one of the officers who had arrested Ray Wilks back in 1988, the boy had said he was there with a group of people when Tate was "sacrificed." Ray also said, "all of the cops were fooled by the way it was done," the officer had testified, and then boasted that he was "the son of the Devil and that no one could hurt him because he had given his soul to the Devil." Ray himself now insisted that he had no memory of telling police officers he had been part of a satanic group that sacrificed Tate Rowland. "I don't remember saying anything because I was so drunk," he explained, then denied any knowledge of Tate's death beyond what he had heard or read.

Not long after this, though, Ray's older brother Darwin had attempted suicide, leaving behind a note in which he wrote that he knew how Teri Trosper had really died and couldn't live with it. After being revived, Darwin said he didn't remember writing the note.

Darwin's best friend, Ricky Bradford, was also still under suspicion in the Teri Trosper case, McCoy and Overstreet separately told reporters, but without a witness who was at the Wilks house on the night of Teri's death, it was impossible to make a case.

The grand jury finished its deliberations just before Christmas without indicting anyone in the murders of either Tate Rowland or his sister Teri. The jurors, though, refused to certify Tate's death as a suicide or Teri's as accidental, recommending that local law enforcement continue to investigate each case.

With Sheriff Bowen's support, Overstreet was still probing both deaths as possible homicides, hoping that the continued application of pressure to Chad Johnston in the Tate Rowland case and to the Wilks brothers and Ricky Bradford in the Teri Trosper case might eventually yield results. And in the Trosper case it finally did.

Just before noon on March 6, 1992, Frank and Darwin Wilks arrived together at the Childress County Sheriff's Department, where they told Bowen and Overstreet that during a barbecue in their backyard during the previous evening, Ricky Bradford had admitted to the killing of Teri Trosper, then threatened to kill them too if they snitched. According to Darwin, Ricky had been provoked by questions he was being asked about Teri's death and had blurted out, "Yes, I killed the bitch." Immediately afterward, the father and son said, Ricky had promised to burn down Frank's house and cut out Darwin's eyes if they breathed a word about what he had said to anyone.

The morning edition of the *Witchita Times Record* reported on March 8 that "a 29-year-old man" had been arrested early the previous morning for the murder of Teri Trosper. In the same story, Kevin Overstreet was quoted as saying he had reached a dead end in his investigation into Tate Rowland's hanging. The people of Childress learned that Ricky Bradford had been arrested for Teri's murder when the *Index* reported it the following morning. The paper also quoted Bradford as claiming that he hadn't said a word to anyone in the Wilks family about Teri Trosper's death and that Darwin Wilks had "set me up" in order to collect the $1,000 reward being offered in the case and to cover his own guilt. In fact, Darwin *did* collect the reward, the *Index* was soon reporting. Also, just weeks before Ricky Bradford's arrest, Darwin had submitted to a polygraph examination in which the examiner found his answers to questions about whether he had been involved in the death of Teri Trosper to have been deceptive. "The cops were trying to frame me," Darwin would tell *Texas Monthly*. "But, hell, I was asleep that whole time she was supposed to have been killed."

As unlikely as it seemed that either the Wilkses or Ricky Bradford would have been part of a satanic cult that had been active in Childress back in 1988, Bradford's arrest had local people wondering if they really knew who anyone in town was. Just days after Bradford's arrest, a white cat with its heart cut out was found on a road just outside the city limits. Bowen and Overstreet drove out to take color photographs of the dead animal. "I don't know what it means," Bowen told *Texas Monthly*, "but it's got to mean something."

The Wilks and Bradford families, meanwhile, traded charges about who was satanic and who was not. Frank Wilks told police that Ricky had once boasted that he was "the Devil." Ricky's sister Leticia

Bloom, Ray Wilks's ex-girlfriend, told a reporter, "I've listened to Darwin say that he works for the Devil and knows the Devil personally." Ricky's younger brother Ronny Bradford chimed in, "Them Wilks brothers have been seen wearing black capes and doing Ouija boards and loading goats into a car. I ain't lyin'." Ronny also said that a group of young men who included Darwin Wilks had once asked him to join them in a graveyard to call up "spirits."

"Oh, shit," Darwin responded to *Texas Monthly*'s Hollandsworth. "Me and Ray do crazy things when we get pissed off at people. We say we're masters of Satan and we say horns are going to come out of our heads. But that's just having some fun. We don't believe in nothin'. We're atheists."

Rumors erupted just a short time later, though, when, while McCoy was preparing the murder charge against Ricky Bradford he would submit to the grand jury, the district attorney's house burned down under what the *Index* described as "mysterious" circumstances. The fire marshal would eventually rule that the fire was accidental, but McCoy wasn't necessarily buying that, telling a reporter, "Anything can be made to look accidental."

ii.

IT PERHAPS SAYS MORE about the problem of evil than anything else in modern history that the person who most effectively answered Voltaire, Diderot, and company was not a priest or a minister or a theologian who opposed their ideas but rather a man who fervently embraced their philosophy, applying it in his life with a commitment that was far more uncompromising than any of them would have dared.

I was sitting under a potted palm tree at a table in the airy bar of Santa Barbara's Biltmore hotel in the late summer of 2009 when it was first suggested to me that Donatien Alphonse François (1740–1814), better known as the Marquis de Sade, had served as the ultimate repudiation of the philosophes. I could not imagine a more unlikely person in a more improbable place speaking with such admiration of Sade than the trim and elegant septuagenarian who was seated across from me in the ludicrously opulent Ty Lounge. Jeffrey Burton Russell was describing the pivotal role he believed Sade had played in humanity's long struggle with the problem of evil. "Sade showed people like Diderot and Baron d'Holbach what they were actually saying," Russell observed with the combination of piercing stare and pleasant expression that was one of the several things I liked about him. "And they were horrified."

As he spoke, the recently retired history professor and I seemed to become isolated from the languid, breathy chatter of the rich and beautiful who surrounded us by some invisible bubble that descended from the palm fronds overhead. A compact man with impeccably groomed silver hair and a matching mustache, Russell was and remains one of the least acknowledged great scholars of the twentieth century. He had been raised in Berkeley and educated there, become a professor of history at Notre Dame, then settled at the University of California at Santa Barbara. In this pastel paradise, Russell took up sailing. One evening, sitting aboard his boat as it floated near the Channel Islands, he watched the sun sinking below the western horizon and was struck by the realization that men had been seeing the same sight for thousands of years. How then, he wondered, could they ever have imagined the world was flat? The answer, he would discover, was that they hadn't. The controversy surrounding the 1492 voyage of Christopher Columbus, Russell's investigation revealed, was not about the shape of the earth but rather about its circumference. Almost no one at the time Columbus discovered the Americas believed the earth was flat, and the few who did were considered cranks. Medieval literature, Russell found, was full of references to a spherical earth. In the middle of the thirteenth century, Thomas Aquinas had used the statement "The world is round" as an example of something so obvious it needed no proof. So where had the idea that our unenlightened forbearers had believed in a flat earth come from? Russell's research led him to the conclusion that the claim had first been put forth during the early nineteenth century by the American author Washington Irving, who had used it to mock the anti-scientific attitudes of religious believers.

In the decades since, millions of schoolchildren, newspaper readers, radio listeners, and television viewers had heard the flat earth story used to illustrate the ignorance imposed upon previous generations by Christian dogma. Anyone familiar with the works of Dante or Roger Bacon, let alone those of Aquinas, knew it wasn't true, but the story had gone not only uncorrected, Russell determined, but largely unchallenged, mainly because people in academia and media found it so useful in demonstrating the dim-witted intellectual bigotry of the religious.

The book *Inventing the Flat Earth* became for both Russell and his readers an astonishing account of how easily a lie can be substituted for truth when it confirms the prejudices of those who control the cultural apparatus. He had observed a similar phenomenon, only in a much more personal and hurtful way, Russell told me, as he worked his way through the magisterial five-volume "conceptual history" of the Devil that was his masterpiece, in the process converting to Catholicism and becoming one of the very few people of his stature in the academic world prepared to state that he believed there was, in fact, an actual Devil. Russell recalled a public address he had made at the university in the 1990s. At one point he had used the word "evil" to describe some mass murderer, Russell said, and was promptly interrupted by loud objections from the audience. I could see the residue of shock and hurt in the professor's face as he described the vehemence of the attack on him. "People told me it was an entirely inappropriate word to use in an academic setting," he remembered, "that it imposed some sort of religious value system that was contrary to the university mission and that offended them personally. They said I should have used the word 'sick.' They were actually angry. Some of them shouted at me."

Russell had used his injured feelings to fuel work on the most compelling of his five volumes, *Mephistopheles*, in which he had offered the Marquis de Sade as the ultimate rebuttal to those who denied moral absolutes. "One must give [Sade] credit for taking the principles of atheistic relativism to their logical conclusions," Russell had written. "Where Diderot and Holbach stopped on the brink of the chasm, Sade enthusiastically hurled himself in."

Sade drew on the horrors he had witnessed in war and in peace to argue that if God exists, "he must be more vicious than the worst of criminals," Russell observed. We should be grateful that this God people spoke of was merely a phantom of the human imagination, Sade had maintained, and anyway, belief in the supernatural served only to divert human beings from their true calling: plumbing the depths of vice.

In an intrinsically valueless world, Sade contended, the only sensible course was the pursuit of pleasure: If you enjoy torture, well and good. If others do not enjoy torture, they need not engage in it, but they have no business imposing their own tastes upon you. Violations of the so-called moral laws are not only permissible but actually commendable, because they demonstrate the artificiality of such restraints, restraints that serve only to obstruct the exalted striving toward the satisfaction of one's appetites.

Sade's philosophy could be boiled down to a single sentence, Russell had written in *Mephistopheles*: "The greater the pleasure, the greater the value of the act." Sexual pleasures should be pursued with absolute abandon, Sade had insisted, and since crime could provide an even more intense experience, the greatest satisfaction one could obtain was to combine sex and crime. For Sade, "the greatest pleasure comes from torture, especially of children," Russell explained. "If one humiliates and degrades the victim, the delight is further enhanced. Cannibalism, for some, may add to the intensity of the experience. And the purest joy, exceeding even sexual pleasure, is to commit crime purely for its own sake in a gratuitous act of what the ignorant call evil."

I found myself simultaneously smiling and shaking my head as Russell seemed to extol Sade for the courage of his convictions. The professor paraphrased what he had written in *Mephistopheles*: "Sade forces us to face the dilemma. Either there are grounds of ultimate concern, grounds of being by which to judge actions, or not. Either the cosmos has meaning, or not. If not, Sade's arguments are right. Sade is the legitimate outcome of true atheism, by which I mean a denial of any ground of ultimate being."

Much as I admired Russell, willing as I was to concede that he was the more learned man, something seemed to be missing from his analysis of Sade. It sounded as if the professor believed that because of the way Sade lived his "philosophy," the marquis had exhibited an intellectual integrity lacking among the likes of Diderot. There might be truth to that, but it was also true, according to any number of the prostitutes whom he abused, that Sade had exhibited a violent opposition to the deity he claimed did not exist. A young woman named Jeanne Testard would testify that as soon as she entered the room to where she was summoned by Sade, he demanded to know if she was a practicing Roman Catholic. When she said yes, Testard recalled, Sade began to hurl a stream of obscene invective her way, masturbating into a chalice as he called Jesus Christ "you motherfucker." Moments later, the young prostitute said, Sade had inserted two communion hosts into her vagina, then entered her himself, screaming at the top of his lungs, "If thou art God, avenge thyself!" This and countless other similar incidents suggested to me a person who did not dismiss the existence of God so much as vindictively defy it. Sade had not simply shown Diderot and the atheist cohort the range of choices available in a world where there was no such thing as a spiritual truth or a moral absolute; he had also demonstrated how a man might live if he was prepared to choose the Devil over God. The Devil, "more powerful than this villainous God, a being still in possession of his power, forever able to brave his author," Sade had written, "incessantly succeeds, by his seduction, in debauching the herd that the Eternal reserved unto himself."

Confronted by Sade, even the most committed of the era's avowed atheists flinched. Those who fell back on ideas such as social consensus and legal tradition to deplore the marquis were ultimately forced to acknowledge that these were arbitrary standards under which the only compelling reason not to commit a terrible act was a fear of being caught. Unable to engage the problem of evil in any penetrating way, they covered their retreat in ad hominem arguments as they withdrew from the discussion. The void this created had to be filled, and so along came the Romantics, who reversed the traditional cosmology by embracing both a God and a Devil who were created in man's image, not the other way around.

DURING THE SEVENTEENTH and eighteenth centuries, Baruch Spinoza and the philosophes who declared the Enlightenment seemed to have achieved a marginalization of the Devil that bordered on eradication. And yet in the early nineteenth century there Satan was again, front and center in the works of the great Romantic poets.

Lord George Gordon Byron (1788–1824) and his friend Percy Bysshe Shelley (1792–1822) had inherited John Milton's Satan from William Blake (1757–1827). Blake's layered, luminous watercolor illustrations of *Paradise Lost*, produced while Byron and Shelley were in their teens, were immensely admired among the rebellious youth of the English aristocracy in the early 1800s. Even more admired, though, were the poetic mediations upon Milton's Satan in Blake's *The Marriage of Heaven and Hell*. What Blake and Shelley especially appreciated was Blake's recognition that the Satan portrayed in the first two books of *Paradise Lost* was a far more compelling literary figure than the God who was the main character in the third and final book. "The reason Milton wrote in fetters when he wrote of Angels and God, and at liberty when of Devils and Hell, is because he was a true Poet and of the Devil's party without knowing it," Blake declared. Blake had framed his proposed union of heaven and hell as an argument that both "good" (reason) and "evil" (passion) were necessary to a full human life, the tension between the two compelling an individual spirit—that is to say, a soul—to the condition of personal excellence.

While Milton's portrait of Satan had become the preeminent one, even among many ministers and theologians, so had his description of hell. In the poetic imagination, however, it was still perhaps superseded by the one offered in Dante Alighieri's thirteenth-century masterpiece *Inferno*. Unlike Milton, Dante (1265–1321) had created a hell with a landscape—more than that, an actual geography: nine circles descending from Limbo at the top, where various unbaptized and virtuous pagans (the poet Virgil among them) dwelled, down through the rings filled with the Lustful, the Gluttons, the Greedy, the Wrathful, the Heretics, the Violent, the Fraudulent, and finally, at the bottom, the Traitorous. Satan himself dwelled in this ninth circle of hell, a gigantic, slimy, pus-filled demon with bat-like wings who was frozen in ice, with three faces in which his three mouths chewed eternally on those Dante had identified as the greatest traitors in history, Brutus, Cassius, and Judas Iscariot.

The hell of *Paradise Lost* was not Dante's frozen realm, but rather a "lake of fire," which Milton described thusly:

> *The dismal situation waste and wild:*
> *A dungeon horrible, on all sides round,*
> *As one great furnace flamed; yet from those flames*
> *No light, but rather darkness visible*
> *Served only to discover sights of woe,*
> *Regions of sorrow, doleful shades, where peace*
> *And rest can never dwell, hope never comes*
> *That comes at all; but torture without end*
> *Still urges, and a fiery deluge, fed*
> *With ever-burning sulphur unconsumed.*
> *Such place Eternal Justice had prepared*
> *For those rebellious; here their prison set,*
> *As far removed from God and light of Heaven*

Dante's Satan had been a rather pathetic figure, sobbing perpetually and unable to speak because he had to chew unceasingly on the great traitors, a sort of passive figure who was little more than the instrument of God's justice—not the one who tempted people to sin, but simply the one who carried out the punishments they deserved. Milton, though, had made the Devil into the ultimate agent of free will, the final proof that God had given both humans and angels the capacity to choose between good and evil, between obedience and defiance. Milton's Satan was an active rebel leader, delivering eloquent speeches that roused the other angels to rise up against the God he called a tyrant.

First Blake and then later Byron and Shelley thrilled to Milton's portrait of Satan, insisting that he, not God, was the true protagonist of *Paradise Lost*. Blake actually dared to offer descriptions of hell that made it seem a rather inviting place. In one passage of *The Marriage of Heaven and Hell*, Blake described "walking among the fires of hell, delighted with the enjoyments of Genius; which to Angels look like torment and insanity." In another passage, hell was a pleasant riverbank with a harpist who sang by moonlight to celebrate the faculty of doubt. Perhaps even more shocking to early nineteenth-century readers, though, was Blake's description of heaven as a house of chained monkeys eternally raping and devouring one another, filled with sanctimony that was a transparent mask over the cynical lust for power that had created the bishophrics and magistratures of the Church.

What Byron, Shelley, and the other Romantics loved best about *The Marriage of Heaven and Hell*, though, were Blake's "Proverbs of Hell." Among these were: "The road of excess leads to the palace of wisdom"; "Prudence is a rich ugly old maid courted by Incapacity"; and "You never know what is enough unless you know what is more than enough." No passage of Blake's poem more inspired Byron and Shelley than these lines:

> *Those who restrain desire, do so because theirs is weak enough*
> *   to be restrained; and the*
> *restrainer or reason usurps its place & governs the unwilling.*
> *And being restrained, it by degrees becomes passive, till it is only*
> *   the shadow of desire.*

Byron and Shelley were even more ardent than Blake in extolling Milton's Satan as a heroic figure. Byron in particular made Milton's Devil into a model for his own protagonists, who were invariably intelligent, moody, passionate, cruel, haunted, alienated, self-destructive,

cynical, conflicted, defiant, and arrogant, even as they struggled he-
roically against tyranny on behalf of hope for a better world. Shelley, in his short essay "On the Devil and Devils," wrote: "Milton's
Devil is a moral being far superior to God as one who perseveres in
some purpose he has conceived to be excellent, in spite of adversity
and torture, is to one who in the cold security of undoubted triumph
inflicts the most horrible revenge upon his enemy—not from any
mistaken notion of bringing him to repent of a perseverance in enmity, but with the open and alleged design of exasperating him to
deserve new torments."

While Blake identified himself publicly as a Christian (even
though most contemporaries saw him as a heretical madman), Byron
and Shelley did not. They rejected outright the dogma of original sin
yet found the evidence of evil in the world so overwhelming that they
felt it had to be accounted for. This led Byron to the belief that the
creator himself was not good. Even as the two young poets rejected
the Christian Devil (on the basis that all one can know is the product
of the human mind), they saw Satan as a necessary figure, for aesthetic
and psychological purposes, if no others, because some actual figure
was required to express the reality of evil. And yet both men insisted
that Satan should also be the symbol of the progressive spirit rising
against the established forces of repression, those who ran the show
in Blake's "dark Satanic mills."

Their "audacious impiety" inspired the poet Robert Southey to
declare that Byron and Shelley were the founders of what he called
"the Satanic School" of literature. While Southey had intended this
as a term of opprobrium, Byron delighted in it, and as well in Southey's description of him as the author of "monstrous combinations of
horrors and mockery, lewdness and impiety."

While England cradled the notion that Satan could be interpreted as a Romantic protagonist, the idea soon began taking root on
the European continent. In Germany, Johann Wolfgang von Goethe's
theatrical reinterpretation of the Faust legend offered not only a protagonist driven by motivations far beyond mere carnality but also a

Devil who was much more ambiguous than any who had taken the stage before him. The play begins with a distant refrain of the Job story, in which a devil (not necessarily *the* Devil) who is called Mephistopheles strikes a wager with God for the soul of the deity's most beloved human being, the scholar Faust, who has set himself the task of learning all that can ever be known. Faust is then found in his study, where he has begun to despair at the vanity of human endeavors and turns to alchemical magic to find infinite knowledge. Failed and frustrated, he contemplates suicide, but rejects the idea when he hears Easter celebrations beginning in the streets outside. He goes for a walk and is followed home by a poodle that transforms into Mephistopheles and proposes an arrangement whereby he will do all that the scholar asks while on earth in exchange for a promise that Faust will serve him in hell.

Faust's Mephistopheles is a character filled with contradictions that he claims do not actually exist, at once the opponent of God and the instrument through which God instructs mankind. He is presented as the champion of a natural world in which good and evil are superfluous concepts on the one hand, and essential ingredients on the other. He is science unsettling religion, creative chaos overturning ossified order. And Faust himself, at the conclusion of Part Two of the play (finished by Goethe a quarter century after Part One), ascends to heaven as angels declare, "He who strives on and lives to strive / Can earn redemption still."

The Romantic Satan was introduced in France by François-René de Chateaubriand, but the Devil that Chateaubriand created in his prose poem *The Martyrs* was a sniveling creature who inspired neither admiration nor astonishment but merely a desire to slap him around a little. The great novelist Victor Hugo created a far more compelling Romantic Satan, embodied by a powerful and monstrous king of Judea named Nimrod, who, after laying waste to the earth, aspires to conquer heaven, building a cage to which he ties four giant eagles, using the meat of dead lions dangling above their heads to draw them upward into the sky. What made the Devil who emerged in

Hugo's epic poem *The End of Satan* so unique was the author's insistence that the characteristics of evil are not simply pride and cruelty but also loss, regret and loneliness. A determined universalist who believed in a God of infinite mercy, Hugo produced a Satan who deep down aspired to a redemption that would ultimately be achieved and served as a metaphor for the human longing to transcend its stupidity and selfishness. A Devil who is on our side.

CHAPTER SEVEN

i.

A CASE AGAINST RICKY LEWAYNE BRADFORD that at first looked open-and-shut was complicated by an almost constant churn of charges and countercharges directed at and from the key witnesses. The sheriff's department and the district attorney's office also were receiving a steady stream of anonymous letters that made criminal accusations against at least a dozen local people in connection to the deaths of Tate Rowland and Teri Trosper. "We knew most of those letters were bogus as soon as we read them," recalled Kevin Overstreet, "but they still forced us to do some investigating, which was exhausting."

More than twenty years later, Brenda Rowland still had a copy of one of those letters, which, based on the grammar and spelling, both she and Overstreet assumed had come from a member of the Bradford family. "But you couldn't be sure, so you had to wonder if there was anything to it," she recalled.

It was a time when paranoia seemed to be a communicable disease, as Reese Bowen recalled it: "Childress was so thick with suspicion and denial during that time that it seemed like everybody in town was either looking over his shoulder or trying to sweep something under the rug."

The main thing that people were denying, in the sheriff's opinion, was the certainty that there truly had been a satanic cult of some sort operating in the community. "There was just too much evidence to deny it," Bowen said. "Too much to deny, but not enough to be sure about just how big the whole thing was. And like Overstreet says, it had mainly moved on from here, so we were chasing something that more had been than was. But a lot of people in Childress, especially in the business community, they wanted to pretend the whole thing was some made-up story."

What the Chamber of Commerce knew to be absolutely real was that people passing through Childress—the economic lifeblood of the town—were stopping by city hall and the police department to ask if it was safe to drive out on Highway 83 after dark. And business owners in town were furious when it appeared in print that a reporter from the Amarillo paper had refused to cover the Ricky Bradford trial unless he was permitted to carry a pistol during the week he would be staying in Childress.

The same people cringed as the media swarmed the small town during the trial. As an article in the *Index* put it, "One newspaper sent four members of its reporting staff. Magazine writers remained throughout the four-day event. Television labeled the trial, on a daily basis, among its top stories."

Reporters from every part of the state who were in attendance enjoyed the way that Billy Don Hinton was made into a buffoon by District Attorney McCoy's interrogation. Hinton was preceded to the standby former police officer Ricardo Campos, who described finding Teri Trosper face down on one of the several mattresses spread out across the living room floor, with "bloodstains near the mouth and vaginal areas" and bruises on her right arm, armpit, and elbow. He and the other officer on the scene immediately assumed Ms. Trosper had been murdered, Campos testified, but did not take photographs or fingerprints, or undertake any real investigation, after being told by Chief Hinton to await the results of Ralph Erdmann's autopsy. When he got Hinton on the stand, McCoy let the ex-chief testify that he saw nothing suspicious about the blood near Trosper's vagina or mouth, or about the bruises, either, because of a suicide note found at the scene. "Everyone in the house told you it was not a murder and you believed them?" McCoy asked. "Yes, sir," Hinton answered. "Is that typically the way you handle an investigation?" McCoy asked. "No, sir," Hinton replied over the audience's giggles. What about when Darwin Wilks had attempted suicide several weeks later and Officer Randall Hendricks, who was called to the scene, found a note written by Wilks that read, "I know something the cops don't know. I know who killed Terrie and I can't live with it"? Had he still been determined not to treat Teri Trosper's death as a murder? asked McCoy. "That's right," Hinton answered.

The most important witness turned out to be a young woman named Betty Lewis, who testified that while lying awake on a mattress nearby she had seen Ricky Bradford smother Teri Trosper with a pillow. Lewis was a party girl who made Teri seem demure by comparison, as Sheriff Bowen recalled it, but "she cleaned up real well, and when she took the stand you'd'a thought she was pure as driven snow. And she spoke pretty good, too. The jury was real impressed by her."

One of Ricky Bradford's cousins, Renee Downing, claimed to possess a tape recording on which Betty Lewis had denied ever seeing Ricky smother Teri. The tape itself was not admitted because much of it was inaudible, but Downing was permitted to testify about what was on it. "The jury wasn't much interested," Bowen recalled. "They liked Betty Lewis."

On September 3, 1992, the Thursday before Labor Day, Ricky Bradford was convicted of capital murder by a jury that had required less than an hour of deliberations. His life sentence made him eligible for parole after fifteen years. Bowen and Overstreet drove him to the prison at Huntsville on September 8.

"On the one hand there was some relief, because a person who was responsible for Teri's death was being sent away to prison," Brenda Rowland recalled, "but on the other hand, I thought, and so did most everybody else, that there was others involved in Teri's death besides Ricky Bradford. And they never did make no kind of case that connected Tate's death to hers. So you had this feeling that things was only partly settled. There was still a lot we didn't know."

ii.

IF FRANCE HAD LAGGED behind Britain in the creation of a Romantic Devil, it would lead the way in ushering in a literary movement that contemplated sin, salvation, and Satan himself at a depth that neither Byron nor Shelley had ever approached. The Decadents, as they would be called, also produced at least one poet who wrestled with the problem of evil so intensely that he made the theologians of his day irrelevant by comparison.

What distinguished the Decadents was the seemingly impossible blend of resignation and fervor with which they embraced mankind's fallen state. Their position seemed to be that they were members of "the Devil's party," as Blake had described it, because it was the only one that would take them as they were. The corollary was that only by savoring the sweet poisons of the nether regions could a man obtain true knowledge of what being himself meant.

Their movement had taken its name from the way various Parisian critics and journalists had scornfully derided them as "decadent." The poet Charles Baudelaire (1821–1867), along with his acolyte Paul Verlaine (1844–1896), was the first to declare that they should wear the label "Decadent" proudly. Baudelaire had previously been considered a Romantic, as had the writer who most fascinated and inspired him, Edgar Allan Poe (1809–1849). Poe became the first American author who was more popular in Europe than in his own country largely as a result of Baudelaire's translations of his work from English into French. Beneath the gloom and morbidity of Poe's tales ("The Fall of the House of Usher" was particularly influential), Baudelaire discovered the most sublime aesthetic of the epoch, one in which the imagination "is a virtually divine faculty that apprehends immediately, by means lying outside philosophical methods, the intimate and secret relation of things, the correspondences and analogies," as the Parisian poet wrote in his slim volume *Further Notes on Edgar Poe*. In "Usher," Poe brought a decaying mansion terrifyingly to life and created an inhabitant whose isolation and melancholy only served to deepen his perception of what was taking place beneath the surface of things. The presence of a supernatural evil was palpable but never ascribed. Poe did not need to mention the Devil to imply his presence.

For all that he adored Poe and the other great Romantic writers who had preceded him, though, Baudelaire was separated from them by the depth and intensity of his preoccupation with a moral dilemma that had been in no way resolved by the supposed breakthroughs of the Enlightenment. He could neither dismiss nor obviate the questions that had been raised in his mind by the Catholicism he had abandoned as a young man, Baudelaire admitted. And the problem of evil was at the forefront. Baudelaire scoffed at the scientific materialism that was the foundation of August Comte's positivism. Comte's formulations ("Induction for deduction, with a view to construction") were to Baudelaire both patently absurd and utterly pathetic, the sort of weak nonsense that could be spouted by only the most pompous boor. And atheism, Baudelaire found, offered no means of addressing what he regarded as both the most disturbing and the most profound aspect of the human condition: the undeniable existence of evil. The terrible images and destructive impulses that arose without warning in his own mind shocked him, and the poet could find no explanation for them other than that they must be the product of some inhuman intelligence or power. "I have always been obsessed by the impossibility of accounting for certain sudden human actions or thoughts without the hypothesis of an evil external force," he wrote to his friend, the great novelist Gustave Flaubert.

Observing the antics of the author George Sand and hearing that she had denied the existence of the Devil, Baudelaire acidly observed that it was to Sand's clear advantage if the Devil and hell did not exist.

During the composition of his masterwork, *Les Fleurs du Mal* (The flowers of evil), Baudelaire seemed to use the Devil alternately as his elusive subject, his leering muse, his fierce opponent, and his sardonic companion. The dedication was written to his friend, the critic and parodist Théophile Gautier:

> *The Devil is at my side;*
> *He swims around me like an impalpable air;*

I swallow him and feel him burning my lungs,
Filling them with an eternal, guilty desire.

The poet began the work with his famous address, "To the Reader," in which he wrote:

It is the Devil who holds the reins and makes us go:
We find charm in the most repulsive objects;
Each day we take one more step into Hell,
Numb to horror, through stinking shadows . . .
If rape, poison, the dagger, arson,
Have not yet embroidered upon us their pleasing designs
The recurrent canvas of our pitiable destinies,
It is that our spirit, alas, is not brave enough . . .
Reader, you recognize this delicious monster,
Hypocrite reader, my likeness, my brother!

Later, in his story "The Generous Gambler," Baudelaire penned what has become the modern era's most quoted—or at least most paraphrased—epigram on Satan and his wiles (and the one from which the title of this book is drawn): "My dear brothers, never forget when you hear the progress of the Enlightenment praised, that the Devil's loveliest ruse is to persuade you that he doesn't exist."

Not only their work but the very lives of Baudelaire and the De-cadents who followed in his wake were fraught with tension between spiritual yearning and attraction to the diabolical. Remarkably, one after another ended with a deathbed conversion. Baudelaire's health began to fail in his thirties, ravaged by poverty, stress, heavy drinking, addiction to opiates, and the syphilis he had contracted from the pros-titute who had been his lover. His life, the poet wrote to his mother on his thirty-third birthday, had been "damned from the beginning." Yet as the life of his body waned, Baudelaire cleaved to the religion he had rejected as a youth, attending Catholic mass almost daily and consulting with various priests. His final journal entry, shortly before his death at the age of forty-six, was a list of the "immutable rules" by which he proposed to find order and comfort: "To pray every morning to God, the source of all power and all justice, to Mariette, and to Poe, as intercessors; that they may give me the necessary strength to fulfill all my appointed tasks." As Baudelaire lay dying after a massive stroke, a priest was summoned to administer last rites. It had been his final request when he still had the power of speech.

Paul Verlaine, who had assumed the mantle of leadership within the movement, and coined the term by which he and the others were best known, *poètes maudits* (cursed poets), was the closest thing the Decadents had to a pedagogue, arguing that a man who would be complete must acknowledge both the angel and the demon that dwelled within him. He was forced to yield his religious impulses to his sensual ones, Verlaine insisted, so that he might "give voice to the Beast within me." Verlaine and his young apprentice, Arthur Rimbaud (1854–1891), made a public spectacle of their homosexual love affair, drunkenness, and drug abuse. The relationship came to a climax when Verlaine shot Rimbaud during a lovers' quarrel in Brussels, and afterward Verlaine was sentenced to two years in a Belgian prison. While behind bars, he experienced a conversion that was even more pronounced than Baudelaire's. Inside, he wrote a book of poems, called *Sagesse* (Wisdom), that included many proclaiming his new religiosity. In one of them, "Écrit en 1875" (Written in 1875), Verlaine celebrated his incarceration as a blessing:

> *O blessed, fortress which I left*
> *Ready for life, armed with sweetness and provided*
> *With Faith, bread and salt and a coat for the road*
> *So lonely, so hard and so long, no doubt,*
> *On which one must strive for the innocent heights.*
> *And may the author of grace be loved, forever!*

For the next twenty years, Verlaine struggled to hold purchase on the renewed Catholic faith he had found in prison. He read Teresa of Ávila and Thomas Aquinas, translated English church hymns, and taught at a Catholic boarding school. He continued to drink himself unconscious nightly, however, and eventually fell in love with one of his male students, then lost his job. On his deathbed, though, Verlaine too would summon a priest to administer last rites, declaring with his final breaths that he renounced Satan and submitted his soul to Jesus.

Rimbaud saw Verlaine only once after the older man's release from prison, and at the time mocked his former lover's religious conversion. The unrepentant apostasy that fueled the most precocious output of poetry in modern literature, all of it written before Rimbaud turned twenty-one, was a large part of what made him the most influential nineteenth-century poet of the late twentieth century, a significant influence on artists who included Bob Dylan. His major work was *Une saison en enfer* (A season in hell). He wrote, "Dear Satan, don't look so annoyed, I beg you! And while waiting for a few belated cowardices, since you value in a writer all lack of descriptive or didactic flair, I pass you these few foul pages from the diary of a Damned Soul."

In it, Rimbaud produced passages that celebrated being damned in ways not even William Blake had dared:

> *I have just swallowed a terrific mouthful of poison.*
> *Blessed, blessed the advice I was given! My guts*
> *   are on fire. The power of the poison twists my arms and*
> *legs, cripples me, drives me to the ground. I die of*
> *   thirst, I suffocate, I cannot cry. This is Hell, eternal*
> *torment! See how the flames rise! I burn as I ought to. Go*
> *   on Devil?*
> *   I once came close to a conversion to the good and to felicity,*
> *salvation. How can I describe my vision, the air of*
> *   Hell is too thick for hymns! There were millions of*
> *beautiful creatures in smooth spiritual harmony, strength*
> *   and peace, noble ambitions, and I don't know what all.*
>
> *And as the Damned soul rises, so does the fire.*
> *O Purity! Purity!*

In this moment of awakening, I had a vision of purity!
Through the mind we go to God!
What a crippling misfortune!

Those who teach his poetry at universities rarely mention that before his death from either cancer or syphilis (or both) at the age of thirty-seven, Rimbaud made a conversion to Catholicism that was every bit as passionate as Verlaine's. The Austrian novelist and poet Thomas Bernhard, writing on the hundredth anniversary of Rimbaud's death, quoted a priest who declared that he had been shaken to the core by the reverence for God that the former *poète maudit* displayed on his deathbed: "I have never seen such strong faith!"

The English Decadents died the same way, almost to a man. Oscar Wilde (1854–1900) had mocked when his former collaborator and fellow Decadent Aubrey Beardsley (the same artist who once remarked that "Nero set the Christians on fire, like large yellow tallow candles; the only light the Christians have ever been known to give") converted to Catholicism while dying of tuberculosis. Wilde had made his reputation by flouting the Judeo-Christian tradition. Along with Algernon Charles Swinburne, W. B. Yeats, and Aleister Crowley, Wilde had joined the occultist Hermetic Order of the Golden Dawn (in which Yeats took the name "Demon est Deus Inversus," meaning "the Devil is God inside out"). During the two years he spent in an English prison after being sentenced for "acts of gross indecency with fellow male persons," though, Wilde devoted himself to reading the works of St. Augustine and Dante's *Inferno*. Immediately upon his release, he asked the Jesuits to permit him a six-month retreat at one of their London houses and wept when he was refused. Despite this, on his deathbed in Paris in 1900, Wilde sent his young lover Robbie Ross to summon a priest who would baptize him as a Catholic. "The contemplation of evil, and of the Devil, was what drove them back to the Church," Jeffrey Burton Russell would write of the Decadents almost a century later.

Perhaps no conversion story offers more proof of Russell's assertion than that of an author not nearly so celebrated today as he was at the height of the Decadent movement. J.-K. Huysmans (1848–1907) is the only man who ever lived to be simultaneously extolled by the *Global Encyclopedia of Gay, Lesbian, Bisexual, Transgender and Queer Culture* (as a man "who exemplified a style of homosexuality at a pivotal moment in the emergence of a gay identity") and by the *Catholic Encyclopedia* (as an unusually pious convert who "fought indefatigably for his faith"). Huysmans was also the founder of the Goncourt Academy, a thirty-two-year employee of the French Ministry of Interior, and the author of an exposé that shook all of Europe with its depiction of a Black Mass orchestrated by a vast cabal of influential satanists.

Huysmans had begun his literary career as a realist, championed by Émile Zola, on whom he turned (rather viciously) when he switched his allegiance to Verlaine and the Decadents. In 1884 he published what was considered at the time the supreme fictional work of the Decadent movement, *À Rebours* (Against nature), a black comedy in which a wealthy aesthete, Duc Jean des Esseintes, celebrates his dissipation with a series of erotic experiments that grow increasingly perverse, dreams of the historical progress of syphilis, withdraws to a house filled with art that he uses as a protection against reality, then abandons himself to perhaps the most elaborate chain of fantasies, nightmares, and visions ever put to paper. Oscar Wilde would write of *À Rebours* that "the heavy odour of incense seemed to cling about its pages and to trouble the brain." In *The Portrait of Dorian Gray*, Wilde would describe his title character as "poisoned by a book." Wilde later admitted that he had been inspired to write *Dorian Gray* after reading *À Rebours*.

Huysmans was perhaps the leading figure in the Decadent movement when he began working on the book that eventually would be published as *Là-Bas* (The damned). He had intended to explore the career of a man who fascinated the Decadents, Gilles de Rais, a fifteenth-century French marshal who was briefly associated with Joan of Arc but became better known as a child molester and mass murderer, eventually executed for satanism. Huysmans researched the book by studying medieval witchcraft and demonology, then moved on to the reported Black Masses conducted during the reign of Louis XIV before eventually deciding that he must involve himself with the satanists of his own time. He proceeded with this part of the project by enlisting the aid of his friend Jules Bois, a journalist who had startled France with a series of reports about an occult subculture of devil worshippers operating in France and Belgium. Bois sent Huysmans to Bruges to visit the infamous canon Louis van Jacke, reputed to practice arcane rites involving obscene sexual practices. Huysmans was unable to gain admission to this "secret world," however, until he began an affair with a woman named Berthe de Courrière, who was a close friend of the most notorious defrocked clergyman in all of Christendom, Joseph-Antoine Boullan (1824–1893).

Boullan was an ordained priest with a doctorate in theology who had become obsessed with satanism by the late 1850s, when he paid a visit to La Salette, France, where two young children had reported what was then and remains today one of the most famous apparitions of the Virgin Mary in the history of Catholicism. In 1846, a pair of shepherd children, fourteen-year-old Mélanie Calvat and eleven-year-old Maximin Giraud, told their family and neighbors that the Virgin had appeared to them while they were watering cattle at a spring, weeping as she told them of terrible things that were to come. Word that Our Lady of La Salette had given each of these children a "secret" began to spread across France. It was believed that Mélanie had shared her secret with a young nun with whom she had grown close, Adèle Chevalier. Chevalier was already claiming to have effected miracles. Soon after she and Boullan met, the two were accused of involvement in "strange sexual practices." The couple promptly formed a group called the Society for the Reparation of Lost Souls and began to travel about Europe dispensing "medications" for "curing devilish illnesses" that they made from human feces mixed with consecrated hosts. When Adèle gave birth to their first child, the two sacrificed it at a satanic mass on December 8, 1860. That crime was not exposed until years later, but in 1861 Boullan was sent to prison for selling fake medicines and served three years.

Boullan was imprisoned again in 1869, this time by the Holy Office in Rome. During his incarceration, Boullan composed the

journal he titled *Cahier rose*. In it, he confirmed all that was rumored
about his satanic methods, and much more. He returned to Paris
after his release, resumed his former practices, and was soon widely
employed in teaching nuns and other women how to receive "incubi"
in secret sexual practices. He was partially exposed in 1875 and defrocked by the archbishop of Paris.

Shortly before he was removed from the Catholic priesthood,
Boullan had met the head of the "Church of Carmel," Eugène Vintras, the onetime foreman of a cardboard box factory who claimed in
1839 to have received a letter from the archangel Michael that was
followed by visions of the Holy Ghost, St. Joseph, and the Virgin Mary.
During these visions, he had been informed that he was the reincar-
nated prophet Elijah, said Vintras, and that he was to found a new
religious order, proclaim the Age of the Holy Ghost, and announce
the true king of France, a German clock and watchmaker named
Charles Naundorff. As he went about the countryside preaching this
news, Vintras enlisted a number of Catholic priests into his new
church. In 1848, though, the Church of Carmel was condemned by
Pope Pius IX, and in 1851 Vintras was publicly accused by a former
disciple of conducting Black Masses in the nude and masturbating
while praying at the altar. Vintras died at almost the moment Boullan
was defrocked, but not before handing over control of the Church of
Carmel to the ex-priest. Boullan was promoting himself as the reincarnation of John the Baptist and supporting himself with fake heal-
ings, fortune-telling, and the staging of assorted erotic rituals when
Berthe de Courrière introduced him to Huysmans.

Boullan successfully seduced Huysmans, sending him reams of
materials on the practice of magic, the summoning of incubi, and the
conduct of Black Masses, but attributing all of these perversions of
the faith to Stanislas de Guaita, the occultist who had established the
Rosicrucian order in France. De Guaita and his partner Oswald Wirth
had early infiltrated Boullan's group, then written an exposé they titled *The Temple of Satan*. Boullan, though, was able to convince Huysmans that this work was slanderous and that de Guaita was the true
black magician. Despite the indignant entreaties of numerous other

occultists, Huysmans refused to model the villain of *Là-Bas* after Boullan, instead using Canon Louis van Haecke.

The novel was almost universally understood to be a roman à
clef in which Huysman gave himself the name Durtel, a writer who
starts out to write a biography of Gilles de Rais. During his research,
Durtal is allowed to observe a Black Mass, and that scene became
by far the book's most famous. It is set in a darkened room lit only by
flickering candles, where a fallen priest named Canon Docre (who is
clearly van Haecke) enters barefoot, with tattooed crosses on the soles
of his feet so that he may tread on the Christ with each step he takes.
Docre feeds the consecrated hosts to mice, mixes feces and urine with
the sacrament, then fondles his genitalia as he recites the Christian
Mass backward. As the smoke of incense fills the darkened room, drugs
are distributed to the congregation, the Devil is invoked, and a hymn
to Satan is chanted. Standing beneath an upside-down cross, the priest
reads a litany of blasphemous insults to Christ, with choirboys inton-
ing the responses. The drugged congregation begins to howl and roll
about the floor while Canon Docre masturbates, using a consecrated
host held in the palm of his hand. As the women step forward to take
bites of the abused host, the men sodomize the choirboys.

Upon its publication in 1891, *Là-Bas* was a sensation throughout Europe and an enormous commercial success, but Huysmans
could not enjoy it. Disgusted with himself and all that he had observed
during the previous few years, Huysmans not only abandoned the Decadent movement but also began a wrenching conversion to Catholicism, gaining readmission to the Church the year after *Là-Bas* was
published, then spending time in a Trappist monastery during 1895,
the year he published *En Route*, the book that chronicled his return
to faith.

En Route was perhaps even more controversial than *Là-Bas*.
Debates raged among the cultural elites of Paris and much of Europe
over what to make of Huysman's purported conversion. What made it
so jarring was that during Huysman's ascendancy within the movement, the Decadents' reputation had darkened steadily. They were
known not only for their devotion to estheticism and sensuality and

for keeping prostitutes as mistresses but also for a fascination with psychosexual aberrations that included incest, sadomasochism, and bestiality. The Marquis de Sade was frequently invoked as a hero of the movement. A letter that Huysmans had written several years earlier to his longtime friend Dutch industrialist Arij Prins, describing a recent visit to a brothel, was widely circulated: "As for news, yesterday I went to the hospitable house where we made a stop one evening. I rediscovered there the two girls we honored with the caresses of our members. I went upstairs with the fortuneteller, a gypsy type, that I had had before, and despite the prodigious heat, I devoured her parts. It was very good!" Now, though, Huysmans was resigning from his position at the Interior Ministry and taking up permanent residence at the Benedictine monastery in Ligugé, where he continued to proclaim his Catholicism (and his rejection of the Decadents) in the book *La Cathédrale*, using a detailed examination of medieval art to describe how he had put away his last doubts about Christian faith.

While Huysman's conversion made him a hero to many Catholics, it did not help his literary reputation. *Là-Bas* in particular was marginalized by the intelligentsia of Paris. Accusations were made that Huysmans's Black Mass scene was pure invention and that he had never actually witnessed one. Huysmans continued to insist that he had in fact observed a Black Mass and that this experience was the pivot on which his turn away from the darkness and back to faith had been made.

By the time of his death in 1907, virtually everyone who knew him, even the people who deplored what had happened to him, believed that Huysman's conversion was sincere. Those who knew him best described how nobly he had suffered when his eyesight began to fail. Even his most severe critics had expressed admiration for Huysman's appreciation of art and his use of color and visual details in his writing. No one they ever met had felt a truer love for the work of Rembrandt and Rubens, his old Decadent friends said. Now, though, Huysmans was being forced to have his eyelids sewn shut, and he told those who visited him that he considered the loss of his eyesight God's way of enforcing penitence.

Whatever anyone made of Huysmans, there was no denying that the Black Mass scene in *Là-Bas* had become the definitive description, one that would be duplicated in countless other books and motion pictures in years to come. Even as admiration for the novel waned among the elites, *Là-Bas* had left a deep impression on the masses of readers who were already inclined to believe that satanic groups were operating all across Europe, and that the Devil was using them to claim countless souls.

CHAPTER EIGHT

i.

"TATE ROWLAND DEATH Remains Big Mystery," read the headline at the top of the front page of the *Index*'s September 13, 1992, edition.

By then, most people in town seemed content—or at least resigned—to let the mystery be. "The business community in particular was happy to see it all go away," Reece Bowen remembered. "They were plumb wore out, and it wasn't just the Tate Rowland and Teri Trosper cases. The Claude Lane deal had put us through so much, and had left such a cloud of suspicion hanging over the town."

Bowen wasn't the only one in Childress who flinched when Lane returned to Childress after serving three years in a federal penitentiary. The former sheriff ran a two-pump gas station for a few months, before being felled by a fatal heart attack. His death came as a relief to many in town. "In some way it was like it marked the end of an unhappy era," Bowen observed.

A bespectacled young man named Clifton Hodges, who had been a friend of Tate Rowland's, told Skip Hollandsworth that in the months following Tate's death he had wanted to check out a book about the occult from the city library but had decided not to for fear of being accused of belonging to the cult. He was anyway, Hodges said, and actually left town for two years, "to get away from all the talk." The atmosphere had cooled considerably by the time he returned to Childress, Hodges said, but only because people had pretty much given up on getting to the bottom of it all.

There was a brief period in the early 1990s when emotions similar to those that surrounded the Tate Rowland case were stirred up by a case involving a woman in town who had been accused of murdering the infant boy she was babysitting. After suffering severe head trauma, the baby had lived for three days on a ventilator while the churches filled with people who prayed for it, and for the child's mother, who blamed herself for having left a sick and crying child in the care of a person who had bashed its head in to keep it quiet.

Sorrowful as it was, the crime had given Kevin Overstreet an opportunity to demonstrate to the citizens of Childress what a properly conducted homicide investigation looked like. Overstreet had arranged for both a detailed autopsy and a thorough forensic examination of the babysitter's home, all of it recorded on videotape. When the autopsy revealed two lateral marks on the back of the dead infant's head, Overstreet spent hours looking at the videotapes of the crime scene, until he noticed a wall heater with a metal vent covering it that was ridged with sharp edges. He performed measurements that showed there was an exact match to the marks on the back of the baby's head "and we had our case," Overstreet remembered.

The babysitter and her attorney, though, claimed that the child's injuries had been caused by the babysitter's husband, a man considered by some to be a hot-tempered fellow. Her husband had come home for lunch and she had gone to the bank while he ate, the babysitter swore; that was when the injuries to the child must have occurred. The timing was wrong, though, according to the forensic evidence. Plus, Overstreet noted, the husband had submitted to a polygraph examination that he passed with flying colors, while his wife had refused to take one. "There was no doubt in my mind that the wife had killed that child," Overstreet recalled. When the case went to court, though, the defense attorney had been successful enough in pointing a finger at the babysitter's husband that he got a hung jury at her first trial and an acquittal at the second.

"We were all just sick," Overstreet remembered. Unsatisfying as its outcome may have been, though, the "Baby Murder Case," as it was known in town, had seemed to mark the point at which the citizens of Childress were released from their obsession with the Tate Rowland mystery. They'd been reminded that evil was a constant of life in both big cities and small towns. That evil was, in fact, ordinary. Satanic cults and secret operations weren't required to make terrible things happen. All it had taken in this case was the whisper of a bad thought in the mind of a sullen woman with a mean spirit and a lack of impulse control. The baby was buried and the woman who nearly everyone knew had killed it left town. Life would go on without them both, and bad things would continue to happen from time to time.

A number of people in Childress, including Chief Deputy Overstreet, thought the "Baby Murder Case" was what had torn it for Sheriff Bowen, who announced his retirement soon after. Bowen, though, said, "It wasn't any one thing. It was all of it. I was done."

Shortly before leaving office, Bowen made a formal declaration that the Tate Rowland case would "remain open," and Kevin Overstreet, who succeeded him as sheriff, vowed to continue pursuing it. "Overstreet worked his tail off, I believe," Brenda Rowland said. "He let me see everything, all the files, and we worked on the case together almost every day. When I'd get off work I would get with him at the sheriff's office and we'd go over it all one more time. I would tell him I heard this, I heard that, I heard this person's involved, I heard this other person was part of it. And he would go bring 'em in for questioning. But he just kept hitting dead ends."

Overstreet admitted his frustration. "We found evidence that Tate's death was no suicide. We found evidence that a satanic cult had been active in the area and was connected to Tate in some way. We found this and we found that, but we couldn't make it all add up to a criminal case." He caught himself reading and rereading the autopsy reports on the exhumed remains of Tate Rowland and Teri Trosper, the new sheriff said, and thinking again and again about how it could have been that Elavil was found in the bloodstreams of both the brother and the sister. "Both Tate and Teri havin' it in their systems, there's no way to explain it," Overstreet said. "You can't make it make sense. There's no way to do it."

Overstreet left Childress just a couple of years later, headed off to a better opportunity in Lubbock. Out at Boxer's Corner, the grass still bent in a breeze that was filled with fine red dust, but one night someone had cut down the horse apple tree where Tate Rowland had been found hanging back in the summer of 1988. When they had lived for a long enough time without answers, folks forgot the questions.

It was as if the town's entire moral force was spent. The evil one had moved among them, all were sure, plucking at strings only he could see, and that continued to reverberate, long after he had stolen away in the night. What he had taken with him no one seemed able to identify, yet all understood to be essential. "Conviction" was perhaps the best word for it.

People could believe what they wanted, but no one could deny it was a devilish outcome.

ii.

THE DEVIL HAD BEEN DESCRIBED more persuasively by literature than by religion since the publication of Milton's *Paradise Lost* in 1667. This trend was only accelerated by the rise of the Reform Church during the seventeenth century. While Martin Luther may have urged his flock to beware of the "old ancient enemy," those who steered Protestantism during subsequent centuries seemed less and less interested in the Devil. As "reform" became synonymous with "progress" and theology was incorporated into philosophy, talk of Satan and his "powers" came to be seen more and more as a relic of the papists. Friedrich Schleiermacher, the most influential philosopher/theologist of the first half of the nineteenth century, went so far as to argue that the doctrine of Satan was traditional rather than biblical and could be discarded (though Schilling did suggest that the Devil be kept as a "symbol" of evil).

Catholics still held sway in France and Southern Europe, though, and the Church of Rome had no intention of abandoning the belief that the Devil was a personage who actively opposed Jesus Christ and worked unceasingly to corrupt human souls. As Jeffrey Burton Russell has observed, it was evident to the Catholic hierarchy that "if one dismisses the Devil (who appears in the New Testament more frequently than the Holy Spirit) as a superstition of the time, then one is entitled to dismiss the resurrection, the incarnation and indeed the whole idea of revelation."

Catholics would be rallied in their faith by one of the longest-reigning (1878–1903) and most influential popes in the history of the Church, Leo XIII (1810–1903). Less than a year after his election to the papal throne, Leo produced an encyclical, "Aeterni patris" (Eternal father), in which he declared Thomist theology eternally valid. In the body of that work, the new pope clearly affirmed the belief in Satan as a personal entity. Perhaps even more influential, at least in regard to the question of the Devil's existence, was the "exorcism prayer" Leo XIII composed in 1884, after a vision in which he believed he had witnessed an exchange between Jesus and Satan. Some accounts have Leo collapsing at the altar after leading a mass, rising from the floor a few moments later, pale and shaking, then retreating to his private apartment, emerging only when his new prayer was written. The pope's private secretary would confirm only the part about Leo withdrawing to his apartment after mass to write the prayer, which entreats the archangel Michael to defend the faithful against "the principalities and powers, against the rulers of this world of darkness, against the spirits of wickedness in high places," as the Letter to the Ephesians had described the forces of supernatural evil. In the next sentence of Leo's prayer, humanity is described as having been "redeemed" by Christ "at a great price from the tyranny of the devil."

Though Leo's exorcism prayer would not be published until after his death, he followed it up immediately with the encyclical "Humanum genus" (The human race), which declared that human beings were "separated into two diverse and opposite parts, of which the one steadfastly contends for truth and virtue, the other of those things which are contrary to truth and virtue. The one is the Kingdom of

God on earth, namely the true Church of Jesus Christ. . . . The other is the kingdom of Satan." Those on Satan's side were "led on or assisted," the encyclical added, by Freemasonry.

Leo XIII's encyclicals, combined with J.-K. Huysman's books, *Là-Bas* in particular, were for many devout Catholics convincing evidence of a real satanic presence in the world. Inevitably, con artists moved in to exploit the credulous. The most audacious of these flimflam men, and by the far most consequential, was another Leo—Léo Taxil.

Taxil had been born in Marseille in 1854 as Marie Joseph Gabriel Antoine Jogand-Pagès. At the age of five the boy had been placed in a Jesuit seminary, where he remained for the rest of his childhood. He never publicly described what had happened at the seminary to turn him into a virulent anti-Catholic, but few people in history have ever humiliated the Church more completely.

Jogand-Pagès had demonstrated his capacity for making fools of the people around him shortly after leaving the seminary, when, at age nineteen, he perpetrated what became known throughout France as "the shark hoax." During 1873, the city of Marseille had been thrown into an uproar by news that the waters just offshore were infested with man-eating sharks. A number of fishermen had written letters to the local newspapers describing in vivid detail their narrow escapes from the jaws of death. A force of a hundred soldiers had been sent to sea aboard a tugboat to locate and destroy the monsters. When the soldiers returned to Marseille and reported that they had searched every cove along the shoreline without finding even a single shark, the letters sent by the fishermen were reexamined and it was determined that they had all been written in the same hand. An official inquiry would conclude that the city had been hoaxed. It says a great deal about Jogand-Pagès's character that he waited twenty-four years to reveal that he had been the author of that hoax.

By the time the shark hoax was proclaimed, Jogand-Pagès had already left Marseille for Paris, where he took the pen name Léo Taxil and began making his mark as an anti-Catholic pornographer and pamphleteer. Parodies of Catholicism had been a literary genre in

France ever since the Revolution of 1789, when opposing the monarchy and defying the Church were considered one and the same. Léo Taxil's work stood out, however, both for its acidic cleverness and for its naughty audacity, a remarkable achievement for an author who was competing with titles like "The Priest's Testicles," "Extraordinary Correspondence of the Ecclesiastical Fuckers," and the unforgettable "Letter from the Devil to the Pope Concerning the Suppression of Menstruation in Girls' Communities." What made Taxil far more widely known than any of his fellow pornographers, though, was his book *La Bible amusante* (The amusing Bible), in which he satirized scripture with a wicked verve.

Attempts to silence Taxil not only failed but added to his reputation. He was accused in court of libel for a book called *Les amours secrètes de Pie IX* (The secret loves of Pius IX) but successfully defended himself by arguing that his work had been satire, not journalism. Later, he was brought up on criminal charges at the Court of Assizes for "insulting a religion recognized by the state" in his pamphlet *À bas la calotte!* (Down with the cloth!). After his acquittal, Taxil founded the magazine *L'anti-clérical* and its umbrella organization, the Anti-Clerical League.

The Church hierarchy, especially in France, regarded the man as a real thorn in their side. It was a period in history in which the spread of republicanism throughout Europe had resulted in a number of countries passing laws that actually outlawed Catholicism, the Second Spanish Republic being most vociferous. Leo XIII had made it his mission to reconcile the Church with modern society, negotiating directly with a number of Latin American governments, persuading Prussia to discontinue its persecution of Catholics, and making a deal with the new Italian state that allowed the Vatican to remain largely independent. Managing all of this while at the same time not only asserting but expanding upon traditional dogmas (in "Humanum genus") was no easy task, and the writings of Léo Taxil only made it more difficult. Taxil became even more reviled among Catholics when it was learned that he had applied for membership in the Freemasons' Paris lodge, the Grand Orient de France. It was therefore with considerable astonishment and delight that Church officials learned, shortly after the publication of "Humanum genus," that the notorious Léo Taxil had announced his return to Catholicism, declaring publicly that he intended to repair the damage he had done to the true faith.

Almost immediately, Taxil began turning out anti-Masonic tracts with the same passion and energy that had fueled his decade-long attack on the Church. Taxil rapidly produced a four-volume history of Freemasonry that was replete with the testimonies of invented eyewitnesses to the various satanic rituals that the author reported were taking place behind the facades of assorted Masonic lodges. Taxil next took on "High Freemasonry," purporting to reveal the existence of Palladism (a "Luciferian occultism dedicated to bringing down the Catholic Church") with a lengthy series of works that were collected as *Le diable au XIXè siècle* (The Devil in the nineteenth century). Taxil wrote that he was drawing upon the vast knowledge of a Dr. Bataille, a learned man who had traveled the globe in search of enlightenment. It was Bataille who had introduced him to Diana Vaughan, a descendent of the infamous Rosicrucian alchemist Thomas Vaughan, Taxil wrote, and Diana Vaughan's revelations were the largest part of what informed *Le diable au XIXè siècle*. This young woman had been chosen by Freemasonry's secret leaders as a high priestess of Lucifer for the purpose of overthrowing Christianity and winning the world for Satan, Taxil informed his readers. He described various of Vaughan's encounters with demons, delighting in their implausibility even as he created them. In one scene, Vaughan told of the demon that had written prophecies on her back with its tail; in another, she described the demon that had played a piano while assuming the appearance of a crocodile.

Taxil's supreme stroke was to announce that Diana Vaughan had been converted to Catholicism, with his personal assistance, of course. In the book *Mémoires d'une ex-palladiste* (Memoirs of an ex-Palladist), Diana Vaughan described how her final break from Lucifer and release from the demons that surrounded her had been achieved, when she publicly professed her admiration for Joan of

Arc, whose name, spoken aloud, had drawn a host of saints, angels, and other heavenly messengers who put the demons to flight. The book was an enormous success, widely read among Catholics not only in France but throughout Europe as well.

Diana Vaughan, now writing from the unnamed Swiss convent where she was living under the protection of nuns, produced a second book, a collection of prayers called *La neuvaine eucharistique* (The Eucharistic novena), which also sold well and was read widely after Pope Leo XIII praised it. She also wrote a monthly journal that was widely distributed across Europe.

Léo Taxil himself had become a darling of the Vatican and in 1887 was received in a private audience by Leo XIII himself, who immediately afterward announced that he was summoning an anti-Masonic council at Trent, famous for the sixteenth-century gathering at which the Church had first confronted the threat of Protestantism. When the bishop of Charleston challenged the veracity of a Taxil/Vaughan pamphlet that purported to identify the leaders of the Masons' worldwide satanic conspiracy, the pope publicly rebuked him.

Among those who adored Diana Vaughan's writings were the Carmelite nuns gathered around the holiest woman in Europe, Thérèse of Lisieux, "The Little Flower of Jesus," whom Pope Pius X would describe as "the greatest saint of modern times." Thérèse's immensely influential autobiography had not yet been published (and wouldn't be until after her death at age twenty-four), but her poetry was widely read and loved among Catholic devotionalists. Her mother superior asked Thérèse to write a poem for Diana Vaughan, and Thérèse agreed to do so, but she found herself inexplicably unable to follow through. What Thérèse *was* able to do, though, was send a photograph of herself and her sister Céline costumed for a play about Joan of Arc, a play Thérèse had written after reading and being inspired by Diana Vaughan's *Mémoires d'une ex-palladiste*.

Taxil was delighted when he received the photograph, knowing it could be put to good use eventually. He was perhaps even more pleased when various other anti-Masonic or pro-Catholic writers began to produce their own books about Diana Vaughan. By the early

1890s, though, certain sober Catholic writers were becoming more outspoken about suggesting that this Vaughan woman might be a figment of Taxil's imagination. In 1896, A. E. Waite, a well-known British authority on mystical cults and secret societies, published a book titled *Devil Worship in France* that systematically debunked Taxil's *Le diable au XIXe siècle*. Citing dozens of factual inaccuracies, numerous instances of plagiarism, and the utter absurdity of many of the claims in Taxil's pulp-fiction narrative, Waite observed that nearly everything Taxil had written was based on the testimony of Diana Vaughan, and he publicly questioned whether the woman actually existed.

Pressure on Taxil to produce Vaughan began to mount, until, in early 1897, Taxil announced that Diana Vaughan would appear in Paris on April 19 for a public lecture in the French Geographic Society's amphitheater. When the date arrived, a crowd of 400 filled the amphitheater's seats. Taxil himself took the stage but was met with a chorus of demands for Diana Vaughan. Taxil replied by pointing to a typewriter sitting on a table nearby. There *was* a Diana Vaughan, Taxil said. She was his typist, a young woman who took his dictation and was delighted to have been made over into a former high priestess of Palladism and the most famous Catholic convert in Europe, especially when he began paying her fifty francs a week for her cooperation. No Dr. Bataille existed, of course, Taxil added, then gloated about having pulled off "the most colossal hoax of modern times." A journalist who was present reported that Taxil "does not hesitate to give himself the title of King of Modern Pranksters. He flatters himself for having used his natural talents, perfected with a gradual training, for the good of a society infected with the virus of superstition." His intent, Taxil told the crowd, was to demonstrate the sheer gullibility of the Catholic Church. As he spoke, the photograph of Thérèse of Lisieux dressed as Joan of Arc was projected onto the wall behind him.

Taxil also took the opportunity to take credit for the shark hoax he had pulled off in Marseille back in 1873 and for another hoax of which he was particularly proud, the one in which he had created a "sunken city" under Lake Geneva that had Swiss and French scholars expounding at length on Atlantis and other civilizations that had existed before the Great Flood.

He regarded hoaxing as "a noble career," Taxil told the crowd, and what proved this was how thoroughly he had taken in not only the pope himself but also the nun regarded by the Church as the holiest human on earth, and in the process exposed the silly superstitions that were the foundation of Catholicism.

The outraged crowd mobbed Taxil as he attempted to leave the hall, compelling a cadre of gendarmes to escort him to a nearby café. He left Paris soon after, resumed his career as an anti-Catholic pamphleteer, and reunited with his wife, to whom (before his "conversion") he had transferred all the rights to his earlier anti-Catholic works. Before long, he had reissued his *Amusing Bible* with a biting letter to the pope as its preface.

Leo XIII excommunicated Taxil and did his best to put the entire affair behind him, an outcome he seems to have achieved, since he is now regarded among Catholics as one of the greatest popes in history. Thérèse of Lisieux, publicly humiliated by the Taxil hoax even as she battled both tuberculosis and a crisis of faith, died five months later. Her autobiography, *L'histoire d'une âme* (The story of a soul), was published a year later and has never been out of print since. Thérèse was beatified in 1923 and canonized in 1925, and she became, along with Francis of Assisi, one of the two most popular saints in Catholicism, with two million visitors to her shrine annually.

Léo Taxil, whose legal name was always Jogand-Pagès, had died with little public note in 1907.

UNTIL THE END of the nineteenth century, the Devil had obtained very little purchase on the American literary imagination. Edgar Allan Poe, arguably the greatest single influence on the Decadent movement, never mentioned Satan by name in the numerous works in which he made serious explorations of evil. The infernal one did appear in a minor Poe short story, "The Devil in the Belfry," a satire set in a town where the dutiful citizens seem to be interested in little beyond clocks and cabbages. The Devil shows up playing a fiddle and introduces chaos to the townspeople by ringing thirteen o'clock in the bell tower of the church. When Claude Debussy adapted Poe's story into a one-act opera, his intent was to "put an end to the idea that the devil is the spirit of evil" and show that Satan was "simply the spirit of contradiction."

Nathaniel Hawthorne, Herman Melville, and Mark Twain each produced just one work in which the Devil was a central character. Hawthorne's protagonist in his short story "Young Goodman Brown" is an earnest lad who wants desperately to believe in the inherent goodness of his family and neighbors in Salem, Massachusetts. He goes for a walk in the woods, where he meets the Devil in the guise of an old man who looks familiar and carries a black serpent-shaped staff. The two of them meet a neighbor who complains about the effort it will take to walk home, and gladly accepts when the old man offers his staff and suggests she use it to fly. Brown meets other neighbors, as well as his father and grandfather, and is shocked when the old man says he knows them all well. The climax comes when Brown and the old man arrive in a clearing at midnight to find all the townspeople assembled for a ceremony that seems to be a witches' sabbath, conducted at a rough altar made of rocks and lit by firelight. Brown and his wife, Faith, are told they are the only people in town not yet initiated. Brown calls to heaven to help him resist, and the scene vanishes. When he returns home, Brown is deeply shaken, his faith in others having evaporated. He grows into a bitter and cynical old man. "And when he had lived long, and was borne to his grave . . . they carved no hopeful verse upon his tombstone, for his dying hour was gloom." Hawthorne's Satan is at once a corrupter and an instructor, one who makes Brown aware that depravity is a central aspect of human nature.

While it can be (and has been) argued that Melville's Moby Dick was a satanic character, the Devil actually appears only in the author's final book, *The Confidence Man*. Satan sneaks aboard a Mississippi River steamboat on April Fool's Day and tests the faith of a series of passengers by challenging those things in which they have placed their trust. He hides behind a confounding array of disguises, appearing as a mute in pale clothing, as a lame beggar named Black Guinea, as an agent of the Seminole Widow and Orphan Asylum, as the president of the Black Rapids Coal Company, as a "doctor" who sells the Omni-Balsamic Reinvigorator and the Samaritan Pain Dissuader, and so on. His central purpose seems to be imparting his motto, "No Trust." Melville's Devil is similar to Hawthorne's in that his function seems to be teaching people lessons they would be both stupider and happier not knowing.

Twain's *The Mysterious Stranger* was his final novel, set in the year 1590 in a remote Austrian hamlet called Eseldorf (*esel* means "donkey" in German and *dorf* means "village"). A handsome teenage boy shows up one day and introduces himself as Satan, explaining that he is an angel and nephew of the great Satan, the Devil himself. Young Satan performs magic for a group of other boys, then tells fortunes, predicting a series of calamities that will befall their loved ones. He isn't believed until one of his predictions comes true. The boys beg him to intercede, but Satan says he must operate under the "technical" definition of mercy and can only do things like allow a person suffering a lingering illness to die instantly. Mayhem and madness rampage through the village in the form of witch trials, burnings, hangings, and various mass hysterias.

At one point Satan seems to speak for Twain, presenting the main theme of the work by bitterly complaining about "a God who could make good children as easily as bad, yet preferred to make bad ones; who could have made every one of them happy, yet never made a single happy one; who made them prize their bitter life, yet stingily cut it short; who gave his angels eternal happiness unearned, yet required his other children to earn it . . . who mouths justice, and invented hell."

When he departs, though, young Satan tells the villagers not to worry, because "you are not you—you have no body, no blood, no bones, you are but a thought. I myself have no existence; I am but a dream—your dream, a creature of your imagination. In a moment you will have realized this, then you will banish me from your visions and I shall dissolve into the nothingness out of which you made me."

Twain's Satan is yet another emissary of radical truths, this one a kind of prophet of the secular humanism that would encroach upon America's religious traditions for the next hundred years following the 1916 publication of *The Mysterious Stranger*. There was a consonance between Twain's novel and what mainstream Protestantism was becoming during the twentieth century. A Christian counterinsurgency was already forming, however.

It was an epoch when the theology issuing from the religion departments of major universities was becoming increasingly a critique of scripture, one that attempted to reconcile the Bible with the scientific materialism ascendant in America. It shocked many of the faithful that these academics often targeted Christ himself. Many prominent theologians were insisting that Jesus should be seen as a man of his time, an uneducated peasant in an obscure corner of an ancient empire who held the same primitive ideas as those around him, and whose statements about the Devil and demons were nothing more or less than his reflection of the prevailing superstitions. The story that Jesus was the divine product of a virgin birth who had walked on water, been tempted by Satan, and risen from the dead was being dismissed as an outmoded relic of traditions that were no longer relevant. Many if not most educated people subscribed to the treatment Thomas Jefferson had given the New Testament, striking out all the miracle stories to leave only the teachings of a great philosopher.

Tens of thousands of devout Christians, though, recoiled at such handling of scripture. They found each other, naturally, most often in places far removed from New York and Boston, and began to form their own churches, institutions that would eventually form the nexus of what became evangelical Christianity. The evangelicals insisted that scripture, and the New Testament in particular, should be read as the Word of God, and that when Jesus spoke of Satan in the Gospels, he was talking about an actual being who was dedicated to the corruption and damnation of human souls.

Some of them—far from a majority, but a significant and dedicated number—saw the Taxil hoax in a very different light than did the newspapers in London, Paris, and New York. The entire affair had been, they said, a sting operation by the Freemasons directed at the Catholic Church. The goal had been an elaborately conceived cover-up of the fact that devil worship *was* the creed of those who occupied the ranks of the hidden, higher ranks of Freemasonry. Virtually everything that was said or written about this claim focused then and still does today on a man who has been at the center of nearly every major conspiracy theory that developed during the twentieth century, the man who had been identified by Dr. Bataille and Diana Vaughan—that is to say, by Léo Taxil—as the leader of the worldwide satanic conspiracy.

Albert Pike was an immense and immensely influential man in the decades before and after the US Civil War. He was until very recently the only Confederate general with a statue on federal property in Washington, DC. Engraved at the base of the Pike monument in Judiciary Square were the words "philosopher, jurist, orator, author, poet, scholar, soldier." Pike's statue was raised to honor him not as a military commander or lawyer, however, but as the southern regional leader of the Scottish Rite of Freemasonry.

Even those who revile him must admit that Pike's is an extraordinary story. He was the son of a Boston cobbler who was forced to drop out of Harvard because he couldn't afford to be a student, and so he compensated with a program of self-education that would eventually make him one of the best-read men in the country. Reputedly, he spoke fifteen languages. That may have been an exaggeration, but its credibility cannot be dismissed out of hand, given that among the written works he left behind were translations from Sanskrit.

Pike arrived on foot in Arkansas during the 1830s, having walked 1,300 miles from a failed exploration of New Mexico. He taught school and garnered local attention with a series of articles written under the pen name "Casca" for the *Arkansas Advocate*, a newspaper he bought (with his wife's dowry) in 1835. He studied law at night and was admitted to the bar in 1837, the same year he sold the *Advocate*.

By the early 1850s he was a prominent advocate of slavery who had renounced the Whigs to join the nativist, anti-Catholic Know-Nothing Party, but quit them too when they failed to construct a sufficiently pro-slavery platform.

After the Civil War broke out, Pike became a brigadier general in the Confederate Army and was given a command in Indian Territory, charged with organizing the Choctaws (slaveholders themselves), Cherokees, and other "civilized tribes" into a military division. Only about a year passed before his own superiors ordered him arrested, after receiving reports that Pike had allowed his troops to scalp enemy soldiers and was misappropriating the money with which he was to pay his men. He escaped while being transported to his court-martial and fled into the Ozark Mountains, which resulted in Pike becoming the only man to be charged with treason by both the Confederate and Union governments. In August 1865, after making his way to Canada, Pike was granted a pardon by US president Andrew Johnson, who was himself a Freemason, as numerous writers have pointed out.

Pike returned to Arkansas and became an associate justice of the state supreme court but left that job to open a very successful law office in Memphis, Tennessee, before eventually moving on to Washington, DC, where he not only practiced law but also served as editor of the newspaper *The Patriot*.

Pike was near the end of his life when Léo Taxil's avatars identified him as the satanic pope, and he had been dead for six years when the Taxil hoax was finally revealed in 1897. Even the Freemasons who have dedicated themselves to defending his reputation have to admit that Pike left behind more than a little material for the generations of conspiracy theorists who have been on his trail for the past 120 years, and who persist in describing him not simply as a keeper of Freemasonry's darkest secrets but also as a founder of the Ku Klux Klan who was singularly responsible for embedding devil worship deep into American society.

Certainly the most solid, if not the most compelling, evidence on the anti-Pike side of the ledger is found in his masterwork, a massive tome titled *Morals and Dogma of the Ancient and Accepted Scottish Rite of Freemasonry*, a book that was explicitly directed to those in the upper, "invisible" ranks of Freemasonry, of which the ordinary lot were not aware. Much of it seems to echo the infamous "Luciferian quote" of the speech Taxil claimed had been delivered as a keynote address to the Freemasons' Supreme Council in Paris on July 14, 1889. It is agreed even by his Masonic defenders that Pike was scheduled to speak in Paris and that he was forced to cancel due to ill health. Taxil had alleged that the speech was read aloud by someone else on the floor of the convention and (in the guise of Diana Vaughan) quoted the entire text. If Taxil made it up out of whole cloth, he demonstrated a remarkable depth of commitment to his hoax, given that the speech ran to 13,000 words. The most famous section of it, though, then and now, was only about 200 words:

> That which we must say to the world is that we worship a god, but it is the god that one adores without superstition. To you, Sovereign Grand Inspectors General, we say this, that you may repeat to the brethren of the 32nd, 31st and 30th degrees: The masonic Religion should be, by all of us initiates of the higher degrees, maintained in the Purity of the Luciferian doctrine. If Lucifer were not God, would Adonay, the God of the Christians, whose deeds prove his cruelty, perfidy, and hatred of man, barbarism and repulsion for science, would Adonay and his priests calumniate him?
>
> Yes Lucifer is God, and unfortunately Adonay is also god. For the eternal law is that there is no light without shade, no beauty without ugliness, no white without black, for the absolute can exist only as two gods; darkness being necessary for light to serve as its foil as the pedestal is necessary to the statue, and the brake to the locomotive . . .
>
> Thus, the doctrine of Satanism is a heresy, and the true and philosophical religion is the belief in Lucifer, the equal of Adonay; but Lucifer, God of Light and God of Good, is strug-

THE DEVIL'S BEST TRICK

gling for humanity against Adonay, the God of Darkness and Evil.

The claims that the speech was fiction created by Léo Taxil are troubled by what Pike most certainly did write in *Morals and Dogma*, in particular those sections that refer to a "Luciferian Doctrine." In one passage Pike excoriated those who worship only "the God of the Apocalypse" and refuse to give Lucifer his due: "Strange and mysterious name to give to the spirit of Darkness! Lucifer, the Son of the Morning! Is it he who bears the Light, and with its splendors intolerable blinds feeble, sensual or selfish souls? Doubt it not!" Equally significant in the eyes of those who insist that the Freemasons were behind the Taxil hoax is a reference to Luciferian Doctrine in which Pike explains that Freemasonry must and does "conceal its secrets" from those in the lower levels of the organization by using "false explanations and misinterpretations of its symbols." In a section of the book he addresses to "Sublime Princes of the Royal Secret," or Masons of the 32nd degree, Pike rhapsodizes about magic as an ancient system that "unites" science, philosophy and "Religion of the Infallible and the Eternal," then advises that "those who accept [magic] as a rule may give their will a sovereign power that will make them the masters of all inferior beings and of all errant spirits; that is to say, will make them the Arbiters and Kings of the World."

Anti-Masonic investigators have produced other tidbits of proof that the "Luciferian quote" speech *was* delivered at the 1889 Paris conclave, among them an article from the main British Masonic publication, *The Freemason*, that noted the reading of the letter on the convention floor. They note as well the report in a Paris newspaper about Léo Taxil's announcement of his hoax. According to that article, at one point a member of the crowd shouted at Taxil, "These Freemasons were your accomplices!" to which Taxil replied, "Tu paries" ("You bet").

Masonic writers have answered by pointing out claims about Pike by Taxil that only the imbecilic could believe, such as the one in which Taxil had Pike meeting face-to-face with the Devil at three o'clock every Friday afternoon at a Freemason lodge.

Even in his day, Pike's character and appearance had provided grist for those who denounced him, and they still do. In his later years, the six-foot-tall Pike weighed more than three hundred pounds and draped his girth in Savile Row suits that encouraged both those who described him as imposing and those who called him grotesque. His appetite for debauchery had been legend back in Arkansas, where he was said to regularly organize bacchanals in the woods in which he sat naked astride a phallic throne surrounded by the prostitutes he had hired to accompany him, consuming copious amounts of food and liquor that were delivered by the wagonload until he passed into a stupor. How true these tales were is impossible to know, but those who believed them were encouraged by the notoriety of his public affairs, including the one he had carried on after leaving his wife for a "wanton" nineteen-year-old sculptress named Vinnie Ream who was forty years his junior.

In the official Masonic photographs he posed for during his middle age, Pike wore an amulet around his neck that students of the occult immediately recognized. It was the figure of a hermaphroditic human body with a goat's head and bird wings, wearing a torch between its horns and with a pentagram emblazoned on its forehead. The creature was the "Sabbatic Goat" drawn by the French occultist Éliphas Lévi that had become identified with the idol Baphomet.

The Baphomet story had been around since the early fourteenth century, when the term was used to describe the deity that the Knights Templar were accused of worshipping. The name had become popular during the nineteenth century, as offshoots of the Decadent movement began to use it in occult practices. Éliphas Lévi had described Baphomet as a "binary" being that represented the "sum total of the universe," male and female, light and dark, good and evil. The accusation that the adoration of this idol was a thin mask over the devil worship practiced by various neopagan cults would be given a measure of credence in the mid-twentieth century, when the Church of Satan adopted Baphomet as its symbol.

The accusations against Albert Pike (and by implication the Freemasons) have gathered force behind the widespread belief that he was a founding father of the Ku Klux Klan. His Wikipedia page asserts that there is "no evidence" that Pike was even a member of the Klan. Reading this, I understood the scorn I've heard magazine fact checkers express for the use of Wikipedia as a source, because there's quite a bit of evidence—compelling evidence—that Pike *was* an early and important figure in the "Imperial Brotherhood."

The earliest claim of Pike's involvement in the KKK came from a man who definitely was a Klan founder, Capt. John C. Lester, one of the six Confederate veterans who assembled in Pulaski, Tennessee, on Christmas Eve in 1865 to create a secret society that would oppose the Union-imposed policies of Reconstruction. In a booklet published nineteen years later, in 1884, Lester and his co-author D. L. Wilson identified Pike as an early and important member of the Klan—the KKK's "chief judicial officer." In a study written by J. C. Lester and D. L. Wilson, with scholarly notes by West Virginia University history professor Walter L. Fleming, published under the title *Ku Klux Klan: Its Origin, Growth and Disbandment* in 1905, Pike (described as standing "high in the Masonic order") was again characterized as the Klan's chief judicial officer, and his photograph was one of seven used to identify the Klan's founding fathers. Fleming thanked as a primary source Major James R. Crowe, the man who organized that first meeting of the KKK in Pulaski and was soon after elected as the Klan's first leader. (Crowe was also a Freemason leader, the "Most Illustrious Grand Master of the Cryptic Rite of Tennessee.") In her 1924 book *Authentic History: Ku Klux Klan, 1865–1877*, Klan apologist Susan Lawrence Davis repudiated the claim that the Klan failed, contradicted Lester on a few small points, dismissed Fleming's work as superficial, and then, on the basis of interviews with more than fifty early Klan members, portrayed Albert Pike as there from the start and the real brains behind the entire operation. Davis praised both Pike's design and stewardship of the KKK during the Reconstruction era.

Freemasons have pointed out that Pike was still living in Little Rock, Arkansas, on December 24, 1865, and so almost certainly was

not present at that first meeting of the Klan. However, the real formation of the Klan as an action network did not take place until
April 1867, when the Pulaski Den held a "reorganizational meeting"
in Room 10 of the Maxwell House in Nashville. By then, Albert Pike
was living in Tennessee and working both as an attorney and as the
editor of the *Memphis Daily Appeal*, for which he wrote an April 16,
1868 editorial that read:

> With negroes for witnesses and jurors, the administration of
> justice becomes a blasphemous mockery. A Loyal League of
> negroes can cause any white man to be arrested, and can prove
> any charges it chooses to have made against him. . . . The dis-
> enfranchised people of the South . . . can find no protection
> for property, liberty or life, except in secret association. . . . We
> would unite every white man in the South, who is opposed
> to Negro suffrage, into one great Order of Southern Broth-
> erhood, with an organization complete, active, vigorous, in
> which a few should execute the concentrated will of all, and
> whose very existence should be concealed from all but its
> members.

Whatever the truth about Albert Pike, ultimately his legacy has
lent more credence to claims of devil worshippers in high places than
that of any other American who has ever lived. Dozens of writers have
placed him at the epicenter of a vast satanic cult that has secretly
steered the course of Western civilization since the late nineteenth
century, and in the process have created an alternative American history that gives the Devil more due than he's received since the time
of the Inquisition.

   Pulling at the loose threads of Albert Pike's mysterious place in
American history was a good part of the process by which theodicy
was reduced to conspiracy theory during the twentieth century. Before the internet, belief in a vast cabal of scheming devil worshippers
was fed mainly by two American authors, William Guy Carr and Edith

Starr Miller. Carr has probably been more influential. Miller is certainly more interesting.

William Guy Carr was a British submarine commander in World War I and a senior officer in the British Royal Navy in World War II who first achieved notice by writing about exploits in the ocean depths. By the early 1930s, though, he had embarked on the career that would turn him into what the folklorist Bill Ellis called "the most influential source in creating the American Illuminati demonology." During his quarter century as a conspiracy theorist— arguably *the* conspiracy theorist—Carr was the first to develop the theme of an international collusion in which the titans of communism and capitalism were being manipulated behind the scenes by Illuminati masters, these being mostly bankers from the Rockefeller and Rothschild families, whose secret nexus was the Bilderberg Group.

The notion of a satanically inspired, Illuminati-led plot against Christianity went back to the immediate aftermath of the French Revolution, which for more than two hundred years has been the signal event of every major derivation of conspiracy theory. The first two to put it forth, almost simultaneously, were the French priest Augustin Barruel and the Scottish physicist John Robison. Barruel was slightly in the lead when he published his book *Mémoires pour sevir à l'histoire du jacobinisme* (Memoirs illustrating the history of Jacobinism) in 1797. His thesis was that the French Revolution had been born out of a conspiracy aimed at the overthrow of Christianity in general and the Roman Catholic Church in particular. Robison's *Proofs of a Conspiracy against All the Religions and Governments of Europe* was published just months later, but Robison's imprimatur made a much deeper impression on intellectuals. The Scot was a noted scientist and mathematician, as well as an inventor who had created the first siren and worked with James Watt to develop the steam car. Furthermore, Robison's missive relied heavily on the testimony of Alexander Horn, a Benedictine monk who had worked as a secret agent for the British government in Germany and France during the run-up to the French Revolution.

Barruel and Robison were also the first to focus on the role of Adam Weishaupt, the German lawyer and philosopher who had founded the Order of the Illuminati in 1776. Weishaupt had, as both Barruel and Robison claimed, joined (or infiltrated) the Masonic lodge in Munich with the purpose of advancing the Illuminati goal of "enlightening understanding by the sun of reason, which will dispel the clouds of superstition and of prejudice." With the words "superstition and prejudice," both Barruel and Robison contended, Weishaupt was taking dead aim at Christian faith. There is little question that Weishaupt did, as Barruel and Robison wrote, establish a network of spies by using Freemasonry to recruit the members of what was meant to be a secret society within the secret society. This mission advanced for eight years under Weishaupt's administration. It was stymied when a dispatch of his writings was intercepted by government officials in Bavaria, who banned the Society of the Illuminati, had Weishaupt removed from his position as a university professor, and chased him to the Thuringian city of Gotha, where he lived until 1830 and produced such works as *A Complete History of the Persecutions of the Illuminati in Bavaria*. While some modern academics have described Weishaupt's Illuminati project as naively utopian, the works of Barruel and Robison (and later Carr) have cemented his outsized place in the popular imagination, demonstrated by his appearances in pulp novels, comic books, video games, and rap songs that have had him, among other things, murdering George Washington and taking his place as the first president of the United States.

William Guy Carr's most original contribution to the conspiracy theory was the same one that would ultimately make him a figure of ridicule: his contention that this age-old, Jewish-led Illuminati banking conspiracy he had described was using radio-transmitted mind control on behalf of the Devil himself to bring into being a global government and the New World Order. A proposition that has since been adopted by generations of schizophrenics resulted in Carr selling more than half a million copies of his 1955 book *Pawns in the Game*.

Carr's most enduring contribution to modern-day conspiracy theory, though, is probably his explication of a plan he said had been developed by Albert Pike for the three world wars that would lead to the establishment of a one-world government ruled by Lucifer. The crux of this claim was and is a letter supposedly written by Pike to Giuseppe Mazzini, an Italian politician and revolutionary journalist who had been instrumental in the unification of the disparate Italian states into a modern country and was among the first to advocate a "United States of Europe." Mazzini was also, supposedly, the Grand Master of the Grand Orient of Italy (a claim Masonic writers have disputed, though not very convincingly).

Delineating the origin of claims about the relationship between Mazzini and Pike is a preposterously thorny task, but the first source seems to have been Professor Domenico Margiotta, a doctor of letters and philosophy who at one time had headed the Freemasons' Lodge Savonarola in Florence but attacked Freemasonry with a vengeance after converting to Catholicism. Margiotta was a primary source for the Chilean cardinal José María Caro Rodríguez, one of the most influential men in the Catholic Church in the period between World War I and World War II, whose 1925 book *The Mystery of Freemasonry Unveiled* was the main work cited by Carr about the Pike-Mazzini relationship.

The prevailing psychological construct of conspiracy theories is that they take root in the yearnings, prejudices, and assorted other frailties of the human psyche, offering the comfort of coherence in a chaotic world. The weakness that conspiracy theorists cultivate in adherents is the wish for a narrative line that can encompass all the evidence of a world gone wrong that people see around them. That is likely why the life and work of Edith Starr Miller fit into nearly every version of conspiracy theory.

MILLER WAS AN AMERICAN society lady who had married into the British aristocracy. Born July 16, 1887, in Newport, Rhode Island, while her parents were residing in their summer mansion, she was the granddaughter of the man who had founded the New York Metropolitan Opera and the daughter of one of the wealthiest industrialists of the late nineteenth century. In 1921, at the age of thirty-three, she married sixty-year-old Almeric Hugh Paget, Lord Queensborough, the grandson of the man who had commanded the British cavalry at the Battle of Waterloo. Paget had already formed a partnership with one of the wealthiest men in the world, Henry Payne Whitney, a partnership that obtained control of coal, steel, and iron conglomerates (all bearing the name "Dominion"). Paget also owned a railroad and an electric company. His first marriage was to his partner's niece, the wealthy heiress Pauline Payne Whitney, in a ceremony attended by President Grover Cleveland. Pauline had died during World War I, however, and Paget married Edith three years later. He was by then the commodore of the Royal Thames Yacht Club, treasurer of the League of Nations, and a Knight Grand Cross of the Order of the British Empire. Point being, marrying Lord Queenborough placed Edith at the pinnacle of European society, a vantage that permitted her to closely observe the operations of power and influence.

For most of what remained of her short life, the woman appeared dedicated to punctilious observation of the duties of her position. The only book of hers published during that time was *Common Sense in the Kitchen*, a volume intended to educate people about "normal rations in normal times." In January 1932, however, she filed for divorce from Lord Queenborough on grounds of cruelty and went to work on a book that would be published in 1933, shortly after her mysterious death in Paris. The title was *Occult Theocrasy*, and it stunned those who had known the woman first as a young socialite and later as a society matron.

"In offering this book to the public," Miller had written in the preface she supplied shortly before submitting *Occult Theocrasy* to a Paris publisher, "I have endeavored to expose some of the means and methods used by a secret world, one might also say an underworld, to penetrate, dominate and destroy not only the so-called upper classes, but also the better portion of all classes."

Miller hastened to state that she had never belonged to any of the secret societies she was describing but had become aware of them by marrying into the upper echelon of the British occult theocracy.

Miller's critics, mostly Masonic, have labeled her an anti-Semite, and not without basis. The occult theocracy, she charged, operated essentially under the control of two groups, Freemasonry and "Pharisee Judaism," which Miller described as a secret society using the Jewish religion as camouflage.

She was not suggesting that all or even most Jews and Freemasons were part of this satanic conspiracy, Miller wrote. The rank and file, or "innocents," as Miller called them, were considered by the adepts to be unfit to know the "ugly truth" and so had to be constantly manipulated with platitudes and deceits. What they most fundamentally did not understand, Miller wrote, was that the theocracy's primary purpose was to advance the goals and maintain the power of the super-rich:

> The power of theocrasy or exercise of government rule over the masses by a hierarchy of priests or adepts [has] rested on its dual system of teaching, namely: Exoterism and Esoterism, the former a code of discipline of the thought and mode of life of the masses; the latter the hierarchic school wherein were trained the chosen adepts destined to safeguard the rules imposed upon the people by the high priests. . . . Regardless of their exoteric objects, the esoteric aims of most [secret] societies are all directed toward the same end, namely: the concentration of political, economic and intellectual power into the hands of a small group of individuals, each of whom controls a branch of the International life, material and spiritual, of the world today.

The section of *Occult Theocrasy* most cited by contemporary conspiracy theorists is Miller's description of the relationship and correspondence between Albert Pike and Giuseppe Mazzini. Miller wrote that the letter was dated January 22, 1870 (Carr would have the date as August 15, 1871, and his date is the one most often cited), and focused her attention mainly on the passages in which Pike had plotted with fellow Illuminati masters to take over Freemasonry:

> We must allow all the federations to continue just as they are, with their systems, their central authorities, and their diverse modes of correspondence between high grades of the same rite, organized as they are at present, but we must create a super rite, which will remain unknown, to which we will call those Masons of high degree whom we shall select. With regard to our brothers in Masonry, these men must be pledges to the strictest secrecy. Through this supreme rite, we will govern all Freemasonry which will become the one international center, the more powerful because its direction will be unknown.

Edith Starr Miller died in Paris on January 16, 1933, shortly after completing *Occult Theocrasy* and just before it was published. The circumstances are mysterious mostly because they are unknown. She was forty-five years old and seemingly in good health. No record of hospitalization, no cause of death, no official certificate of any kind pertaining to her demise has ever been produced. During her young adulthood and her marriage to Lord Queenborough, she had been a prominent person, and yet, as her one and only biographer, Richard Evans points out, "No newspaper article or obituary was published. . . . Details of her life have been expunged, save for a *New York Times* clipping announcing her wedding in 1921." The only document Evans could find was a record in the files of the Masonic Grand Lodge of Canada noting that she died "under suspicious circumstances."

During the decade following her death, Miller's reputation would suffer owing to her marriage and because she was conflated with Nesta Helen Webster, a British author and contemporary of Miller's who also wrote about the alleged conspiracy of the Illuminati. Webster agreed that the secret society's members were occultists, but she tended to emphasize their satanic origins far less than their political and economic aims. Webster maintained that the Illuminati were committed to using communism to achieve world domination. She also added the Jesuits to the Masons and Jewish bankers as the three fronts upon which the conspiracy was advancing, beginning with the French Revolution in the late eighteenth century and culminating with the Bolshevik Revolution of 1917. Like Miller, Webster was well educated, prominent socially, and associated with various men of influence. She was also a charismatic public speaker whose admirers included Winston Churchill, the author of an article (titled "Zionism versus Bolshevism: A Struggle for the Soul of the Jewish People") in which he praised Webster lavishly and wrote that a "world-wide conspiracy" among certain wealthy Jews bent on "the overthrow of civilization and for the reconstitution of society on the basis of arrested development, of envious malevolence, and impossible equality has been steadily growing." Webster's own anti-Semitism grew steadily more strident ("What mysteries of iniquity would be revealed if the Jew, like the mole, did not make a point of working in the dark!") as she became a darling of the British Fascists and publicly dismissed reports of the persecution of the Jews by Nazi Germany. For obvious reasons, World War II and its aftermath would lead to the decline and fall of her reputation.

Lord Queenborough also had been a Fascist sympathizer who railed against the Bolsheviks and was overtly anti-Semitic. Those who dismissed Edith Starr Miller's claims regularly used her husband against her, despite the fact that she had fled from him after filing for divorce and seemed to have written *Occult Theocrasy* to expose what she had observed during their marriage.

Miller's admirers believe she was referring to herself when she wrote in the preface of her book: "Irrefutable evidence of a particular example of underworld tyranny has come into my possession. The victim's guilt was her reluctance to step from virtue into the mire of evil which surrounded her. Moreover, she was intolerant of evil and sought to oppose and destroy it. The case of her persecution at the hands of her foes is complete. She belonged to what is termed Society as did also some of the other actors in this bewildering drama."

Richard Evans, who calls Miller an "unsung heroine," writes of her, "Occult and New Age sites label Edith Starr Miller as an anti-Semitic, pro-fascist, Christian fundamentalist who believes in the 'Jesuit-Masonic, Illuminati-Bolshevik conspiracy theory.' This is how Satanists classify the vestiges of decent humanity who resist them."

Miller's description of the victim of "underworld tyranny" caught in a "bewildering drama" is haunting, but even more remarkable is an observation she put into print in 1932 that at once echoed Justin Martyr's second-century remarks about moral relativism and sounded remarkably like what Christian traditionalists were saying and writing in the twenty-first century: "Today, most of the good people are afraid to be good. They strive to be broadminded and tolerant! It is fashionable to be tolerant—but mostly tolerant of evil—and this new code has reached the proportions of demanding intolerance of good."

The sad fact was that William Guy Carr's writings had become more central to the conspiracy theory than those of Edith Starr Miller. Not only had what Miller reported about the Pike-Mazzini correspondence been subsumed into Carr's work, but Carr's book *Pawns in the Game* had included a purported passage from Pike's letter to Mazzini that Miller hadn't mentioned, a description of the plan by the secret powers to instigate three world wars in order to create a global government and the kingdom of Satan on earth. The "three world wars" plan would become a central feature of the conspiracy theory in the second half of the twentieth century, owing in large part to the startling prescience about future events that it ascribed to Albert Pike. Illuminati agents planted in the British and German governments would foment the first of these world wars, Pike had written (according to Carr). The purpose would be to facilitate the overthrow of the czarist regime in Russia and make that country a fortress of atheistic Communism, in the process weakening the grip of Christianity on the European continent. The underlying dynamic of the second of these world wars, Pike had added (again, according to Carr) would be to pit fascism against Zionism, with an aim to the establishment of a Jewish state in Israel, an outcome that would create the basis for the third world war. The second world war would also increase the power of international communism and further weaken the influence of Christianity. The ostensible focus of the third world war, Pike had written, would be a battle between the new Zionist state in the Middle East and "the Moslem Arabic World." The other nations of the earth would be not only divided by this conflict but inevitably drawn into it. Both Zionism and Islam would be destroyed in the process of a war that might well last decades, and the planet's surviving nations would be utterly exhausted, materially and spiritually. The Illuminati masters would then unleash "the Nihilists and Atheists" to provoke a social cataclysm that would discredit both Christianity and atheistic materialism, leaving people desperate for something to believe in. At that moment, the "true light" of the Luciferian Principle would be shined on the peoples of the entire planet, offering the dispirited human race a path not only to survival but also to salvation, and a one-world government would be established. For anyone who has ever read the Book of Revelation, the correspondences to the biblical time of the Antichrist will be manifest.

The provenance of Carr's version of the Pike-Mazzini letter has been the subject of investigations conducted on three continents. Masonic writers have sought to discredit the book by Cardinal Caro Rodríguez that includes the alleged correspondence between Pike and Mazzini, noting that Caro Rodríguez's book had been published more than seven years after the end of World War I. Caro Rodríguez's version of the Pike-Mazzini letter was obviously a fabrication that offered not foreknowledge but hindsight, these writers claimed. A reasonable enough argument, but I had to ask: how could a Chilean cardinal have known in 1925 that the second world war would involve an attempt by Fascists to eradicate Zionism?

Eventually, separate researchers from South Africa, France, and the United States would conclude that the version of the Pike-Mazzini letter Caro Rodríguez cited in his 1925 book was nearly identical to the version Léo Taxil had included in *Le diable au XIXè siècle*, published in 1894. Taxil was, as the Masons pointed out, the most notorious hoaxer in history. But how was it possible that Taxil, writing in the nineteenth century, could have concocted eerily accurate descriptions of the Bolshevik Revolution in the context of World War I and the attempt by the Nazis to kill off the Jews during World War II, resulting ultimately in the establishment of Israel? Even putting that aside, various contemporary conspiracy theorists have asked, was it not ominous, given the current state of the world, that Caro Rodríguez, writing in 1924, and Carr, writing in 1954, had forecast a third world war that would be ignited by a clash between Islam and Israel?

It seemed ominous enough to me. Feverish and dizzy from a survey of the conspiracy theory's vast literature, one that had me exploring tangents that went off on the Mormon Church and Henry Wadsworth Longfellow, the disappearance of Ku Klux Klan records from libraries all over the country, and the various interpretations of Albert Pike's 1874 book *Irano-Aryan Faith and Doctrine as Contained in the Zend-Avesta*, I was looking over my shoulder mainly for whoever might catch me immersed in this muddle, simultaneously fearing such a humiliation and yet still troubled by the eureka moment I might be missing if I stopped now.

Who or what does all this serve, I found myself asking at one point, this crazed obsession with an equation of implicit and/or imaginary connections that grows increasingly fractal the more desperately one tries to solve it? And the answer was obvious: in the modern age, the Devil had managed to hide in plain sight, dancing on the head of a pin right in front of our eyes, his gleeful shriek drowned out as much by the clamor of people who believed he existed as by those who did not. And yet it was in the moment of this revelation that I seemed to see him most clearly, strutting amid the words and thoughts and deeds of us all, arms outstretched in triumph. For the Devil, I thought, this really was the best of all possible worlds.

PART TWO

The Door He Hides Behind

CHAPTER NINE

ON A SUNNY AFTERNOON in September 2014, just before the rollover from summer into autumn and a little more than two months after my first trip to Childress, Texas, I returned from a five-mile hike through the hills surrounding my home, stopped to collect what was in the mailbox, and felt my gut clench when I saw the envelope on the top of the pile.

The only visible cue for such apprehension was that, while my own name and address had been handwritten in large, well-formed letters on the front of the envelope, there was no return address. Yet I felt so wary that I held the envelope at arm's length as I opened it and pulled out a single sheet of notebook paper that was covered with the same handwriting that appeared on the envelope. My dread was justified by the first paragraph of the letter:

> R,
>
> *My hand is not my own in this missive. You are afraid and with good reason. You have been working for ɯıH for a goodly time. ǝH likes the status quo.*

The sheet of paper was already fluttering in my hands as I read on:

> *It is easy for ɯıH to operate anonymously in this age when for many, all seems settled. You have been asked to throw open the door ǝH hides behind.*

You have lied to yourself about what you believe conveys his work and evil deeds. Oh yes, He enjoys a splashy blood bath, for it breeds fear and helplessness. He breathes these like the air. However, His best work is far more subtle. It is in the unkindnesses, the pettiness and unfair acts of spite that we mete out to one another every day. It is in the prideful judgements we make of one another and our inability to forgive even ourselves. To forgive ourselves requires humility.

This may be your last best chance to save your soul and as God has created you, it is worth saving, even as you act as though it is not.

I pray that you seek His protection and do what has been asked of you. Save yourself, if only for a chance for happiness. You have not had this for a long long time.

This may be your last and only chance.

By the time I finished the letter, my heart was pounding so violently that I couldn't organize anything remotely like a rational response to what I'd just read. This person didn't just know things about the book I was writing; he or she knew things about *me*. The few people I spoke to about the letter during the next couple of days all seemed astonished that I had been so affected by it; there was a hint of either mockery or condescension in some voices. How could I take an anonymous letter from some stranger who was obviously a lunatic so seriously? Interestingly, each of the friends I spoke to about the letter imagined its author in a different way. One referred to the writer as "a religious nut." Another thought the letter could have been sent by one of the satanists connected to the Childress case, trying to frighten me off. There was also a suggestion that it had come from someone with a personal vendetta who had heard about the book and had decided to mess with my mind.

That last idea was the easiest to dismiss. Apart from the fact that I didn't think anyone in the world hated me enough to make such an effort, this explanation seemed to suppose that I had been sharing details about the book with some number of persons when in fact I hadn't spoken to a single soul about how I was approaching what I called "the Devil book." I hadn't even shown the nearly two hundred pages I'd written so far to my publisher, and I had never once used the internet—not even Google Documents—to save those pages. The woman who was my closest confidante tried to convince me that someone could have hacked into my computer to read the manuscript, but that seemed ridiculously farfetched, unless the letter *had* in fact been written by some satanist who'd heard I was looking into the Tate Rowland case and wanted to scare me into taking another direction. That explanation was so convoluted that even I couldn't follow it, and anyway I doubted a satanist would urge me to seek the protection of Jesus.

So only the "religious nut" idea made any kind of sense to me. I found myself going through the letter a sentence at a time to try to understand who the writer might be. *My hand in this missive is not my own.* This person was claiming, I had to assume, to be the vehicle of some supernatural entity, and to be drawing upon that authority. And then there was the use of the word "missive," with its implication that the message being delivered was in some way official. I pictured someone older, with what was by my standards an exaggerated sense of formality. *You are afraid and with good reason.* This attempt to seize my attention had been terribly effective the first time I read the words, but I began to grow defiant as I reread them. Did the writer mean I was afraid of him (or her)? Or that I was frightened in a larger way by some circumstance in which I had either placed myself or been placed? But then I began to demand to know by what right this person dared to claim knowledge of what I felt. Anger, I noticed, brought instant relief from the anxiety I experienced whenever I picked up the letter. The next sentence—*You have been working for ɯıH for a goodly time*—disturbed me in a much deeper way. It was crazy, I knew, but I couldn't stop wondering what I had ever done that made me deserve such a thing being said about me. There was no mention, I realized eventually, of what the work was that I had done for *ɯıH*. It was as if the writer was counting on me to fill in that blank. Then: *ɘH likes the status quo.* What could that mean other than that the Devil wanted me to keep doing what I was doing?

This seemed even clearer when I considered the next paragraph: *It is easy for ɯıH to operate anonymously in this age when for many, all seems settled. You have been asked to throw open the door ɘH hides behind.*

Baudelaire could have written that first sentence, it occurred to me. The next sentence, though, was one I kept returning to in my mind for the first week after the letter's arrival. *When* had I been asked? I wanted to know. And by whom? Well, I knew whom the writer meant. But the idea that God or his heavenly emissaries had selected me for the task of throwing open "*the door ᴐH hides behind*" jammed in my brain. I'd received no messages, no instructions, no requests, other than the ones that existed in my own mind. And how would this person know about those? Was this an appeal to my sense of sacred duty, or to the grandiosity it would require to imagine I had been chosen for such an immense task? Whatever, I couldn't get over feeling at once daunted and indignant whenever I reflected on that sentence, which I admit was often in the days immediately after I received the letter. I found myself asking God when exactly I'd ever suggested I was capable or courageous enough to accomplish such a task. God, though, was leaving me to figure that out on my own.

The last part of the letter was what made the greatest long-term impact on me. Satan's best work, the author had written, *is in the unkindnesses, the pettiness and unfair acts of spite that we mete out to one another every day. It is in the prideful judgements we make of one another and our inability to forgive even ourselves. To forgive ourselves requires humility*. I had never killed anyone or, for that matter, committed any serious crime. Unkindness, pettiness, spite, and prideful judgment, though, were evils with which I was all too familiar. I didn't understand the line about how forgiving ourselves requires humility, but I sensed some kind of truth behind it, and I found this a terrible concession to have made when I read the last part of the letter, filled as it was with warnings so dire they felt like threats:

> *This may be your last best chance to save your soul and as God has created you, it is worth saving, even as you act as though it is not.*
>
> *I pray that you seek sIH protection and do what has been asked of you. Save yourself, if only for a chance for happiness. You have not had this for a long long time.*
>
> *This may be your last and only chance.*

I was physically ill the first couple of times I read the last sentences of the letter. Being threatened with damnation was not an entirely unfamiliar experience for me. I had been warned my soul was at risk many times in Medjugorje, but never since, until now, in a letter that made it sound as though my chances of salvation hung by a thread. Do what has been asked of you, or else.

Eventually, reacting to and against this last part of the letter was the process that freed me from the stress I had experienced the first few times I read it. It finally registered with me that by sending it anonymously, the author of the letter had forfeited any claim to credibility. Maybe God was the kind of tyrant who would send me to hell for failing to complete an assignment I'd never been given, but I wasn't going to take the word of a coward for it.

I put the letter back in its envelope and stuck that in a box filled with research materials I was finished with. Gradually I was able to go a day or two or ten without thinking about it.

ONE SECTION OF THE LETTER not only lingered, though, but persuaded me to make a major change in the book I was writing:

> *You have lied to yourself about what you believe conveys his work and evil deeds. Oh yes, ∂H enjoys a splashy blood bath, for it breeds fear and helplessness. ∂H breathes these like the air.*

At the time, the first half of this book included lengthy sections on my personal encounters with evil, and in particular with the serial killers I had been assigned to report on while working for newspapers in New York and Los Angeles during my twenties. In the weeks after reading the anonymous letter, I began to tear those sections out of the book. But then there were two I felt compelled to keep. One was on the most frightening person I've ever been in the presence of, Lawrence Bittaker.

With his partner Roy Norris, whom he had met in the late 1970s while they were locked up in the California Men's Colony, Bittaker had devised a "game" in which, after their release from prison, they would snatch a girl for every teen year, from thirteen to nineteen, then rape, torture, and finally murder her. Behind bars, Bittaker and Norris devised a scenario in which they would see how long each victim could be kept alive and screaming. A month after Norris was released from prison in 1978, they met at a seedy hotel in downtown Los Angeles and agreed to play the game for real.

It was Bittaker, now working as a machinist, who purchased the pair's "Murder Mack," a silver GMC cargo van that he liked because it had no side windows but was equipped with a large sliding door on the passenger side that would allow the two of them to "pull up real close and not have to open the doors all the way" while snatching a young woman off the sidewalk. Bittaker and Norris spent four months cruising up and down the Pacific Coast Highway, stopping at beaches and taking pictures of girls who interested them. Detectives later would find more than five hundred photographs of smiling young women among Bittaker's possessions. They were saving the rape and murder, explained Norris, who would be the main witness at Bittaker's trial, until they found the perfect isolated spot. This the two discovered in June 1979 at the end of a remote fire road in the San Gabriel Mountains.

During the next three months, Bittaker and Norris abducted, raped, and murdered five teenage girls. As planned, they began to see how long they could keep their victims alive and screaming, torturing them with Bittaker's pliers and Norris's sledgehammer, taking Polaroid photographs and making audiotapes for their later enjoyment. One girl's agony lasted almost two full days.

It was my misfortune to be in court on January 29, 1981, when an audiotape was played of Bittaker and Norris torturing a sixteen-year-old named Lynette Ledford. Norris testified that Bittaker had played the tape constantly during the last weeks before they were captured and considered it to be "real funny." The tape began with Bittaker slapping Lynette and shouting, "Say something, girl!" "What do you want me to say?" Lynette whimpered. The slapping continued, with the girl alternately crying, gasping, shrieking, and pleading.

Bittaker's frustration was audible as he shouted, "You can scream louder than that, can't you?" Then he went to work with the pliers, repeating, "Scream, baby!" several times. "Make noise there, girl!" Norris could be heard shouting a moment later. "Go ahead and scream or I'll make you scream." There was the sound of Norris hitting the girl's elbows with his sledgehammer (detectives counted twenty-five blows) as he chanted, "Keep it up, girl, Keep it up! Scream till I say stop!"

Deputy District Attorney Steve Kay, a veteran prosecutor who had convicted dozens of murderers and rapists, wept openly. So did most of the jurors. The only two people in the courtroom who displayed no distress were Bittaker and Norris. Norris's expression was blank, but the corners of Bittaker's mouth curled into a tight-lipped smile; he was enjoying himself.

I refused to return to the Bittaker trial the next day and could barely make myself skim the stories about the case filed by other reporters. I did take time to inspect the probation reports that were produced before Bittaker and Norris were sentenced, but there was nothing important in them I didn't already know. A certain rootlessness that had resulted from Bittaker, who had an IQ of 137, being adopted by a couple who moved constantly because of the husband's job was the only thing remotely like an antecedent to the criminal career he began as a teenager, primarily shoplifting and stealing cars before he met Norris in prison.

What the examiners in the probation reports found most notable about both Bittaker and Norris was a lack of feeling for their victims, an utter absence of compassion or remorse. Not caring was an essential quality of evil, I remember thinking, in a vague sort of way. But I sensed that there was more than Plato's "absence of good" going on here: Something had moved in to fill the moral vacuum of Bittaker's soul, something alien, radically inhuman, something that took pleasure in suffering and found affirmation in fear. I didn't know what it was, and didn't want to know, yet needed to.

I felt no satisfaction when Bittaker was sentenced to execution in the gas chamber. Not that I didn't think the world would be a better place without Lawrence Bittaker in it. After listening to the Lynette

Ledford tape, I was still an ostensible opponent of the death penalty, but for different reasons than before. Death wouldn't be punishment enough for the likes of Bittaker, I had decided. I didn't want him killed; I wanted him erased, nonexistent, never was and never will be. That being an impossibility, so was justice. It was a grim realization.

In the three decades since Bittaker was sentenced to the gas chamber, he has made himself at home on San Quentin's death row. For a number of years, he shared a daily bridge game with three fellow serial killers, Randy Kraft, Douglas Clark, and William Bonin, who between them claimed an estimated ninety-four victims. Then Bonin was executed in 1996 and left the game shorthanded. In addition to the ongoing appeals of his death sentence, Bittaker has entertained himself by filing dozens of lawsuits against the state prison system. He forced state officials to pay $5,000 to obtain the dismissal of a suit claiming he had been subjected to "cruel and unusual punishment" by the delivery of a lunch tray with a broken cookie on it. In the late 1990s, Bittaker began to earn spending money by selling his fingernail clippings to murder groupies through a prison memorabilia catalog. He still regularly receives fan mail, most of it sent to him by women. Bittaker reportedly answers every letter, signing off with his prison nickname, "Pliers."

My conversation with Jeffrey Burton Russell in the Ty Bar was what had first persuaded me to tell the story of Lawrence Bittaker. At one point, Russell had segued into a description of the shock and horror he'd experienced as he read about Bittaker's crimes, and how deeply it had convinced him that the word "evil" was an essential part of the human vocabulary. And now, strangely, another fragment of my conversation with Russell, recalled in the context of the anonymous letter I had received, was having the opposite effect. At one point I'd asked Russell about his personal encounters with evil. It seemed pretty weak to me at the time that all Russell could come up with was the childhood memory of a woman who lived across the street and had been both relentless and remorseless in spreading false stories about her neighbors. Perhaps, I thought now, Russell was simply a much more sensitive being than me, and only needed exposure to a nasty gossip to comprehend the reality of evil.

Perhaps a consideration of how souls were corrupted by everyday evils—*the unkindnesses, the pettiness and unfair acts of spite*—might be more powerful than the tale of a "splashy bloodbath." Only that book had already been written by C. S. Lewis.

The disturbance the anonymous letter had produced in me did yield at least one good result, this being that it sent me back to *The Screwtape Letters*. Lewis's central conceit was to compose the book as the correspondence sent by a senior demon, Screwtape, to a young nephew, Wormwood, who is still learning about how human beings can be induced to damnation. In *Screwtape*, Lewis had created a lowercase-*d* devil who could easily be imagined as an amiable neighbor or co-worker, a man with a quick wit and a winning smile, one who would instruct his nephew that "the safest road to Hell is the gradual one—the gentle slope, soft underfoot, without sudden turnings, without milestones, without signposts." Screwtape was the sort of fellow who would happily join those who deplored warfare, not on moral grounds, of course, but because "the continual remembrance of death which war enforces" renders useless "one of our best weapons, contented worldliness."

The enduring power of Lewis's book was demonstrated to me by the fact that much of the advice Screwtape gives Wormwood seemed more relevant in late 2014 than it did when I had first read it decades earlier: "The great thing is to direct the malice [of a man] to his immediate neighbors whom he meets every day and to thrust his benevolence out to the remote circumference, to people he does not know. The malice thus becomes wholly real and the benevolence largely imaginary."

In the preface to *The Screwtape Letters* that Lewis composed more than fifteen years after the book was first written, he told his readers that because "I live in the Managerial Age," he was compelled to observe a world in which the greatest evil was not done in Dickens's crime dens or even in Hitler's concentration camps but rather in "clean, carpeted, well-lighted offices, by quiet men with white collars and cut fingernails and smooth-shaven cheeks who do not need to raise their voice." The Hell he imagined, Lewis, added, was "something like the bureaucracy of a police state."

I could never have written *The Screwtape Letters*, I realized. Talent and imagination aside, Lewis had drawn on a faith that was both sturdy and rigorous, one that adhered strictly to Anglican theology. My faith was shakier, my doubts more pronounced. My experiences in life had compelled me to contemplate the source of the evil I witnessed nearly everywhere I went in the world, but I hadn't even resolved the question of whether God himself should be held responsible for it. The way I had reacted to that anonymous letter showed me how deeply the idea of a Devil was embedded in my psyche, but I was quite capable—intellectually, at least—of conceiving of Satan as no more than the personification of the Jews' *yetzer ra* or even as a Jungian archetype.

Two very basic questions were what had motivated me to undertake this book, I decided after rereading *The Screwtape Letters*. The first was whether the Devil actually existed. Only if my answer to that was yes did I come to the second question: Who or what are we describing when we refer to "the Devil"?

I had felt compelled to pursue those questions in the way that addressed them most directly. "A splashy bloodbath" made the reality of evil unavoidable. Those who wanted to describe a Lawrence Bittaker as "sick" were insipid, of that much I was certain. But then, in the one article I'd written about his trial, what I had called Bittaker was "depraved." Did I imagine that was truer?

NO MATTER HOW THOROUGHLY the modern mind may dismiss the idea of the Devil as an actual being, the problem of evil has persisted right up to the present moment, repeatedly surfacing in ways that compel people from all across the planet to address it. The ghastly cruelty of Nazi Germany's concentration camps, the mass slaughter of Tutsis by Hutus in Rwanda, the internecine atrocities in what was once Yugoslavia—these and other events demand some kind of explanation, some sense of a source from which they emanate.

So it is inevitable that our age should produce psychological theories of evil. The most notable has emerged from the work of Stanford professor Philip Zimbardo, whose attempts to explain evil as something created by systems and situations is compelling up to a point. The problem is that past that point his argument attenuates into meaninglessness.

Zimbardo is best known for his infamous 1971 Stanford Prison Experiment. This was largely an iteration of research that had been conducted ten years earlier by the psychologist Stanley Milgram at Yale, where Zimbardo had taken his PhD. At Yale, Milgram had recruited participants for a "study of memory" that was really a study of how people became obediently evil—evil enough to perform the duties of, for instance, concentration camp guards.

Only when they arrived at the site were the participants informed (by a "scientist" wearing a white lab coat and horn-rimmed glasses) that the purpose of the study was to test the effects of punishment on learning.

They would be divided, by drawing straws, into "teachers" and "learners," the participants were told. But this wasn't true; all of the learners were working for Milgram and only pretending to be study participants.

Each teacher was seated in front of a console on one side of a partition and given a list of word pairs. They were instructed to read aloud the first word, then tell the learner on the other side of the partition to choose the second word by pushing one of four buttons. If the learner's answer was incorrect, the teachers were told, they would push a button to administer an electric shock that they were to increase by 15 volts for each wrong answer. In front of them were buttons marked with letters and colors ranging from a yellow button delivering a "slight shock," 15 volts, up to the purple "danger severe shock" button, delivering 450 volts. Milgram made sure the teachers understood what they were doing by giving each of them a "sample" 45-volt shock before they began working with the learners.

The learners wouldn't be actually receiving electric shocks when they gave wrong answers, and what the teachers would hear from the other side of the partition was actually a tape recording of an actor's voice. But from the perspective of the teachers, it was all really happening.

As the shocks administered by the teachers increased in fifteen-volt increments, what they heard at first was shouts and protests from the other side of the partition. At 120 volts, the learner was heard screaming, "Hey, this really hurts!" Nearly every one of the teachers by that point was expressing concern for the unseen learner. The scientist in the white coat, though, stolidly told them, "The experiment requires that you continue. Please go on." Almost without exception, the teachers did just that. Even when, at 270 volts, they heard the learner screaming in agony, "Let me out of here! Let me out of here! Let me out! Do you hear?" the vast majority of teachers continued. At 300 volts, the learner stopped answering the word pair questions and began to simply shriek in pain. A refusal to answer was the same as a wrong answer, the scientist in the white coat told the teachers, and so an elevated shock must be administered.

When Milgram had earlier described his experiment to an audience of thirty-nine psychiatrists, the group predicted that maybe one participant in a thousand would continue until he or she delivered the 450-volt "severe shock." The actual result was that nearly two-thirds of the participants—62.5 percent—administered the 450-volt shock.

Zimbardo's experiment was more elaborate, even though he was making essentially the same point about the human capacity for evil given the right circumstances. At Stanford, Zimbardo recruited (at $15 per day) twenty-four male students who would be evenly divided between "prison guards" and "prison inmates." The twelve inmates went through an initial shock of being picked up at their homes by actual Palo Alto police officers, then abruptly taken to the basement of a campus building, the "Stanford County Jail," where they were stripped, deloused, and put into rough muslin smocks, without underwear. As Zimbardo described it, "We dehumanized the prisoners, gave them numbers, and took away their identity. The guards were outfitted in khaki uniforms, given silver reflecting sunglasses to wear indoors, and instructed to demand that the inmates address each of them as "Mr. Correctional Officer."

What happened during the next six days was not only shocking but immensely influential, mainly because of the single most consequential decision Zimbardo made, which was to film the experiment as it happened, resulting in a documentary that has been viewed by millions of American high school and college students, among them me. A full one-third of the guards seemed to relish the opportunities for sadistic abuse they were given, a number of them actually working extra hours just for the fun of inflicting fear and humiliation upon the prisoners under their supervision. Among the punishments they meted out was removing the prisoners' mattresses to make them sleep on the floor and refusing to let them empty the buckets they used as toilets. One guard, the son of a Stanford engineering professor, was particularly relentless, encouraging the prisoners to harass one another with increasingly cruel innuendos about their sexuality and throwing them into solitary confinement for the most minor failure to follow orders immediately and without question.

What he had demonstrated, Zimbardo would declare, was that even "good ordinary college students" would become barbarous bullies if given permission. The holes in his conclusion were as gaping as the flaws in his experiment. Zimbardo seemed to imagine that his most significant deviation from Milgram was to dispense with the "authority figure" that had demanded pitiless obedience from the test subjects at Yale. All he had really gotten rid of, though, was the white coat; Zimbardo himself had played the role of prison superintendent in the Stanford experiment. Academic critics would fault him for various other methodological shortcomings, such as "selection bias" or "inadequate sample size." The results of the Stanford Prison Experiment were further tainted when the most abusive of the guards, the one who called himself "John Wayne," said in an interview years later that he had been playing a role, much as in the drama productions he had performed in during high school and college. He had modeled his "character" on the prison warden in the movie *Cool*

Hand Luke, he said: "It was something I was very familiar with, to take on another personality before you step out on the stage. I was kind of running my own experiment in there."

All of that was probably relevant, but it had been obvious to me even as a nineteen-year-old college student that both Zimbardo and his critics were missing the main point. What I was curious about was the other two-thirds of the guards who hadn't become sadistic, who had in many cases shown concern for the prisoners under their control, asking what they needed or if there was anything they could do to help. I wanted to know what separated them from the guards who had been indifferent to or even enjoyed the suffering of the prisoners. But this was a question that didn't interest Zimbardo. His commitment to the idea of evil as a product of environmental conditions was total, and the film of his Stanford Prison Experiment spread it to the point of cultural saturation. Zimbardo achieved even greater notoriety when he testified before Congress about the torture of prisoners at the Abu Ghraib prison by US military personnel. He could sum up his theory of evil very simply, Zimbardo would say: "Evil is the exercise of power. . . . [And] the power is in the system. The system creates the situation that corrupts individuals, and the system is the legal, political, economic, cultural background. And this is where the power is of the bad-barrel makers. So if you want to change a person, you've got to change the situation."

What "situation" did Zimbardo imagine could produce the likes of Lawrence Bittaker? The only system that had failed in his case was the legal one that had repeatedly released this demonic character back into society. It's true that those who study serial killers have found that an unusually high percentage of them are, like Bittaker, adoptees, but it's also true that millions of people who are adopted as children don't become any kind of criminal, let alone one has heinous as Bittaker. There was no explaining Bittaker. He was beyond understanding, and that was really the most significant thing about him. What Bittaker's existence suggested was the starkest and scariest answer to evil I had ever considered: There is no why. It just is.

CHAPTER TEN

ONE THING PHILIP ZIMBARDO *had* accomplished, albeit unintentionally, in his Stanford Prison Experiment was to bolster the "just following orders" Nazi excuse. Only a third of his prison guards had taken it all the way, becoming the merciless martinets Zimbardo was so focused upon. In the Stanley Milgram experiment at Yale, on the other hand, *two-thirds* of the teachers had pushed the "severe shock" button, fully conscious of the agony they were inflicting. The only obvious difference between the two situations was that while Zimbardo had only encouraged his guards to do evil things, Milgram had commanded his teachers to. Yet both Zimbardo and Milgram had largely ignored the most salient question raised by their experiments: Why had one-third of Milgram's teachers and two-thirds of Zimbardo's guards refused to keep doing harm? In my mind, even if just one of the teachers in Milgram's experiment had said no, this would have introduced the issue of volition. Those 37.5 percent of teachers in the Yale experiment who refused to keep going, to continue torturing the learners, had made a moral choice. They had known right from wrong.

I wondered after reading about the Zimbardo and Milgram experiments how the guards and teachers who had done the worst had been affected by it afterward. Had they recoiled and become more conscious, or merely shrugged it off and moved on with their lives? What I most wanted to know, I realized, was whether evil could be undone.

*   *   *

AS I BEGAN TO CUT the serial killer sections out of the first draft
of this book, I paused for a long time at the end of the one I had written about Westley Allan Dodd.

I had begun to consider Dodd in late 1989, while staying in the
snug and cozy Portland, Oregon, home of my oldest friend, celebrating the recent birth of his son. As the Dodd story began to unfold amid
the community around us, we two followed it in the newspaper
and on television with a sickened fascination. The part of us that
wanted to will the facts into nonexistence was being slowly battered
into submission by a mounting realization that such creatures existed, even here. And yet we couldn't look away.

Dodd was a small and scrawny young man with black hair and
dark eyes whose features could have been called delicate. At twenty-
eight, he looked as if the thick mustache on his upper lip had been
pasted in place. His puniness engendered a sense of helplessness and
bafflement in those who interrogated him—and probably had helped
him gain the trust of the children he raped, tortured, and murdered.

As in the case of Lawrence Bittaker, I had been bewildered by
the absence of anything that came close to explaining how Dodd had
developed into Dodd. His parents' constant bickering and inability
to connect with him emotionally were the best explanations he had
for growing up as an isolated boy who was intimidated by girls. A meek
and obedient child, Dodd first got into trouble at age thirteen when
neighbors complained that he was standing naked in the upstairs
bedroom window of his parents' home, his face hidden behind a
curtain, whenever grade school children passed by. Soon after, he began exposing his genitals in random encounters with children. He
got his first job, as a babysitter, at sixteen, and molested the kids he
was supposed to be caring for as they slept.

Another similarity to Bittaker was that Dodd had been caught
and diagnosed as deviant multiple times before committing his most
horrendous crimes. In Bittaker's case, it was the absurdly lax California
penal system of the 1960s and 1970s that had failed to stop him. The

first state prison psychiatrist to examine him in 1961 acknowledged his "superior intelligence" and described him as a "borderline psychotic." A second prison psychiatrist who interviewed him in 1964 also gave Bittaker a diagnosis of borderline psychosis. Nevertheless, he was released again from prison in 1966, only to return in 1967. In 1976, the famous forensic psychiatrist Robert Markman examined Bittaker and deemed him a "classic sociopath," as close as a shrink ever comes to calling someone evil. Bittaker was "a highly dangerous man, with no internal controls over his impulses, a man who could kill without hesitation or remorse," Markman warned. Despite this, and two more psychiatric evaluations that labeled him "a sophisticated psychopath" who was "more than likely" to commit new crimes if let go, Bittaker was released from the California Men's Colony in late 1978, followed to the streets two months later by his prison friend Roy Norris.

In Dodd's case, the passes he received from the criminal justice system seemed to even more clearly echo what Jeffrey Burton Russell had said to me about the inability of educated people in the contemporary world to comprehend that there actually was such a thing as evil. In 1981, while enlisted in the navy, Dodd had gotten off with a warning after attempting to abduct a pair of little girls. Less than a year later, while still in the navy, Dodd was taken into police custody after offering a group of boys $50 each to go with him to a motel to play strip poker. Yet even after he admitted that he intended to molest the boys, the charges were dropped because the parents didn't want to put their sons through the ordeal of a public trial. Just months later, Dodd's approach to a young boy in a public restroom resulted in his conviction for "attempted indecent liberties" and a jail sentence of nineteen days. The navy gave him a general discharge and sent Dodd on his way. Within the year, he was arrested for molesting a ten-year-old boy, but somehow drew a judge who gave him a suspended one-year sentence, on the condition that he receive counseling.

Westley Allan Dodd was twenty-six and living once again in Vancouver in 1987 when he chose an eight-year-old boy as his first intended murder victim. Working as the security guard at a construction site, Dodd spotted the child in the neighborhood and tried to lure him into one of the vacant buildings by claiming that he needed help to find a "lost little boy." Sensing danger, the boy said he was going home to get some toys for the lost boy and would come right back. His mother phoned the police a few minutes later. Dodd went to trial, where the judge reduced the charge to a "gross misdemeanor" and sentenced Dodd to just 118 days in jail. The psychologist who examined Dodd during his custody reported that while he was struck by the remarkable "history of deviant assaults" in someone so young, he did not consider Dodd to be capable of violence. When Dodd talked about his crimes, the psychologist explained, "he did it in baby talk, like a kid. He fit right in with them. He didn't want to hurt them."

Dodd was back out on the streets in the early autumn 1989, working as a shipping clerk at a paper company, where he told his fellow employees that he had a second job, having been hired by the sheriff's office to "stand on the corner and watch children." He spent a good deal of his time in Vancouver's heavily wooded David Douglas Park, walking the paths and looking for isolated spots behind shrubbery where he thought a child might venture. By then Dodd was carrying what he called his "hunting gear," a fillet knife that he wore strapped to an ankle and the shoestrings he would use to bind his victims. In his diary Dodd chronicled his frustration with the ways in which he was thwarted—by a parent following a child on the path, by a kid's abrupt turn down a different trail, or by the sudden appearance of a potential witness. He began eating his lunch in the park, so as not to miss any "opportunity," and by the week after Labor Day was returning to the park each evening to walk the trails.

He "got lucky" as Dodd put it, when he spotted eleven-year-old Cole Neer and his ten-year-old brother Billy pedaling furiously through the park, taking a shortcut because they were late for dinner. The two had spent the afternoon at the golf course, where they collected and sold lost balls. Dodd stepped out into the path, blocking their way, then ordered the boys off their bikes and told them to "come with me." When Billy asked why, Dodd answered, "Because I told you to." Why the boys obeyed is impossible to know, but both brothers remained quiet when a pair of teenagers walked past, and let Dodd lead them to the spot he had previously selected, hidden by thick brush on all sides. Dodd got the boys to stand back-to-back while he tied their wrists together with the shoelaces. The older boy, Cole, kept asking, "Why?" All he said in reply, Dodd would recall, was that one of them needed to pull down his pants. Cole asked, "Will it hurt?" "No," Dodd told him. "Why are you doing this to us?" Cole asked when Dodd began to assault him. He turned then to the younger brother, Dodd said, but Billy was crying so hard that it was impossible to finish with him. So he forced both brothers to their knees, Dodd said, and cut the shoestrings with his fillet knife. Billy asked if he could go home and tell his father that they would be late. "No," Dodd answered. "I'm almost done." He then ordered Billy to sit and watch while he raped Cole. Both boys were sobbing and pleading by then, remembered Dodd, who told them, "There's just one more thing," and then stabbed Billy in the stomach with the fillet knife. Cole leaped to his feet and tried to run, but Dodd caught the boy and forced him to the ground, stabbing him once in the side. Billy somehow was able to stagger toward a street that bordered the park. Still struggling with Cole, Dodd stabbed the older brother two more times, until the boy stopped moving, then went after Billy, catching the younger boy just before he made it to the road. The only part of this horror that Dodd would admit to being haunted by was that Billy had begun to sob, "I'm sorry! I'm sorry!" That the boy would apologize as he was about to be killed made him feel "strange," Dodd admitted, but that hadn't stopped him from stabbing Billy two more times before fleeing the scene, leaving both boys to bleed to death.

As we read about the murders of the Neer brothers in *The Oregonian*, my friend Steve and I speculated about who could possibly commit such a crime. Most people have terrible thoughts pass through their minds, Steve and I agreed, and then wonder where *that* came from. Likely there are more than a few who follow one of those thoughts to the rim of the abyss. How many look over the edge is impossible to know, but it seems a safe bet that the number is greater than we want to believe. Some turn away immediately in shock and never return to that place, whether constrained by fear or conscience.

Some look longer, until they start to see shadows moving below them. They may come back for another glimpse, or maybe more than one, but eventually most withdraw. A few perhaps sit and dangle their legs over the side; maybe they stay there a long time, maybe the rest of their lives. Those are the people who can be called "sick" or "twisted." There are others, though, who look down until they find their own shadows in the void, then lean forward. Whether they slip over the side (as Steve wanted to think) or take a headfirst dive (as I suspected) probably mattered very little.

Off the cliff and over the side—feet-first or headfirst, who could possibly say?—Dodd embraced his depravity with a new and terrifying enthusiasm. Alone in the room where he spent nearly every bit of time he wasn't working or "hunting," he clipped newspaper articles about the killings of the Neer boys, and filled his diary with fantasies that became more hideous by the day.

He was both frightened and thrilled, Dodd wrote, when the parents of Vancouver began to organize into "sentry committees," watching over the city's parks and paths, warning children to avoid isolated areas.

On October 29, 1989, Dodd drove his mustard-colored Pinto station wagon across the Columbia into Portland and parked next to the Richmond School playground. There were a group of boys playing football, while another, younger child watched. Dodd waited until the little boy, four-year-old Lee Iseli, wandered off to climb a concrete play structure that the older kids called "the volcano." When blond, blue-eyed Lee came down the slide, Dodd was there waiting with a smile. "Hi! How you doing?" he asked. When Lee smiled back, Dodd asked him, "Would you like to have some fun and make some money?" The boy got scared and said no, but he didn't resist when Dodd took him by the hand and led him toward the road. Little Lee began to pull away when he saw Dodd's car, and said, "I don't want any money," but Dodd told him in a soothing voice that it was okay, that "your dad sent me to get you." Lee let himself be placed in the car but protested, "I live the other way," as Dodd drove off. He told the child they were going to his house to play some games, Dodd recalled: "Just do what I tell you and I promise I won't hurt you. But you'll have to be quiet when we get there. My landlady doesn't like little kids." He chatted with the boy all the way back to Vancouver, Dodd said, and managed to get the boy into his apartment without any struggle. Once the door was closed behind them, Dodd took some Polaroids of Lee, told the boy to get undressed, and then tied him to the bed with ropes. He took more pictures, molested the boy, then untied him and let Lee watch cartoons on television while he recorded what had just happened in his diary. After telling the boy he was going to spend the night, Dodd, incredibly, drove Lee to a nearby K-mart to buy him a toy. In the store, the boy began to cry, and an employee approached, concerned. It was okay, Dodd said, he was babysitting his nephew who wanted to go home. After leaving K-mart, Dodd drove Lee to McDonald's for lunch, then took the child back to his apartment. While Lee played with his new toy, Dodd wrote in his diary, "He suspects nothing now. Will probably wait until morning to kill him. That way his body will be fairly fresh for experiments after work. I'll suffocate him in his sleep when I wake up for work (if I sleep)." He molested the boy on and off all during that night, taking breaks to make more entries in his diary, fantasizing about how to kill the child and hide the body while he was at work. At one point Lee awoke with a start and Dodd whispered to him, "I'm going to kill you in the morning." "No, you're not!" Lee cried. He convinced the child it was just a joke, Dodd said, and eventually Lee fell back asleep. He watched until the boy was breathing rhythmically, Dodd said, then strangled the child into unconsciousness.

I'm not going to describe the things Dodd did next; they're too horrible. And yet he felt not the slightest remorse about any of it, Dodd would claim. He was again alone in his room, filling page after page of his diary, working on the "torture rack" he was building out of boards and ropes, and planning his next "hunting expedition." He chose as his venue the New Liberty Theater in nearby Camas, where *Honey, I Shrunk the Kids* was playing.

He sat in the back row during the seven o'clock showing, Dodd would recall, and watched the audience, not the movie. Less than an hour into the show, a six-year-old boy named James came up the aisle alone, headed for the bathroom. Dodd got out of his seat and followed. At the door to the men's room, he smiled, Dodd remembered, and told the boy to go first.

Only a couple of minutes later, theater employees in the lobby heard a child's piercing screams. Two of them ran toward the men's restroom, just as Westley Dodd came bursting through the door with a writhing, screaming little boy thrown over his shoulder. The employees followed, but lost sight of Dodd in the dark. At the Pinto, Dodd fumbled for his keys, and James got loose, sprinting back up the sidewalk straight to a young woman who worked as a ticket taker at the theater, grabbing her by both legs and holding tight. "That man was going to hurt me," the boy said. The young woman led James back to the theater to find his mother, while Dodd, who had chased the boy a short distance, turned back to his car. The boyfriend of James's mother was out on the sidewalk by then, having heard what happened. Someone said they had seen the abductor in a yellow or orange Pinto station wagon. Within moments, the boyfriend spotted a mustard-colored Pinto wagon stalled in the road. He approached the car and asked the driver if he needed help. Westley Dodd answered that he could use a push. The boyfriend moved closer, asked the driver to get out and help, then grabbed Dodd in a headlock and dragged him back to the theater.

After less than an hour in police custody, Dodd was confessing everything. His statement went on and on, far more detailed and graphic than what I've reported here. The two detectives who questioned Dodd each had to excuse themselves to go to the bathroom and vomit.

At Dodd's apartment, police investigators recovered the "torture rack," along with the X-Acto knives that Dodd planned to use as his surgical tools, and the ropes that were still tied to the headboard and footboard of his bed. There were four books on the parent-child relationship and a copy of the New Testament in which Dodd had written "Satan Lives." Under the bed was the briefcase that contained Dodd's diaries and a photo album bearing the title "Family Memories" on its cover. Inside were iconic images of Jesus as a baby, neatly clipped advertising images of children in underwear, and Polaroids Dodd had taken of himself naked, Polaroids he had taken of himself assaulting Lee Iseli, and Polaroids he had taken of the boy hanging in the closet after he had been killed. On top of all this was the neatly folded pair of Ghostbusters underpants that Lee had been wearing when he was abducted.

Less than two months after his capture, Dodd pleaded guilty on all counts. A trial to determine his punishment was necessary, anyway, and how the jurors must have suffered as they heard Dodd's diaries read aloud one can only imagine. Dodd told *The Oregonian* he was bored by the testimony: "I've heard it so many times now, it's kind of old, really."

On July 15, 1990, Dodd was sentenced to death. How he responded to that was something Steve and I discussed for days afterward. "I didn't offer any mitigating evidence during the penalty phase," Dodd told the court, "because in my mind that's just an excuse. . . . It really doesn't matter why the crimes happened. I should be punished to the full extent of the law, as should all sex offenders and murderers." Washington state law allowed an inmate sentenced to death to choose the method of his execution, either lethal injection or hanging. He wanted to hang, Dodd said, "because that's the way Lee Iseli died." Was Dodd reaching for some sort of redemption? Could he imagine that was possible?

Even as the American Civil Liberties Union was opposing his execution on the grounds that hanging was cruel and unusual punishment, Dodd was urging the judge to kill him as quickly as possible and joined the state in opposing the appeal of his sentence: "I must be executed before I have an opportunity to escape or kill someone within the prison," he said in court. "If I do escape, I promise you I will kill and rape and enjoy every minute of it."

It seemed some grotesque form of grandstanding when Dodd began to market himself to the media as a real live monster, appearing on numerous television shows (including a CNN special), phoning radio programs from his cellblock, and welcoming print reporters to visit him at the Washington State Penitentiary in Walla Walla. He was trying to help by telling his story, Dodd insisted, and wrote a pamphlet advising parents how to keep their kids safe from child molesters. At the same time, he wrote letters such as the one he sent to a forensic psychiatrist who wanted Dodd to try to explain his cannibalism fantasies: "I was mainly interested in eating the genitals while kids watched. . . . I was going to do this as a form of torture more than anything else."

The ACLU strung the ordeal out for nearly three years, until January 5, 1993, when Dodd became the first inmate to die on the gallows since 1965, when Perry Smith and Richard Hickock, the subjects of Truman Capote's *In Cold Blood*, were hanged in Kansas. His last words were these: "I was once asked by somebody, I don't remember who, if there was any way sex offenders could be stopped. I said, 'No.' I was wrong. I was wrong when I said there was no hope, no peace. There is hope. There is peace. I found both in the Lord, Jesus Christ. Look to the Lord, and you will find peace."

I took my finger off the delete button and reread Dodd's final statement. Even as most of me dismissed his words, something in me wondered: What if it was possible that even a Westley Allan Dodd could escape the grip of evil and achieve deliverance? What if Clement was right and even the Devil himself could be saved?

I went back to the news stories about Westley Allan Dodd's execution, and in one read a passing reference to the close relationship Dodd had developed with the chaplain at the Washington State Penitentiary. More than two decades later, I began to try to find out who that chaplain—now retired—had been. His name, I learned, was Ron Willhite. A former real estate investor, Willhite had made millions rehabilitating distressed properties before going to work for fifteen years as the chaplain at Walla Walla. I eventually tracked down an interview Willhite had given, shortly after his retirement from the chaplain's job, to the alumni magazine at the University of Puget Sound, where he had graduated in 1967. In that article, there was a brief mention of Westley Allan Dodd: he had baptized Dodd about two months before the execution, Willhite said, and spent a good deal of time with the condemned man during his last days. I was flabbergasted to discover that Willhite (who was close to the evangelist Billy Graham) had been quoted as saying that "when Westley Allan Dodd died, he was cleaner spiritually than any man I have ever met."

Willhite repeated almost those exact words to me when I found him. It was not the only thing about the former chaplain that astonished me. Willhite was a big, beefy fellow who had grown up poor and unprotected in tough towns and developed into a legendary bar fighter, famous throughout a certain stratum of Northwest society for both the frequency and the degree of the beatings he gave those who dared to test him. His conversion to Christianity had coincided with his recovery from alcoholism and a subsequent pledge to stop pounding people senseless. His business based on the rehabilitation of decayed commercial buildings had made him a rich man by the time he turned forty, when Willhite was recruited into prison ministry. Inmates incapable of listening to anyone who was afraid of them, he was told, might respond more favorably to a pastor who could credibly threaten to mop the floor with them. This had proven so true that Willhite was offered the position of chaplain at the Washington State Penitentiary in 1986, even though he lacked the master of divinity degree that was part of the official job description.

Westley Allan Dodd had come to him through another notorious inmate, one Danny Yates, Willhite recalled. It was probably just as well that I didn't know the nature of Yates's crimes when Willhite told me his story, because I would never have believed it otherwise. The ex-chaplain described Yates simply as "a motorcycle gang murderer who had killed people in most Western states," and said that his conversion was the most complete he'd seen among the inmates at Walla Walla: "He just was on fire for the Lord, and his spirit turned from a hard-core biker personality to a gentle, sweet guy. I mean a 100 percent turnabout. He led more men to Christ than anyone I've ever known, men you'd think could never be converted." Yates had described to him, in detail, every one of his crimes, Willhite recalled. "He told me, 'I murdered people here and I murdered people there.' But he didn't just say it. Danny *dealt* with the pain he'd caused. He would cry and cry. In order to get a new Bible from me, or any of the books in the catalog I used, I'd make them write a thousand-word paper about wanting to be forgiven for their sins. Usually it was only toward the end of that thousand words that most guys would get in touch with the magnitude of what they'd done. The child molesters, a lot of 'em couldn't get there even at the end of a thousand words. But the others, they'd give their paper to me and come in a week later to hear what grade they got. Some I'd have to tell, 'You got a D-minus. You're lyin' to me. Don't try to lie to me. If you wanna lie, go talk to the counselors. They get paid $3,000 a month to listen to lies.' Then I'd tell 'em, 'If you wanna try again, write a 5,000-word paper, and I'll buy you any book in the catalog.' And by the end of a 5,000-word paper, any man that wrote one was beginning to see where he was going and where he came from. But, anyway, Danny earned every book I had. Danny probably wrote fifteen of those papers, and he wrote them from his heart and his mind in all purity. Absolutely phenomenal."

Not everyone at the prison was so impressed. "The lieutenant who ran Five Wing, where Danny was, he just hated Christians, myself included," Willhite recalled. "Danny was sitting outside his window one day, waiting to talk to him about something, and some other young man was waiting too, so Danny started talking to him about Jesus. And Butch, the lieutenant, came out and started cussin' and swearin' and accused Danny of trying to start a riot. He threw him in IMU—put him in Intensive Management Unit, that is, which is basically solitary. So I went out to see Danny, and he asked me, 'How could God do this to me?' I said, 'God doesn't make any mistakes. There's somebody out here that needs to know the Lord.' And Danny says, 'Yeah, but I've been so good. How come I have to be out here where I get my food through a hole and can't talk to anybody?' I said, 'Danny, you need to pray. God knows where you are. Nothing happens by accident. He allowed you out here for a purpose that's above anything you and I know.' 'All right, chaplain, I believe you,' he tells me, though he doesn't sound like it. But the next thing you know, Danny's got a Bible study group goin' out there, one that he and the others conducted by tapping on walls and knocking on plumbing. And that was the way Danny led Westley Allan Dodd to Christ."

Converted or not, "Dodd was very standoffish when I first met him, like just about all the guys in IMU are, especially the guys who are sentenced to death," Willhite recalled. "They're pretty guarded about who they talk to and what they say. But Danny told him I was a good guy, so we'd have conversations. They weren't supposed to be let out of their cells for anything, but I convinced the lieutenant to let me take Dodd to the counseling room, so I could hold his hands while I prayed with him. Pretty soon I'm going out there more and more frequently, because Dodd chose to pass up all of his court options and was asking to be put to death. Even after he became a Christian he wanted to be put to death. Westley knew that if he had been let out of prison he would have committed more terrible crimes. He couldn't change what he was, even by becoming a Christian. At least a third of the inmates at Washington State Penitentiary were men who should never be let out of prison ever, and Westley was one of them. Westley told me very clearly that he wanted to die, and he never wavered. All he wanted was to be baptized first.

"So I told the head of IMU, Lt. Van Skyke, 'Look, you're a Christian. I wanna baptize this guy.' And he said, 'I can't let you do it. There's no place for it.' And I said, 'Yep, there is. We're gonna use a plastic laundry cart, that one right there. It's four feet deep.' He said, 'You'll have to see the superintendent.' I went to see [Superintendent James] Blodgett, and he said, 'Well, I don't care. If you think you can do it, knock yourself out.' So I went in there on a Saturday with a Catholic chaplain. The lieutenant had told his men to fill the laundry cart with warm water, but they'd filled it with straight cold water, and it was freezing. I said, 'That's okay. I've baptized people in rivers and lakes that are colder than this. Cold doesn't hurt.' And the lieutenant's face turned bright red, and he personally bailed out about a third of that water by hand and refilled it with warm water and said, 'Now you can baptize him.' So I baptized Westley Allan Dodd. The Catholic chaplain cried for two days afterward. He thought it was the neatest thing he'd ever seen. And I can tell you that it was a very high spiritual experience for me. But it was nothing compared to what was gonna come."

Refusing all appeals or stays, Dodd's time was growing short as the year 1992 approached its end. "He was doin' three or four Bible studies at a time," Willhite recalled. "He'd mail 'em in to me through the interprison mail and I'd mail back, but I couldn't mail fast enough to keep up, because he was writing that much and sending that many." Yet Dodd gave no indication he was a changed man in the interviews he granted during December 1992, telling a reporter from a Seattle television station that he felt no remorse for his crimes—felt nothing at all about anything, really. "I don't know what love is—for myself or anyone else," he explained. He wrote a letter to the *Seattle Times* in which he stated, "I do not want to die. But I have been completely honest in saying that I must die, because I know I will kill again." He scorned those—the ACLU and the Catholic Church in particular— who were trying to prevent his execution. If successful, Dodd told the TV interviewer, "they will be named as a co-defendant at my next aggravated murder trial." Dodd also repeated his threat to kill a prison guard if he was not executed as planned on January 5, and revealed that (as prison officials eventually admitted) he had tricked a guard into entering his cell by feigning unconsciousness. The point was to prove that he could attack a guard even in the IMU, Dodd said, and that the sane choice for everyone was to put him to death.

"I never tried to talk Westley out of letting himself be executed," Willhite said, "and I think that had a lot to do with why he trusted me." Willhite spent eight hours alone with Dodd in his cell from about four in the afternoon on January 4 until just after midnight on January 5. "I had promised to give him communion that night. I remember tellin' my wife it might take as long as half an hour, since Westley had never taken communion before. Well, it took four hours. The confession he made was that detailed, and that deep. He told me everything he'd ever done. He told me, 'You know, Ron, some people wonder—and maybe you do too—why it's okay that I'm gonna go in a little while. Every night I still have dreams. The dreams make me sick. I wake up and I have to throw up in the toilet. What I have done in my life makes me physically ill. I know that God has approved of me and loves me and I want to go be with him in a place where I won't have these horrible thoughts and dreams.' Westley told me how much he loved his mom and dad—I don't think he'd ever told them—and how he'd abused their love, how his dad used to take him camping and he'd go find little boys to molest. I don't believe he held anything back. We prayed together a very long time. And when we took communion, I can tell you—" Willhite's voice, which had been thickening ever since he began to talk about that night, was choked to silence. He was unable to speak for several minutes, managing only deep breaths and barely suppressed sobs. When he finally squeezed out half a word, he choked up again, gasping for breath. Finally, between deep sighing breaths, Willhite got out the words, "I can tell you that Westley Allan Dodd that night left the earth as clean as any man has ever left this earth. He didn't lie to himself or to me or to God about one tiny thing."

At midnight, the captain and his guards came to escort Dodd to the gallows. "I said, 'Captain, we're gonna pray,'" Willhite recalled. "When we stepped out of the cell I said, 'Westley, don't close your eyes. I'm gonna look at you while I pray.' Now the officers all had bets that he was gonna wet his pants or faint or this or that. They all thought he was a big baby and a sissy. He looked in my eyes and I looked in his, and I said, 'Lord, please give this man the courage and the strength to walk out there with dignity.' He looked me in the eye and said, 'Ron, I'll be there in a minute.' And he walked out through that second door to the scaffold without a flinch or a hesitation."

Among the sixteen witnesses in the death chamber were the mother of Lee Iseli and the father of Cole and William Neer. It was reported that the former shook her head and the latter hissed when Dodd made his speech about finding hope and peace in Jesus Christ, and that some others present booed. The consensus among the twelve "media witnesses" seemed to be that the speech was the final outrage of a man who lacked all conscience. Dodd's "voice was broken, but he displayed no sorrow, regret or remorse," the *Seattle Times* reported. Still, all present agreed, Dodd had remained perfectly calm, standing motionless as the black hood was placed over his head and the waxed Manila noose was tightened around his throat.

Willhite wasn't watching. "I didn't see any purpose," he explained. "I can tell you, though, that I did not feel bad. I did not cry. I did not have any heavy feeling. It was just okay. And it was more okay as time went by, and it was never not okay. We had two more executions after that while I was at Walla Walla, and they were much more difficult to go through. One of them was Charles Campbell [convicted of cutting the throats of two women and an eight-year-old girl as revenge for their testimony against him in a sexual assault trial], and he left grinnin' and callin' us all filthy names. If there was ever a totally evil man, he qualified. Westley Allan Dodd, though, he's in good shape. Trust me, he is in the front of the line, ahead of me and ahead of you. He was a man that left here who knew who he was and knew who Christ was. It was a privilege to be there with him. It was the highlight of my spiritual life," Willhite got out before he choked up again.

I waited until prompted to admit to Willhite that I had a very difficult time believing in Westley Allan Dodd's salvation. He knew why without my needing to say. "You think there are some things that just can't be forgiven," Willhite said. I tried to obviate: "It's more like I don't see how someone who has gone that far could ever come back." Willhite didn't bother to point out that I'd simply rephrased his accusation. "Here on earth we have categories of sin," he pointed out. "And we need to. But God sees it all as something we have to come to him about, if we really want to change." He waited out my silence for a moment, then added, "There's no judging sins when you are a sinner." I felt my face redden slightly, but still said nothing. "I've met hundreds of Christians that never came clean with themselves," Willhite went on a moment later. "And I've met many more that never became Christians, because they didn't want to even think about coming clean. Westley Allan Dodd and Danny Yates were rapists and murderers, but they are among the few men I've ever known who came clean all the way."

I felt myself plunging into rumination. It happened so swiftly that, within seconds, I wanted to be done with the interview. Willhite began to talk about meeting Billy Graham during his crusade in Spokane. I barely heard the first part, but tuned back in when he told me,

"I can tell you that if Westley Allan Dodd had stood at the microphone that night, he could have said something about grace and mercy and forgiveness that would have brought seventy thousand people to their feet. Because he knew whereof he spoke. It came from deep. Deep! He knew that he had been forgiven and he was absolutely thankful. As thankful as any man could ever be."

My conversation with Ron Willhite troubled me almost as much as the anonymous letter. I was unable to accept what he'd told me about Westley Allan Dodd "coming clean," but I couldn't bring myself to reject it, either. Stymied, I had no idea what to do next or who to seek out. Then, right after I decided to put this book aside, it struck me that what I needed to continue might be found in a part of the world where people accepted the reality of good and evil unimpeded by any fog of modernity that obscured the meanings of the words. Some place where God's existence was a given and where the Devil was not a symbol or a concept, but an actual being from whom one might either flee or seek favors. I had heard of such a place.

CHAPTER ELEVEN

THE FIRST MENTION of the Mexican jungle village Catemaco I heard was during the longest and most satisfying interview I conducted with Antonio Zavaleta, a cultural anthropologist at the University of Texas–Brownsville, regarded as the foremost expert on the subject of Mexican witchcraft to be found in the US academic community.

I was intrigued by Zavaleta's background. He was the son of an Anglo mother from Southern California and a Mexican American father from a Texas border town who had met and married at the end of World War II. His parents raised him in Texas, Zavaleta told me, but made sure he was educated "in a way my California mother's family approved of, in Catholic boy schools." He was isolated enough from his surroundings growing up that he did not really become aware that witches were a big part of life on the border, Zavaleta said, until, as a young academic, he began to focus his research on the delivery of health care among the Mexican immigrants living along the Rio Grande: "I found that many—probably most—of the people in this area were seeing *curanderos* and *curanderas* [white witches]. And a lot were seeing *brujos* [black witches]." He did not really understand how dangerous *brujos* could be until he was almost thirty and became involved in local politics, Zavaleta said: "In the late seventies and early eighties, I was a candidate for public office, and I found myself being warned by people involved in my campaign that my opponents were using witches to destroy me. And they were quite insistent that I needed to go see my own Mexican witch, to get protection and retaliate. I learned the hard way that they were right, that you have to fight fire with fire in this world."

Rather than a *brujo*, Zavaleta said, he used a *curandero* during the years he served two terms on the Brownsville City Council. His allies advised that those opposing him saw this as weakness and gloated about it when he ran for mayor and lost the election by 127 votes. "I saw with my own eyes that this is real stuff, that it actually makes things happen," Zavaleta told me, "but I don't think I ever truly understood it. Even after more than thirty years of studying, I still don't understand it."

He not only didn't understand the attitudes of the people who practiced as magicians, Zavaleta said, but couldn't comprehend, either, those who employed them. "What I discovered early on, and have been shown repeatedly ever since," the professor told me, "is that in the Mexican, and Mexican American, and really in the Latino culture as a whole, the concepts of making well and making ill go hand in hand. But I still don't really get it.

"The main thing I've had trouble sorting out is how exactly these people justify in their minds hiring someone to kill someone, hiring an agent, a spiritual agent, to do the ultimate harm to someone. That clearly is defined by me and by you as evil. And the use of a supernatural medium to accomplish someone's death would clearly be considered evil by American standards. But here at the border not only does it exist, and it is part of everyday life, yet people don't see it as evil, or in terms of good and evil, or right and wrong. What I've found is that if you ask the witch who conjures up the spirit or whatever to do it, ask him or her, they will just respond with a puzzled look. They just don't understand it in those terms. Christianity, Catholicism, is overlaid on top of this ancient and very different mentality."

But the people he was talking about understood what he meant when he described something as evil, didn't they? I asked. "Well, yes, the concept of evil means something to them," Zavaleta allowed, "but generally when it is placed in the concept of trying to do something to someone by using curses, hexes, or spells, it doesn't apply. That isn't to them one of the categories of evil. It's just part of their cultural reality. If you're able to manipulate the spiritual or supernatural world, then you have a right to, as they see it. This is a power you possess, and you can use it if you want."

Zavaleta, a burly man with thinning black hair and tiny wire-rimmed spectacles, chuckled ruefully at how flummoxed I was by what he described. "I've been hunting around in this world for almost forty years, and still, whenever I'm confronted by this mentality—which is frequently—I'm shocked by it," the professor told me. "I just haven't gotten used to it. It's such a juxtaposition to what I believe and what I think that I just can't comprehend it."

He had seen any number of visitors from places like New York and Los Angeles suffer terribly for their failure to appreciate the danger that *brujería* represented, Zavaleta told me. "I worked on this *National Geographic* piece on Mexican witchcraft," he said, "and I know that many of the people who worked with *National Geographic* on that got very sick and are still sick. This is serious stuff. You start trying to break the curse a *brujo* has put on someone, that power can turn on you. It's dangerous work."

I asked Zavaleta if at any time he had suspected that the effects of witchcraft he observed had more to do with the power of suggestion than with supernatural agency. "I've seen some people who thought that," he replied, "and then they got close and said, 'Okay, I'm out of here.' And besides, do we even know the difference between a psychological effect and a magical or spiritual effect? All I know is that any effect is an effect. If you're sick, you're sick."

There had been a bifurcation among the *brujos* in recent years, a result largely of the rise of the drug cartels, Zavaleta told me. "There are those who do what witches have always done. They break up marriages, they drive neighbors away, they make people ill. Money is their motive. But now you have some of the most powerful witches working for the drug cartels. Sometimes the second-most-powerful person in a cartel is a witch. They like power even more than money, and they are very, very dangerous. The ones who are involved with *narcotraficantes*, they don't place any value on lives. Killing someone is like cleaning a window. Those witches, they're very stealthy, very secretive. They like to stay in the shadows and they look at anyone who would probe them as an enemy to be eliminated. They would probably never go to the *brujo* convention, at least not out in the open."

When I asked what *brujo* convention he was talking about, Zavaleta told me that it was held in a village called Catemaco on the first Friday of every March. Catemaco was in the Mexican jungle, about a six-hour drive south from Veracruz. During early March, witches from all over Mexico gathered there along the lakeside, Zavaleta said.

The moment I heard about it, I knew I was going to the Catemaco event. Eventually I would realize that if Zavaleta had actually been in Catemaco at the Hour of the Witches (which I doubted), he hadn't looked very deep beneath the surface. When I first spoke to him, I imagined the professor to be not just an authority on the subject but also the kind of intrepid adventurer that becoming an expert in this field would require. When I suggested a trip to Catamaco together, though, he flatly dismissed the idea. "I have no interest in taking the kinds of risks that would involve," Zavaleta told me. "You need to understand, there's a huge liability to involvement in this area. You want to go to Catemaco, you're on your own."

Well, not entirely on my own. When I suggested that Michelle Gomez join me on an expedition to Catemaco, she readily agreed. "You're not afraid?" I asked her.

"No, I'm excited," she answered. "Evil can only enter in if we let it," Michelle added a few moments later. "And I won't be doing that."

I would have liked to share her confidence.

IF NOT CONFIDENT, I FIGURED, at least I could be prepared. So I spent much of the nearly three months before my planned departure for Catemaco by doing some of the historical research that Antonio Zavaleta had suggested. The starting point seemed obvious: the violent collision between Spanish colonists and the Aztec civilization centered on what is today Mexico City. In particular, of course, I was interested in how the Catholic Spaniards had perceived the religious practices of the Aztecs (or Mexica, as they are more commonly called today, at least among academics) and how the beliefs underlying them had been absorbed into what became Mexico. The perspective of one Catholic Spaniard in particular mattered most. His name was Hernán Cortés.

Cortés was born in 1487, the same year that the giant pyramid temple in the great Mexican city of Tenochtitlan (meaning "Cactus Rock," today Mexico City) was dedicated with four days and nights of human sacrifices. Cortés knew nothing of that, of course, but was enraptured by tales of the New World (many produced by the voyages of Christopher Columbus) that filtered through the southern Spanish port cities of Cádiz and Seville. Cortés was just seventeen when he sailed for Hispaniola, where Columbus had established the first Spanish settlements. Seven years later, the young colonist was with Diego Velázquez de Cuéllar during the conquest of Cuba, where Cortés would become a man of wealth and influence, in large part due to the rights he was granted to supply Indian labor—slave labor—for mines and cattle ranches.

What would make Cortés into a major historical figure, though, was that in 1518, at the age of thirty-one, he had been placed in command of an expedition to explore and secure the interior of Mexico ("New Spain" at the time) for colonization. Velázquez, now the governor of Cuba, revoked that charter at the last moment, but the defiant Cortés sailed anyway, arriving in what was once Mayan territory on the Yucatán Peninsula with ten ships and a few more than five hundred men.

Bernal Díaz del Castillo, the soldier whose chronicle of the Cortés campaign would become the primary historical source, had also been part of the first Spanish expedition to Mexico, one year earlier, in 1517. In his memoir *The True History of the Conquest of New Spain*, Díaz described how shocked the Spaniards were by the abandoned Mayan temples they discovered: "There were clay idols made of pottery, with the faces of demons or women, and other evil figures that showed Indians committing acts of sodomy with each other." The Spaniards also found temples where the walls were covered with bas-reliefs of snakes and the altars showed dried blood and hanks of long black hair.

Díaz was with the second Spanish expedition to Mexico in the spring of 1518, among those who spotted a pretty girl running along the beach as their ship approached the shoreline and brought her aboard. The young woman was from what is today Jamaica, where she had been fishing with her husband and ten companions when they were caught in currents that carried them all the way to the Yucatán, as the Spaniards understood it. When the party came ashore, they had been quickly captured by a band of warriors who killed her husband, then sacrificed all of her other companions on the altars of their "devil-gods," the young woman would explain.

With Díaz aboard, the Cortés expedition made landfall in the Yucatán during the spring of 1519 and quickly found good fortune in the person of Gerónimo de Aguilar, a Spanish Franciscan priest who in the course of surviving both a shipwreck and captivity had learned the Mayan language. Aguilar was with Cortés as the Spanish commander and his men made their way west (passing about a hundred miles north of what would become Catemaco) into the Tabasco region. There they were confronted by and defeated a native army. In the truce that resulted, Cortés was presented with twenty young native women, all of whom he converted to Christianity, by the account of Díaz. One of them, known as Malinche, would become the mother of his son Martín. Malinche spoke both Mayan and the Nahuatl language of the Aztecs, which would permit Cortés to communicate with nearly all the natives they encountered through the team of her and Aguilar.

In the summer of 1519, Cortés met with the leaders of two tributary Aztec tribes and through them sent a request for a meeting with the ruler of the Aztec Empire, Montezuma II. Montezuma refused the request, but Cortés proceeded anyway toward the Aztec capital city, Tenochtitlan, under his banners of red and black, trimmed with gold, accompanied by 508 Spanish soldiers and another hundred sailors, sixteen horses, thirty-two crossbows, thirteen muskets, and four small cannons. Along the way, Cortés forged alliances with several lesser tribes by taking their warriors prisoner, then releasing them. He and his men had been learning day by day how hated and feared the Aztecs were among their neighbors, mostly due to the bloodthirst of their "devil gods."

Among the two principal Mexica deities was Huitzilopochtli, the "Hummingbird Wizard," who was also known as the "Lover of Hearts" and the "Drinker of Blood." When the Aztecs made a human sacrifice (and they made many) to the Hummingbird Wizard, Cortés and the Spaniards learned, the victim would be placed face up on a stone slab before the priest cut through the chest with an obsidian dagger to remove the still-beating heart and raise it to the sky. Afterward, the body was often returned to the warrior who had captured the victim, who would cut it into small pieces either to be distributed as gifts or to use in cannibalism rituals. The news that the Aztecs ate human flesh terrified the Spaniards like nothing else they had heard.

The Aztecs' second main deity was Tezcatlipoca, the demiurge of creation, who was also known as "the Enemy" (to stress his love of conflict and discord) and as "He Who Is at the Shoulder" (as a tempter). Tezcatlipoca was the god of night, of sorcery, and of destiny, nearly all-powerful and utterly indifferent to human suffering. Another of this god's many names translated to "We Who Are His Slaves."

The Aztecs also worshipped a fire god called Huehueteotl, who preferred as his sacrifices newlywed couples who were thrown onto a fire, then pulled out just before death to have their hearts removed. Tlaloc was the Aztec god of rain, who drank the tears of children, requiring that only the very young be sacrificed to him.

As the other tribes described it, the Aztecs not only sacrificed thousands of prisoners and slaves every year to their gods, but actually waged war for the sole purpose of capturing those who could satisfy their gods' appetites for human blood. This approach to warfare had over time resulted in a military weakness that might permit an army of a few hundred to defeat an opposing force that numbered in the thousands. This the Spaniards would discover when they were met in the field by the warriors of the large Tlaxcalan tribe (second only in power to the Aztecs). The Tlaxcalans first sent forth a force of 3,000 warriors against the Spaniards, whose fighters numbered fewer than 300, according to the account of Bernal Díaz del Castillo. The next day, the Tlaxcalans sent 6,000 warriors, and the day after that they sent more than 30,000. The Tlaxcalans also practiced human sacrifice, however, and because they had been trained to capture rather than to kill, they were far less formidable than their numbers suggested. Fighting mostly with swords and crossbows, the Spanish were able to hold off the Tlaxcalans with the loss of just forty-five men, whose bodies, according to Díaz, were buried so deep that the Tlaxcalans could never find them.

The Tlaxcalans finally proposed a truce when they realized that the Spanish intended to take the Aztec capital, and more than a thousand of the tribe's soldiers were with Cortés as he marched his men twenty miles south to the ancient religious center of Cholula. In Cholula, it was said, there was a temple for every day of the year. What happened there is a source of controversy that has endured for more than 500 years and serves as a vivid example of how historians so often choose to believe what they wish rather than what they know. The account of Cortés and Bernal Díaz del Castillo is that the conquistadors marched unknowingly into a trap laid by the Aztecs, who had instructed the Cholulans to make a show of welcoming the Spaniards, in order to lull them into complacency. They were lodged in a palace, according to Díaz, and fed well for two days. But then the food stopped coming. Malinche was warned by a Cholulan woman that the Spaniards were to be murdered the next day, except for those who submitted to capture; those would be taken back to Tenochtitlan for sacrifice. She should escape now and save herself, Malinche was told. Instead she informed Cortés, who immediately ordered his men to attack the Cholulans. According to Díaz, a few more than 250 Spaniards killed 3,000 armed warriors in the ensuing battle.

The central revisionist version of what happened at Cholula was published thirty-three years later by the Spanish Dominican friar Bartolomé de Las Casas, who was thousands of miles away when what he called "a massacre" took place. According to Las Casas (an opponent of slavery and an advocate for native peoples—a well-meaning man, but not an entirely credible witness), Cortés decided shortly after arriving in Cholula "to organize a massacre . . . in order to inspire fear and terror in all the people of the territory." While the Cortés/Díaz version of events held sway for hundreds of years, the Las Casas story began to be preferred by twentieth-century historians (especially south of the border), inclined as they were to see the indigenous peoples of the Western Hemisphere as innocent victims and Europeans as a murderous invading force.

Shortly after whatever it was exactly that happened at Cholula, Montezuma sent emissaries to the Spanish to present them with a feast of the finest food the Aztecs had to offer. The conquistadors spat it out in disgust when they realized the food was sprinkled with human blood. An enraged Cortés ordered the emissaries placed into chains and positioned next to a cannon loaded with a maximum charge. When it was fired off, the emissaries collapsed into a dead faint.

The Spaniards' conviction that they were headed to war with a nation of devil worshippers mounted. Cortés sent a senior officer, Pedro de Alvarado, ahead to perform reconnaissance and gather food from the villages on the approach to Tenochtitlan. The Indians had fled their villages, on orders from Montezuma to avoid contact with the Spaniards at all costs, Alvarado reported, leaving behind them scenes of horror such as he had never seen: the trunks of dozens of human bodies were piled in the blood-splattered temple rooms of each village, the arms and legs cut off and carried away to be eaten. Cortés sent a courier back to Veracruz with the message that the human sacrifice his men were seeing was "the most terrible and frightful thing they have ever witnessed."

The terrain flattened and their march became easier as the Spaniards came down out of the mountains toward Tenochtitlan. They entered a town called Zacatlan, where every building, all the idols, and even the defensive walls were painted white. "White Castle," the Spaniards called it, until two of them discovered a pyramid constructed entirely out of human skulls. There were racks of human skulls inside the temples of Zacatlan, according to Bernal Díaz del Castillo, who wrote that he and some of the other men counted more than 100,000 skulls: "I say again, *one hundred thousand*."

As the Spaniards looked down on the plain of the Valley of Anahuac, they recognized for perhaps the first time that the Aztecs were an actual civilization. Thirty separate communities were clustered around two lakes spanned by bridges in what Cortés and his men could see even from a distance was an engineering marvel. The whitewashed adobe houses sparkled in the sun, while cubic temples unlike any they had ever seen towered above.

Though Montezuma had repeatedly attempted to persuade Cortés not to come to Tenochtitlan, offering immense treasures when all else failed, the Aztec emperor welcomed the Spaniards into his capital city on November 8, 1519, as honored guests. His plan, as the Aztecs' own records reveal, was to study the Spaniards at close range, in order to learn their weaknesses before annihilating them. Cortés and his men were provided with the use of a palace, where they were startled by opulence that included a private bath for each of the hundred rooms.

The Spaniards' new residence was directly across from the spectacular pyramidal temple of the Hummingbird Wizard. The temple had been dedicated just thirty-two years earlier by the man regarded as the architect of the Aztec Empire, Tlacaelel. The highlight of the ceremony was the greatest human slaughter in the history of the Mexica—eighty thousand sacrificed, according to a sixteenth-century Aztec historian; the lines of those who would die stretched for miles, he recalled, and the killing went on without interruption for four days and nights. The Aztec nobility were provided with seats in boxes covered with rose blossoms intended to mask the smell of drying blood and rotting flesh. The stench was overwhelming, though, before even a thousand were dead, and by the second day nearly every one of the boxes was empty. Yet the eighty-nine-year-old Tlacaelel remained the entire time, personally observing each and every sacrifice. It was Tlacaelel who had instituted Aztec worship of Huitzilopchtli, the Spaniards would learn, and who had invented the "Flower Wars"—contrived conflicts with neighboring tribes that were intended only to take prisoners for sacrifice to the Lover of Hearts and Drinker of Blood.

Tlacaelel died at age ninety just a year after the dedication of the temple, but the Mexica practice of human sacrifice continued unabated, as the Spaniards discovered almost as soon as they settled into their luxurious rooms in the palace. They smelled the carnage even before they went to inspect the temple, climbing the 114 steps of the pyramid to the terrace at the top, where they entered doorways that led to a honeycomb of apartments inhabited by more than a thousand priests, many of them wearing clothes stained with human blood as if it were a decoration. Carved images of snakes were everywhere, covering entire walls and crawling all around the Aztec gods. The most exclusive temple in Tenochtitlan was the House of the Serpent, where Montezuma had retreated for eight days after learning that Cortés and his men had set fire to Cholula. The Aztec emperor spent much of that time contemplating the severed head of a Spanish soldier.

Sacrifices at the great pyramid began the morning after the Spaniards' arrival. Quails had been offered at first light, then men and boys were led to the stone altars, accompanied by the boom of a giant snakeskin drum. Though they could not know the number of those killed, the Spaniards reported later that they had seen blood running down the temple walls. The Aztecs' own records show that they saw the weeping of the Spaniards in the face of human sacrifice as a shocking display of weakness and vulnerability.

Behind the great pyramid was the city zoo, where the animals kept in captivity fed on the entrails of sacrificed men. When the beasts smelled their breakfast, Bernal Díaz de Castillo recalled, the cacophony of shrieks and roars they let loose in anticipation was both hideous and deafening. "Infernal," Díaz wrote. "It seemed like Hell."

Cortés set off to meet with Montezuma, accompanied by men who included Díaz. The Spanish leader immediately informed the emperor that his primary mission was to bring the Aztecs word of the One True God and the good news of Jesus Christ. Montezuma replied that his people worshipped their own gods and would allow the Spanish to worship theirs, then asked Cortés to drop the subject, for the time being.

That became impossible after the Spaniards toured the city's main plaza. They were astonished at the quality of the merchandise in the markets, until they found themselves inside a building that seemed to have been literally made out of human skulls. The walls, stair steps, and benches all were constructed of stones and skulls held in place with mortar. There were towers made entirely out of skulls and mortar, and the main decorative items were seventy tall poles studded with spikes, each holding five skulls. Two Spanish soldiers would say they counted 136,000 skulls, not including those in the towers.

At that point, Díaz would recall, Cortés climbed the steps to the top of the main temple and addressed his men: "Truly, my heart tells me that from here many kingdoms and dominions will be conquered, for here is the capital wherein the Devil had his main seat; once this city has been subdued and mastered, the rest will be easy to conquer."

The depredations, of course, were not all on the Aztec side. Montezuma's attempt to buy the Spaniards off with gifts of gold and gemstones had aroused an appetite for plunder in many of the conquistadors, who were far more interested in what treasures they could steal from the Mexica than in bringing the natives word of the One True God.

When Cortés learned that Spanish soldiers supporting the Totonac tribe on the coast south of Veracruz had been killed by Aztec warriors, he placed Montezuma under what amounted to house arrest, then ordered that sixteen Aztecs believed to have been responsible for the death of a Spanish commander should be burned at the stake, an event that shocked and horrified the citizens of Tenochtitlan. After this, Cortés became the de facto ruler of the Aztecs' capital city, either convincing or compelling Montezuma to permit the installation of a cross, an altar, and an image of the Virgin Mary in a room within the great pyramid. The priests from the pyramid temple came to visit Montezuma a short time later, though, and informed him that the Hummingbird Wizard had spoken to them, declaring that the cross, the altar, and especially the image of the Virgin Mary must be removed, or there would be war. When the Aztec emperor informed Cortés of this, the Spanish commander responded by marching with his men on the great temple, then climbing with his officers to the top of the pyramid, where he stood face-to-face with the Hummingbird Wizard. Cortés stared at the carved image for a few moments, then picked up a metal bar. "I pledge on my faith as a gentleman, and swear to God that it is true," a young officer named Andres de Tàpia would write, "that I can see now how [Cortés] leapt up in a super- natural way and swung forward holding the bar midway until he struck the idol high up on its eyes, and broke off its gold mask, saying: 'We must risk something for God.'"

Cortés did not stop there. Over the next week, he forced the priests to remove every idol from the great temple, then ordered their shrines cleaned. In the process, the Spanish discovered the ashes of Tlacaelel and, more significantly to most of them, a hidden chamber filled with a fabulous treasure of gold and gemstones.

For three months, there were no human sacrifices in Tenochtitlan. In April 1520, though, Cortés learned that Governor Velázquez had sent a second expedition after him, made up of 1,100 men led by Pán- filo de Narváez, who had been ordered to arrest Cortés as a mutineer. Cortés left 200 men in Tenochtitlan under the command of Pedro de Alvarez, then led the rest of his army, including hundreds of Tlaxcalan warriors, toward the coast to confront Narváez. Cortés not only easily subdued Narváez but also convinced nearly all of the opposing force to join his side. He headed back toward Tenochtitlan with an army that was more than twice the size of the one he had led out of the city a few weeks earlier and now included 1,300 Spanish soldiers.

The situation in Tenochtitlan, however, had deteriorated in Cor- tés's absence. Before departing, Cortés had granted a request from Montezuma that the Mexica be allowed to celebrate Toxcatl, a festival honoring the Hummingbird Wizard, so long as no human sacrifices were made. Once Cortés was gone from Tenochtitlan, though, the Az- tecs grew increasingly bold. A new idol of Huitzilochtili was carved, then the Hummingbird Wizard was outfitted in a vest decorated with dismembered human body parts: skulls, ears, hands, and feet. The Az- tec priests warned the Spaniards that they intended to offer human sacrifices, as they always did during Toxcatl, and that the conquistadors had better not try to stop them. When the ceremonies of the festival began, Alvarado grew alarmed by the pounding of the giant snakeskin drum, and the chanting and dancing that accompanied it. The captives who would be sacrificed were not even assembled when Alvarado, frightened that the Aztecs were working themselves into a frenzy that would climax in an attack on the Spanish, ordered his men to strike first. Hundreds of unarmed Mexica were slaughtered before they organized a counterattack in which thousands of wailing Indians drove the Spaniards back into their palace, then laid siege to the building.

Cortés returned to Tenochtitlan only a few days later, on June 25, leading his swollen army into an ambush he did not see coming until it was almost too late. As Cortés would describe it, just as the Spanish reached the palace they had been calling home, "there came upon us from all sides such a multitude that neither the street nor the roofs of the houses could be seen for them. They came with the most fearful cries imaginable, and so many were the stones that they hurled at us from their slings into the fortress that it seemed they were raining from the sky, and the arrows and spears were so many that all the walls and courtyards were so full we could hardly move in them."

The siege continued all day and night; at one point the Spanish palace was set on fire. Montezuma approached to negotiate a truce but was killed by a hail of stones hurled by his own people, who accused him of betraying them. Eventually Cortés and his men fought their way to the pyramid temple, then up the steps to the high terrace. Cortés rallied his men by urging them to protect the Virgin Mary icon they had installed earlier, but found when he arrived that it had already been removed and replaced by a Hummingbird Wizard idol surrounded by human hearts, along with seven Spanish helmets, to make clear who the most recent sacrificial victims had been. The Spaniards hurled the images of Huitzilopochtli and Tezcatlipoca down on the Aztecs from above, set fire to whatever would burn, then fought their way down the steps and moved toward the water. The Aztecs had raised all their bridges, to keep the Spanish inside the city, so Cortés ordered the construction of a portable span, built by men who worked under the shields of their comrades. Many of the Spanish drowned anyway, weighted down by the gold they had attempted to carry away. By the time they made it to dry land, half the Spanish force was dead.

One week later, the Aztecs trapped the Spanish on the plain of Otumba, with their backs to the desert the Indians called Mictlan, an expanse so vast and barren that men could not survive there for more than a few days. Vastly outnumbered, their guns gone, with just a few horses, a half dozen coats of mail, and their steel weapons, the surviving Spaniards fought their way through the Aztec horde to the mountains and made it back to Tlaxcala.

Within a few weeks, Cortés returned to Tenochtitlan with six hundred Spanish soldiers, forty horses, nine cannons, and a huge Tlaxcalan host, then laid siege. The Aztecs' new emperor, Montezuma's nephew Cuauhtémoc, was repeatedly offered the chance to negotiate a truce, but refused after the priests told him the Hummingbird Wizard had forbidden it. The fighting that ensued lasted ninety-three days. Cortés lost dozens of men in the battle for the marketplace at Tlatelolco, and the Aztecs flung the severed heads of Spanish soldiers at retreating columns of conquistadors. The next day, Cortés and his men awakened to the booming of the giant snakeskin drum, then watched as the seventy soldiers who had been captured in the battle for the marketplace were stripped naked, then made to dance before the Hummingbird Wizard on the terrace atop the pyramid temple before being flayed, sacrificed, and dismembered, all within sight of the Spanish position. Most of the Tlaxcalans fled at the sight.

In the end, Cortés used the cannons that had been carried across the mountains in pieces, then reassembled on Lake Texcoco, to sustain a bombardment that cut off the supply of food and water to Tenochtitlan. The starving, desperately thirsty Aztecs finally surrendered, this time for good.

FOR MORE THAN A CENTURY and a half, the definitive account of the Cortés expedition has been William H. Prescott's masterly *History of the Conquest of Mexico*, which drew on a vast array of sources, none more important than Bernal Díaz del Castillo, who was witness to every moment of it. Revisionist histories, produced by both Mexican and US academics, have challenged the Spanish version of events, largely relying on theories supported by weak evidence and a determination to vilify Cortés and make the Aztecs into a great and misunderstood civilization. This has been most exaggerated in the arguments of these scholars that stories of Aztec cannibalism are "mythology." The evidence that the Aztecs did in fact eat the flesh of sacrificial victims is overwhelming* and includes the archeological recovery of human bones showing human tooth marks (there is also anecdotal evidence that the Aztec upper classes regularly substituted turkey meat for the human flesh with which they were presented). The sheer horror of the Aztec sacrifice rituals conducted at what is today Mexico City shocks everyone who studies them, just as they shocked the Spanish in the sixteenth century. For Christians, Catholics in particular, it was for hundreds of years an article of faith that what Cortés and his men confronted at Tenochtitlan had been the Devil's own empire. As the Catholic writer Warren H. Carroll observed of fifteenth-century Mexico, "Nowhere else in human history has Satan so formalized and institutionalized his worship with so many of his own actual rites and symbols."

As it has been told to millions of Mexican Catholics, the struggle between the forces of light and those of darkness for the national soul not only continued but actually came to a climax in the decades following Cortés's conquest of the Aztecs. Those who doubt that religious conviction was part of Cortés's makeup haven't read their history. Among the very first actions the conquistador took after the fall of Tenochtitlan was to send a request to Spain's King Charles V that Franciscan and Dominican friars, rather than diocesan priests, be sent to convert the indigenous population to Christianity. "If [the natives] were now to see the affairs of the Church and the service of God in the hands of canons or other dignitaries, and saw them indulge in the vices and profanities now common in Spain, knowing that such men were the ministers of God, it would bring our Faith into so much harm that I believe any further preaching would be of no avail," Cortés wrote to his king. When the first group of Franciscans arrived in June 1524, after walking barefoot the entire 200 miles from Veracruz to Mexico

* See Appendix A for a further consideration of this subject and of how I have characterized the Aztec gods and the rituals of sacrifice to them.

City, Cortés performed what one of them, Gerónimo de Mendieta, would describe as his greatest deed: kneeling at the feet of the friars when he greeted them. It made an enormous impression on the Indians, Mendieta would write, seeing a man they saw as all-powerful prostrate himself before spiritual leaders.

One of "the Twelve Apostles of Mexico," as that first group became known, was Toribio de Benavente Motolinia, who wrote the most important early history of Mexico. Motolinia also vied with the Dominican leader Bartolomé de Las Casas to define what it was Cortés had accomplished in Mexico. "A grievous man, restless, importunate, turbulent, injurious and prejudicial," Motolinia would describe Las Casas to the king, in a letter that defended Cortés as a hero whose military conquest of the Aztecs had made their conversion and salvation possible. Motolinia, though, also contended with Nuño de Guzmán, who the king had named the secular ruler of all Mexico, and Juan de Zumárraga, who had been appointed bishop of Mexico City. Motolinia's attempts to protect the Indians from the brutal oppression of Guzmán were so bold that Zumárraga warned he might be considered to have encouraged revolt among the native peoples.

Zumárraga was only slightly more sympathetic than Guzmán to the natives, but Motolinia left enough of an impression on the bishop to make possible what many Mexicans, more than four centuries later, continue to regard as the most important event in the nation's history: the appearance of the Virgin Mary (as Our Lady of Guadalupe) on the hill of Tepeyac, overlooking Mexico City.

The man who reported that appearance, as the story goes, had been born Cuauhtlatoatzin ("he who talks like an eagle") in 1474. He was thirteen years old when Tlacaelel organized the three days of unceasing human sacrifice that had dedicated the great pyramid temple in Tenochtitlan, forty-five when Cortés and the conquistadors defeated the Aztecs and captured the city. He had been witness to unspeakable horrors and breathtaking transformations. Among those transformations was the baptism that had given him a new name, Juan Diego, and a new faith, Catholicism.

The oldest reliable account we have of what took place on Tepeyac comes from an Indian scholar named Antonio Valeriano, who
claimed to have known Juan Diego, and told the former Cuauhtlatoatzin's story in a document known as the *Nican Mopohua* that was
written (in Nahuatl) in 1556, twenty-five years after the events. According to Valeriano, on Saturday, December 9, 1531, Juan Diego was
on his way to Tlatelolco for morning mass when he climbed Tepeyac
and was met at the summit of the hill by singing and then a dazzling
white cloud inside the aureole of a rainbow. A beautiful young Indian
woman emerged from the cloud, Juan Diego said, shining so brightly
that the dull gray rocks around her seemed to become giant gemstones
and the cactuses were plated with gold.

She spoke to him in Nahuatl, Juan Diego said: "My son, Juan Diego, where are you going?" When he told her, she said, according to
Juan Diego, "You must know and be very certain in your heart, my son,
that I am truly the perpetual and perfect Virgin Mary, holy mother of
the True God through whom everything lives, the Creator and Master
of Heaven and Earth. I wish and intensely desire that in this place my
sanctuary be erected so that in it I may show and make known and give
all my love, my compassion, my help and my protection to the people.
I am the compassionate mother of you and of all you people here in this
land, and of the other peoples who love me, who cry out to me, who
seek me, who have confidence in me. Here I will hear their weeping,
their sorrow, and will remedy their suffering and misfortunes." She directed Juan Diego to go to the bishop and tell him what he had heard.

Bishop Zumárraga met the Indian's story with skepticism and
suggested he come back at "a better time." Juan Diego returned to
Tepeyac just before sunset and found the lady of light waiting for him.
He pleaded with her to send someone more distinguished to the
bishop, according to Valeriano, someone more likely to be believed.
"I have chosen you," the lady replied.

Juan Diego approached the bishop the next day after mass, and
this time Zumárraga seemed a bit more disposed to listen, but said he
needed proof—"a sign." The Indian headed off to seek the evidence
that Zumarraga had asked for, trailed by two of the bishop's attendants,

who lost him along the way. In fact, by Valeriano's account, Juan Diego did not return to Tepeyac for two days. He had been distracted by the illness of his favorite uncle, Juan Diego had explained, feeling that somehow it was his fault. Walking to church, he actually tried to go around Tepeyac, but the shining lady who said she was the Virgin Mary came down the hill to meet him. The lady reassured him, said Juan Diego, who claimed he had been most affected when she asked him, "Am I not of your kind?" She asked him to climb the hill, collect flowers, and bring them to her, Juan Diego said. All that grew on the hill so far as he knew were cactus, thornbush, and thistle, and yet on that day he found a bush that was thick with Castilian roses (which do not grow in Mexico) glistening with dew and gloriously fragrant. It was the woman who took the roses from him, wrapped them in his *tilma* (an Indian cloak, made of cactus fiber), then told him, "This is the sign you must take to the Lord Bishop."

He was kept waiting for a long time at the bishop's house, Juan Diego told Valeriano. Zumarraga's assistants insisted upon seeing the roses and then tried to take some, but they could not, because it was "not roses that they touched, but [something that was] as if painted or embroidered," in Valeriano's words. Eventually, he was admitted to the bishop's presence, Juan Diego said, and when he opened his cloak the roses cascaded to the floor and on the *tilma* was the image that is known today as Our Lady of Guadalupe.

For the Catholic Church, the miracle would be confirmed by the nine million baptisms in Mexico during the next seventeen years, up to the time that Juan Diego and Bishop Zumárraga died within a few days of each other. The faithful celebrated the spiritual victory over the Devil and his followers that followed the martial one accomplished by Hernán Cortés. The basilica built on the spot where Juan Diego said he had first met the Virgin Mary would become the most-visited pilgrimage site in all of Catholicism, but the way was hardly smooth, even in the immediate aftermath of the Guadalupe miracle, and became increasingly rocky and treacherous in the epoch of revisionist history that dawned during the twentieth century.

I was surprised to discover that the earliest opponents of Guadalupe were the Franciscans themselves. Their main criticism was that the cult of devotion growing up around the apparition site encouraged the natives in idolatry and superstition. Many of the Indians who came to Tepeyac to worship referred to the image of the Virgin Mary as Tonantzin ("our revered mother" in Nahuatl), the Aztec goddess of love and fertility. This sort of syncretism was seeping into the Church from all over the New World, the Franciscans complained, abetted by the Dominicans, who were the main supporters of the Guadalupe shrine. The Franciscans also claimed that the image of the Virgin had been painted by an Aztec known as Marcos, an accusation that has been made repeatedly by critics and opponents over the past several hundred years. And in fact much of the image of the Virgin on the glass-encased cloth that is the central feature of the shrine *was* added to it by artists working under the direction of priests during the sixteenth and seventeenth centuries; the angel and the moon at the Virgin's feet, as well as the starburst that surrounds her and the stars on her cloak, all were painted, according to the single scientist who was permitted by the Church to conduct an infrared photography study of the *tilma* in 1979. That scientist, Philip Serna Callahan (a renowned biophysicist, a United States Department of Agriculture entomologist, and a NASA consultant), also discovered, however, that there was an older, original image under all the paint. How it had been made, Callahan was unable to determine. What Callahan could say, though, was how remarkable it was that the unretouched areas of the image on the *tilma* had managed to remain perfectly preserved, while the painted details that were added later all had cracked and faded. And there was no preliminary sketch beneath the image, Callahan found, which the artists who were consulted found incredible. Callahan's study also confirmed that the purported cloak of Juan Diego was apparently of maguey cactus fiber, as had been claimed since the sixteenth century. Only this was impossible, because a cactus fiber cloak would have disintegrated within a couple of decades at most, and this one had already lasted well over four hundred years.

CHAPTER TWELVE

THERE WAS BOTH COMFORT and inspiration in believing that what happened was meant to be, I reflected on the afternoon of March 3, 2015. If not for the conversations between Michelle and Brenda, I almost certainly would not have been aboard an AeroMéxico flight headed from Mexico City to Veracruz at this moment, and Michelle Gomez definitely would not have been sitting next to me. Whether it was meant to be was beyond the limits of both my faith and my understanding. All I could say for sure was that I was glad to have Michelle beside me, because what I knew was going to be a perilous expedition would have been hopelessly doomed without her.

Michelle's fluency in Spanish was what I most required of her for the time being. At the Mexico City airport, after I asked her for the tenth time, "What did they just say?" the jokes I had been making to friends and family about being protected by a four-foot-eleven-inch bodyguard sounded a lot less funny to me.

At least after Mexico City I was able to stop fretting about the ridiculous prices I had paid for our plane tickets, purchased at the last minute when we abandoned our plan to drive from Texas in Michelle's SUV. It seemed insane now, but our original intent had been to take the shortest route by road to Veracruz, entering Mexico at Matamoros and then heading down Mexico 101 along the Gulf of Mexico. Only a couple of weeks before our scheduled departure had I discovered that no one called that highway 101 anymore. It was better known now as "the Highway of Death," though "the Devil's Road" was also a popular name for what 101 had become. The highway was almost totally deserted these days, and absolutely no one drove it after dark. The bloated bodies of dead cattle that lay amid the cactus and prickly pear were now far outnumbered by the burnt-out shells of various vehicles that had been attacked by bandits or kidnappers or psychopathic killers and left like litter along the roadside. What inspired more profound terror, though, were the mass graves that had been discovered next to the highway during the past several years. The largest such grave was just outside a town 200 miles south of Matamoros called San Fernando, where we had actually considered stopping for the night: 145 bodies had been found compacted into a single hole in the ground, and dozens more had been discovered in graves nearby. Not a single Mexican television station, I had been told, was able to convince a camera crew to venture out onto 101 to capture footage of the exhumations.

There were now more than a dozen government roadblocks between San Fernando and Ciudad Victoria, each one manned by squads of marines and federal police armed with .50-caliber machine guns and grenade launchers, but still almost no drivers ventured onto Highway 101. The problem, I had been told, was that the criminals, dressed in green uniforms and armed with the same weapons, also were setting up roadblocks.

After considering all this, Michelle and I decided to change our route, entering Mexico through Nuevo Laredo and taking Highway 85 south into the interior of the country, through Monterrey, before turning west on Highway 70 at San Luis Potosí until we reached the coastal highway, 180, at Tampico, then continuing south to Veracruz. I became less enthusiastic about that idea, though, when I received by email a 2014 article from *The Guardian* that described how Tampico, "the New Orleans of Mexico," which had only recently been a spring break destination for US college students, was now best known for the grenades thrown into bars and restaurants that had been sprayed first with machine gun fire, and also for a series of "ultra-violence" shootouts in the streets that had left dozens dead.

While the drug cartels were blamed for only most of the murder and mayhem on Highway 101, they were entirely responsible for what had happened to Tampico. Life in that seaside city of 300,000 had been generally tolerable until 2007, as I understood it, when twelve tons of cocaine had been confiscated from local members of the Gulf Cartel. The cartel bosses, who lived mostly in Reynosa, a city of nearly 700,000 just across the Rio Grande from Hidalgo, Texas, demanded that their Tampico operatives cover the loss. This had set off a wave of kidnappings, including one that made news all over Mexico, the victim in that case being the city's former mayor, whose cousin was the CEO of the country's biggest media empire, Televisa. When the truly wealthy fled Tampico, the cartel began to target members of the upper middle class—doctors, lawyers, and small business operators—and they left town, too. "Those who flee the city usually can't sell their homes and businesses, so more and more buildings, including some of Tampico's largest and most impressive ones, lie abandoned," *The Guardian* article had reported. "Buildings that could easily survive for another century are mere empty shells, with huge trees growing through the roofs and out of the windows. Such levels of abandonment are rarely seen in the centre of a major city."

The situation had grown even more dire around 2010, when the Gulf Cartel's enforcers, nearly all of them recruited from Mexico's most elite military unit, the paratroopers, decided they had become powerful enough to challenge their bosses and formed what was now considered the most murderous cartel in all of Mexico, the Zetas. The turf war that resulted had become violent almost beyond imagining. In the spring of 2010, the Gulf Cartel announced they would begin enforcing a curfew in Tampico, and that ordinary citizens who ventured out after ten in the evening should not blame them if they were caught in the resulting gunfire. The carnage escalated dramatically, month after month. Hundreds of hired guns were killed on both sides, along with scores of civilian bystanders. In October 2010 alone, more than twenty military and police installations in Tampico were bombed.

The Gulf Cartel had won control of Tampico and the rest of Tamaulipas state, which was their home turf, but they had been forced to surrender the far wealthier and more desirable state of Veracruz. The two cartels actually installed tollbooths on both ends of the Moralillo

Bridge, which connected Tamaulipas and Veracruz—the Gulf Cartel on the north side and the Zetas on the south, each either collecting money ($232 per month was the going rate) or stealing the vehicles of those who refused to pay.

So the route through Tampico was out. Michelle and I briefly considered following Highway 85 all the way into Mexico City, then heading east on another major highway, 150, which would take us almost all the way to Veracruz. Then we consulted Michelle's brother Mario, a US Immigration and Customs Enforcement agent, whose reply was, "You know what we call people who drive vehicles with US license plates into Mexico? Organ donors."

Our plane tickets, purchased on the morning we departed, cost just about four times what they would have if I'd bought them even a few days earlier. And the only seats we could get were on a jet that left San Antonio in the late afternoon, routed us through Mexico City, and got us into Veracruz at around midnight. The taxi driver who took us from the airport to our hotel on the *zócalo* issued the first of what would become an unending series of warnings about the danger in which we were placing ourselves. At least after advising us never to open car windows, to refrain from walking more than a few blocks beyond the main plaza after dark, and to avoid speaking English outside tourist areas, our driver gave us some good news: things had become much improved in Veracruz during the past eighteen months.

The Zetas had placed the city in a virtual lockdown beginning in early 2011, our driver said; no one went out after dark and "the city lived in fear." That situation had been changed in late 2013 and early 2014 by the arrival of the marines, the branch of Mexico's military and law enforcement apparatus most resistant to corruption. Determined to secure the nation's most vital port, the Marines had established patrols that forced the Zetas into hiding and freed the citizens of Veracruz to begin venturing forth (though only on well-lit streets) even after the sun went down. Several times during the next two days, Michelle and I would see a convoy of Marine vehicles pull up in front of Our Lady of the Assumption Cathedral next to the *zócalo*, bristling with weapons that always included a .50-caliber machine

gun mounted in the bed of a pickup truck. Each time, the people on
the sidewalks and in the cafes would respond to this apparently menacing show of military authority with celebratory waves and a palpable air of relief, as if it had suddenly become easier to breathe and
safer to smile.

Even after losing control of Veracruz city, the Zetas had continued their campaign of terror throughout the rest of Veracruz state.
This had become especially effective when the Zetas began to post
videos on the internet in which they executed cartel enemies (two
years before the Isis Army began posting the same sort of videos from
their caliphate in Syria and Iraq). Two Zeta videos had particularly terrified the ordinary citizens of Veracruz. In one, a group of masked
men had beheaded four women who were accused of consorting with
the Gulf Cartel. Just a single woman had been decapitated in the other
video, but the manner in which the Zeta who had done the deed held
her head in front of the camera, as a trophy, was shocking even by
Mexican standards. During the first twenty-four hours I spent in Veracruz, I would hear stories about the thirty-one bodies discovered in
a mass grave outside the town of Tres Valles, just west of Catemaco
and about the three headless corpses found long after this in the trunk
of a taxi on a highway running through the nearby village of Yanga.
Four different people told me about the two pickup trucks that had
stopped rush hour traffic on a highway in Boca del Río, just outside
Veracruz city, in order to dump forty-nine bodies out onto the road.
The taxi driver, hotel bellman, and restaurant waiter who shared these
tales had ostensibly done so in order to impress upon me the risks I
was taking in venturing beyond Veracruz, but I could see in their eyes
that each of them took some pleasure in making a gringo squirm. *You
can never know what we know*, I heard them telling me, although no
one ever spoke these words.

An intimacy with evil was characteristic of the people of this region long before the arrival of Hernán Cortés. The Spaniards, I
learned, had established Veracruz immediately after their first discovery of two Aztec temples located on offshore islands. According to
Bernal Díaz del Castillo, this was the initial Spanish encounter with

the primary Aztec deities, whose hideous, grinning faces had been carved into the stones overlooking the altars. That Huitzilopochtli and Tezcatlipoca had an appetite for human blood Díaz and the others in his party understood when they saw that five natives from local tribes had been sacrificed on the altars, their hearts torn from their chests and their bodies dismembered; the walls of the temples were splattered with human blood that was still drying. Naming the first Spanish city established in Mexico "True Cross" had been their answer to this horror, Díaz would explain.

The Zetas' decapitation videos raised the question of what, really, had changed during the five centuries since the Spanish conquest of Mexico. Was there any fundamental difference, I wondered, between cartel members beheading people for the purposes of power and profit and Aztec priests ripping out the hearts of captives and slaves to satisfy the appetites of the Hummingbird Wizard and We Who Are His Slaves? I found some grim humor in the thought that there were probably some up north who would argue that killing for something real (money) rather than for something imaginary (supernatural protection), represented progress.

Progress was no easy thing to measure in Mexico, however, let alone prove. At our hotel, I had picked up a booklet titled *Tip's de Veracruz* that was distributed by the Mexico Tourism Council for the purpose of introducing the city to foreign visitors. The contents had been organized around a single story that the Tourism Council apparently believed to be emblematic of local history and culture. It was called "The Countess of Malibran" and recounted how the beautiful young wife of an early nineteenth-century Spanish nobleman had taken up the practice (when her husband was attending to business inland) of promenading along the docks of Veracruz as ships arrived and inviting whatever sailors struck her fancy to parties at her mansion that lasted until the wee hours, at which time the countess retired to her chambers in the company of the young man she found most appealing. Those young men all disappeared afterward without a trace, the story explained. Inevitably, of course, the count himself returned home early on one occasion, only to find his wife bedded with her latest young man. He impaled both his wife and her lover with his sword, then summoned a servant who described how the countess had done this same thing many times before, sleeping with and murdering at least a dozen young men whose bodies had been disposed of in the pit of crocodiles located at the bottom of the property. The count did the same with the corpses of his dead wife and her young lover, but lost his sanity in the process, the story finished, and spent the last years of his life stumbling through the streets of the Port, shouting "Justice, justice, and death to the Countess of Malibran."

I couldn't begin to comprehend a mind that imagined such a story would be an enticement to tourists. Antonio Zavaleta's description of the shock and confusion experienced each time he encountered the "ancient and very different mentality" that existed just under the surface layer of Christianity in Mexico gave me something to relate to, but added nothing, really, to my understanding. The number of views that the decapitation videos posted by cartel members on the internet had achieved, though, made a convincing case that the Devil was running the show in this part of the world.

IT TOOK THE ENTIRE MORNING of March 4 to rent the subcompact Ford Ikon with a shrieking high-rev engine and balky manual transmission that I was going to drive to Catemaco. There's no such thing as a rapid business transaction in Mexico.

I made a couple of potentially fatal miscalculations before we even passed beyond the city limits of Veracruz. My worst decision by far had been to take the scenic shortcut of Highway 44 that ran along the Gulf of Mexico. We passed the fortified beachfront mansions of various cartel leaders as I threaded through the traffic into Boca del Río, stopping for a red light at the very intersection where those forty-nine bodies had been dumped three years earlier. From there it was just a twenty-eight-kilometer drive to the town of Antón Lizardo, according to my map, and only about another ten kilometers beyond that to the connection with Highway 180, which would allow us to continue south down the Gulf coast and then into the jungle toward

Catemaco. What no one had told me was that this stretch of Highway 44 went through villages ruled by bandits who had intentionally torn up the road, creating crater-sized potholes in the hope that some idiot like me would blow a tire or break an axle and turn himself into a sitting duck. By the time we realized our situation, this part of the drive had turned into an agonizingly slow weave around holes in the pavement that were not only broad but deep enough in spots to swallow our tiny vehicle, with us constantly watching the sides of the road and our rearview mirrors for armed men. The Ikon proved to be a tough and durable little vehicle, but the half dozen times when I gave in to the impulse to hurry, Michelle shouted in my ear that we were dead people if the car became undriveable. After the third or fourth time she called me a *pendejo*, I suggested she could get out and walk anytime. Our only serious scare came when two motorcycles, each carrying both a driver and a passenger, came zooming up behind us. "Oh shit," Michelle said. "Randall, I think you've gotten us killed." Within seconds, the motorcycles were on both sides of the car and the passengers riding behind the drivers were peering into our windows. They rode next to us for perhaps thirty seconds, then sped away, slaloming through the potholes at twice the speed we were traveling. "What just happened?" I asked aloud. Michelle only shook her head and we drove for another hour in silence, not speaking again until we had reached the highway.

Good fortune turned my second mistake into little more than a colorful comedic episode. I had made the thoughtless assumption that, as in the United States or any other place I'd rented a car, it was given to you with a full tank of gas. It was just about an hour later, on an empty stretch of 180, that I noticed the gas gauge needle sitting on empty and realized I had been given a car with maybe a quarter tank of fuel. We were fortunate enough to sputter into a filling station on the outskirts of Lerdo de Tejada with nothing but fumes left in the tank, only to discover that my credit cards were being denied and that the station wouldn't accept American currency. The attendant actually drove with us into town, where the auto parts store that also served as the community's informal bank traded me pesos for a $100 bill and allowed me to pay for the tank of gas that was already in the car. In no apparent hurry to get back to the station, the attendant directed us down a gravel road to a wobbly suspension bridge that was essentially a long rubber mat strung between steel cables. His purpose was to show us the marvelous sight of several dozen iguanas lazing above a flowing tributary of the Laguna de Alvarado on the branches of the largest ficus tree I had ever seen. I was exchanging stares with a lizard that was maybe twelve feet away when a family of four clambered onto the bridge, causing it to sag and sway so extremely that I gripped the single-wire railing with both hands. A boy of about eight holding a sandwich in one hand peeled off a thin strip of ham and tossed it into the river, where the water began to boil within seconds. This stretch of the river had been taken over by piranhas, which had eaten all the other fish, the filling station attendant explained to Michelle, in a tone that was slightly sad but mostly matter-of-fact.

"No more stops until we reach Catemaco," I told Michelle when we had dropped the attendant off at his station and were back on the highway.

I COULDN'T HAVE KNOWN IT at the time, but our departure from Veracruz had coincided almost exactly with the Mexican government's most aggressive attack ever on the Zetas and their power structure. On March 4, 2015, the day Michelle and I drove to Catemaco, the federal police arrested the Zetas' supreme commander, Omar "Z-42" Trevino, at a house just outside Monterrey. Dozens of Zeta regional bosses would be taken into custody during the next ten days, and I watched a strange succession of emotions play across the faces of the Mexicans who followed the government campaign through television news coverage: first there was shock, then relief, and finally a kind of free-floating dread of what would replace the Zetas, because in Mexico there was always some new faction to fill the breach caused by the takedown of this or that cartel operation. The Devil they knew was always preferable to the Devil they didn't. Just hours after Trevino's arrest, while Michelle and I were driving toward Catemaco, police officers in the town of Emiliano Zapata, also in Veracruz state, had found three naked bodies on the side of a road; after a brief search, three more bodies wrapped in plastic bags were discovered nearby. Though I could understand almost none of what the television reporters and commentators were saying when I watched the television coverage of these events, I had been taken aback to see the regular cutaways to images of a black-robed female skeleton holding a scythe and a globe—Santa Muerte. No Mexicans were surprised; "Saint Death" was the main figure of worship in what had become the virtual religion of the drug cartels and had been featured for years in television reports of various *narcotraficante* atrocities.

Santa Muerte first became widely known in 1998, following the arrest of Daniel Arizmendi López, the leader of Mexico's most notorious kidnap ring, when news reports mentioned that he kept a shrine to Santa Muerte in his home. An impression was created that criminal organizations south of the border had invented Santa Muerte. The cult's origins, though, extend deep into Mesoamerican history, where the worship of death has been a feature of many cultures, before and after the Aztecs. Historians have found references to Santa Muerte that date to eighteenth-century Mexico, and the figure of Saint Death was certainly a devotional object in some homes before the dawn of the twentieth century. I recall seeing a Saint Death statue for the first time in an East L.A. *botánica* in the early 1980s. There had been an explosion in the popularity of the Santa Muerte cult since the beginning of the twenty-first century, however, and by the time of my arrival in Veracruz estimates were that it claimed between two and three million adherents in Mexico alone. David Romo Guillén, leader of the Church of Santa Muerte, said there were five million members.

Santa Muerte devotion was as complex as it was controversial. The enormous number of Black slaves who had passed through the port of Veracruz between the sixteenth and nineteenth centuries left a deeper imprint on Mexican culture than most Mexicans liked to acknowledge. My friend the writer Kambon Obayani had described to me the hostility he experienced when he tried to report on the elements of the Yoruba religion he found in the shamanistic "traditions" of Mexico. Suggesting that a large percentage of Mexicans living along the Gulf of Mexico had African blood in their veins, though, was what had gotten him thrown out of the country. Nevertheless, the Santa Muerte cult clearly had been influenced by Santería. The hierarchy of the Catholic Church in Mexico was among those who had said as much, but what Catholic leaders added was that this served only as stronger evidence that Santa Muerte devotion was satanically inspired. The Vatican had described the church of Saint Death as a "degeneration of religion" that was especially blasphemous in the way it attempted to mix Christianity with devil-worshipping occultism. The antipathy of Mexico's bishops to the worship of Saint Death had grown more acute a few years into the twenty-first century when David Romo and his followers decided to rebrand their organization as La Iglesia Católica Tradicionalista Mexicana Estadounidense (the Traditionalist Mexican American Catholic Church). The Roman Catholic Church charged that this was outright fraud and persuaded the federal government to impose a ban on the Church of Santa Muerte that stayed in place for several years. The ban, however, failed to put a dent in the popularity of the Saint Death cult; by 2008 there were more than thirty-five locations in Mexico where Santa Muerte was publicly venerated and twelve towns and cities where Santa Muerte "pilgrimages" were staged. Santa Muerte figures appeared in shop windows in virtually every town along the US-Mexico border, and all along the routes of illegal immigration and drug trafficking between the two countries. By 2009, Santa Muerte devotion was no less popular in Los Angeles than it was Mexico City.

The Catholic Church had imagined this might change when David Romo was arrested in December 2010 on charges that he had been doing the banking for a kidnapping gang linked to a drug cartel. Yet even when Romo was sentenced in 2012 to sixty-six years in prison after being convicted of crimes that now included active participation in kidnapping, robbery, and extortion, the Church of Santa Muerte continued to thrive. In part this had to do with the fact that the cartels were running what were arguably the most profitable businesses in Mexico. It certainly didn't hurt, though, that Santa Muerte devotion was increasingly identified not just with criminal enterprises but also with societal outcasts in general. Large swaths of the homosexual, bisexual, and transgender communities had adopted Santa Muerte as their "protectress," and soon the Church of Saint Death was the only significant organization in Mexico that recognized gay marriage and performed wedding ceremonies for homosexual couples.

When you asked Mexican people about their devotion to Santa Muerte, though, they almost always answered that they worshipped her because she was so much more generous about dispensing favors than the saints of the Roman Catholic Church. "Prayers to Santa Muerte get results," a woman operating a stall on the *zócalo* in Veracruz told me.

The first real dip in Santa Muerte's popularity did not occur until March 2012, when the Sonoran state police arrested eight people for murder for allegedly having performed the human sacrifice of a woman and a pair of ten-year-old boys.

"Now finally people will see for themselves: Santa Muerte is the Devil's daughter," a Catholic priest told the Mexico City newspaper *Excélsior*.

CHAPTER THIRTEEN

IT WAS DIFFICULT TO REMEMBER to be afraid during the final two hours or so of the drive to Catemaco. The terrain was magnificent and every high point of the narrow broken road offered views that were breathtakingly lush. On the last stretch of highway along the Gulf Coast, Michelle and I agreed that we'd never seen a more beautiful place to live in poverty. Tiny crooked houses that were little more than four plywood walls and a tin roof commanded 180-degree ocean vistas to the east, and to the west they looked out onto the canopy of a jungle rainforest, with guava, papaya, and banana trees growing in between. I was transfixed by the sight of a man on a bicycle and one on a donkey in conversation along the side of a lonely stretch of road, with no one else in sight for as far as I could see in either direction.

The atmosphere became even more exotic when we turned southwest on the narrow two-track road that would take us into what was known as the Los Tuxtlas region. The constantly rising and falling road twisted through the foothills of two immense viridescent volcanoes, San Martín Tuxtla and Santa Martha, each thickly covered with rainforest from base to summit. San Martín was still active—its last major eruption had been in 1793—and the volcano's summit crater was a full kilometer wide, more than 150 feet deep. The Olmec civilization that thrived on the Gulf Coast of Mexico a thousand years before the birth of Christ had hauled the huge basalt boulders that they carved into their famous "colossal heads" out of the San Martín lava flows. Tiltepetl ("black mountain") was what the locals called San

Martín, whose magmatic eruptions had also provided the town where we were headed with its name, Catemaco, derived from the Nahuatl phrase meaning "place of burned houses."

Between the volcanoes, the going was torturously slow. We were constantly backed up behind big trucks. Some carried as many as twenty or thirty young men who stood in a plywood-sided bed, singing and smiling after a day of cutting sugar cane in the lowlands. They seemed to me to exist in a dimension that was utterly removed from the cartels, but that was likely my limited point of view. The same trucks carried the actual cane, stalks stacked more than twenty feet high, lashed with rope and swaying absurdly as vehicles climbed uphill at five or ten miles per hour. Michelle gasped and groaned and cursed me every time I decided to pass one, the puny engine of our tiny car issuing a squeal of desperation as I floored it and just managed to squeeze in between the truck in front of us and the one coming at us head-on. "I want to get there before dark" was my only defense, and it had worn thin fast. I was down to "We made it, didn't we?" by the time we approached our destination.

Catemaco was more like a small city (population 26,000) than the dusty village I had imagined. Curving roads wound past *supermercados* and *farmacias* on the outskirts of town, through a couple of blocks where sketchy-looking commercial operations and low wooden houses with peeling paint were interspersed, then into a circle maze of tiny stores and stalls that peeled off in opposite directions toward the two main features of the town, the lovely and imposing Basilica of Our Lady of Mount Carmel, which anchored the *zócalo*, and Laguna Catemaco, the immense freshwater lake that was the primary source of the town's existence.

The best hotel in town, where I had reserved a room, was right on the lake. Drained from the drive, I gave myself until morning to begin a serious exploration of Catemaco. The helpful guest who had advised that Michelle and I make sure we weren't followed whenever we left the hotel encouraged my decision to wait for daylight to go looking for trouble. Instead, I sat in a plastic chair under a palm tree on the thin strip of sandy beach that bordered the lake and watched the sun dissolve into a smoky mist as it sank behind the hills on the opposite shore. There were a half dozen volcanic islands out there that looked like mounds of tropical rainforest floating on the gray-blue surface of the water. On three of the islands lived colonies of macaque monkeys, left behind by an abandoned University of Veracruz research project. Scores of small boats offered themselves for hire to ferry tourists from the north shore of the lake to the islands where the monkeys lived, though few if any would actually take people ashore, given the macaques' reputation for attacking human visitors.

There was also an island called El Tegal, where, according to local legend, the Virgin Mary had appeared during the seventeenth century in the avatar of Our Lady of Mount Carmel. I was unable to discover if Mary had delivered any message back in 1664, but she had, according to the local diocese, left behind a statue of Our Lady of Mount Carmel that was the centerpiece of the shrine to the Virgin inside the basilica. The pilgrims who visited nearly all came bearing fresh flowers, which they rubbed all over their bodies after making the sign of the cross on the glass case that held the statue. In answer to the prayers they then offered, it was said, many miracles had been granted.

I wondered, based in large part on what I'd heard from Antonio Zavaleta, whether some of the same people who brought flowers to the statue of the virgin also sought help from *brujos* who had offered their own souls to El Diablo. I supposed that the answer was yes and then a moment later was struck by a thought I found deeply unsettling: It was human nature to try to have it both ways; the Devil knew that, and it was his great advantage over God.

Assuming there was a Devil, of course, which I seemed to be doing a lot of since arriving in Mexico.

I WAS BACK on the little strip of beach early the next morning. It was Thursday, March 5, 2015. At midnight it would become the first Friday in March and what was known as the Hour of the Witches would be celebrated with Black Masses held at various locations in Catemaco. The best explanation I ever got to my question "Why the first Friday in March?" was that this had marked the first "moment" of creation, the beginning of time, when the Devil had made his choice to separate from God and declare his own principality. At midnight, the Devil's demons would gather in Catemaco for the celebration of their power and of the souls they had claimed during the previous year. For those who wished to make a bargain with El Diablo, this was considered the optimal time. Now that I was here, I found it more rather than less difficult to say why I had come. "To see what a deal with the Devil looks like," I told Michelle at one point. She merely nodded, with a sober expression.

In full sunshine, the lake was much more vast than I had imagined it at dusk. Through the silvery haze of evaporation, I could see the mountains in the distance, but not the actual shore where the water ended. A young fisherman in a small boat was spreading his net not far from where I stood. There were several varieties of fish in Laguna Catemaco, but the main catch, I had been told, was a snail called *tegogolo* that was sold at little stands lining the breakwater on the southern edge of town. "Muy sabroso," the waiter at the hotel's restaurant had assured me the night before; he appeared disappointed when I passed.

The Spanish word *laguna*, just like the English word lagoon, technically describes a body of water exposed to the sea. Laguna Catemaco was actually a freshwater lake, the third-largest in Mexico, but only the professors from the University of Veracruz referred to it as Lago Catemaco, I had been told. While waiting for Michelle to awaken, I had read an article by one of those academics, who asserted that, based on its "high rate of endemicity," Lago Catemaco most likely had been "biogeographically isolated" since its formation two million years earlier, caused by a lava flow that had blocked what was now the north shore. I could only imagine that this isolation also had something to do with why and how Catemaco had become Mexico's capital of *brujería*.

It was almost nine by the time Michelle and I sat down for breakfast.

The most popular local dish, said the same waiter who had served us the night before, was called *carne de chango* (monkey meat) but was

actually smoked pork. Michelle refused resolutely to even try it, telling me she had been warned that the locals sometimes substituted
actual monkey meat in the meals they fed to tourists. Feeling bad about
refusing the snails, I ordered *carne de chango* anyway and found it delicious. The person who had told Michelle to be careful about eating
monkey meat was a client of hers, a wealthy Mexican oilman who
kept his main residence on the US side of the border near McAllen.
When he learned that Michelle was joining me on a trip to Catemaco,
he discouraged her, asking, "Why would you ever want to go to such
a dark place?" My annoyance with him for that was mitigated when
he said he knew the owner of our hotel and would call ahead to ask
that we be treated with special consideration.

Over breakfast, when Michelle asked me what the "plan" was,
I elected not to answer with the plain truth, which was that my only
plan was to walk around town looking for people with interesting faces
and ask them questions. Instead, I proposed that we begin by driving
into downtown and parking near the *zócalo*, then check in at the parish office of the basilica. The people there almost certainly would have
strong opinions about the *brujos* and their deals with the Devil.

No one followed us as we left the hotel, but as soon as we turned
into the long road that ran along the breakwater we were surrounded
by men who came running toward the car, shouting that they could
take us to the *brujos*. As I maneuvered through them, several young men
on motorcycles pulled up alongside our car, urging me to follow
them if I wanted to meet the most powerful *brujo* in Catemaco. I ignored them and continued in the direction of the basilica.

We didn't even have to go inside the church to find one of the two
most helpful people we would meet in Catemaco. All along the street
on the south side of the Basilica were tiny stands selling crosses, rosaries, and assorted religious medals. Michelle, who scorned Catholicism
whenever her devout mother pushed the subject, now insisted upon
loading up with what she called "protection." Specifically, she wanted
St. Benedict medals, which her mother had advised were the best for
warding off evil. The woman operating the stand closest to the *zócalo*
had not only the nicest collection of trinkets but also the strongest

face and clearest eyes we had thus far seen in Catemaco. I was impressed also that, unlike all of the other stand operators on the street, she did not call or wave us to approach, instead watching us patiently, as if she knew we would come back to her. When we did, she introduced herself as María, asked where in the United States we were from, then said she had lived in San Diego for four years, had liked it there, and wanted to go back someday. It would have to be someday soon, I thought, reckoning the woman's age to be about sixty.

Sixty-one, it turned out. I picked up that much, though not much else as I listened to María and Michelle converse in Spanish while sorting through the stall's several dozen St. Benedict medals. Not until the sale was completed more than ten minutes later did Michelle fill me in on what had been discussed. "Good news, bad news," she began. "We're in a very dangerous place. The Zetas have been running the town for the past couple of years and they've made things a lot worse. They were out in force just a few nights ago, putting people in sequester, which basically means pulling them off the street and making them surrender their valuables and identify police informants."

"Making them how?" I asked.

"Beatings and torture," Michelle said. "And threats against people's families. María said all of the older people and the women and children just stayed indoors, but some young men wanted to be macho and went out even when they were warned not to. Several of them have disappeared. Their families hope they were just forced to join the cartels—that's what usually happens, but if someone says no, the cartel people kill them as an example. So people are worried." Michelle paused to look around, like she thought someone might be eavesdropping. Other than María, who didn't speak English, there was no one within twenty feet of us. "María says most of the men who say they will introduce you to the *brujos* are really just low-level cartel guys who work as bandits. She said if you go with them they'll lead you into the dog traps."

"Dog traps?" I asked. "What are those?"

Michelle spoke to María in Spanish for a few moments, then told me, "They keep kennels of pit bulls up the dirt roads into the mountains. They put stupid tourists in there and let the dogs tear them up until they turn over all their financial information, including their PIN numbers and passwords."

"So plenty of evil around these parts, with or without witches."

"That's the other thing you won't like to hear," Michelle replied.

"What?"

"María said the *brujos*, the real *brujos*, died years ago."

"What is she talking about? There are at least a dozen *brujos* practicing in Catemaco, including a couple of famous ones."

Michelle and Mara chattered for a few moments, then Michelle told me, "She says the new ones are not like the old ones. They don't have the same power. They aren't respected or feared in the same way. They don't know the Devil personally like the old ones did. The only ones people are afraid of now are the *brujos* who work with the cartels."

"Who were the old ones?"

Michelle and María spoke again for a minute. "There were two. The famous one that first attracted people to come here from Mexico City and other places was Gonzalo Aguirre. He was called the *brujo mayor* and was the first one that politicians and movie stars and athletes came to visit. He was powerful and respected. And feared. He could kill people with a spell if he wanted. But the one who taught him was even more powerful and more feared. No one wanted to be against him."

"When did these men die?"

"Gonzalo died in the eighties," Michelle told me after conferring with María. "His teacher died long before that, in the nineteen-sixties."

"What was the teacher's name?"

Michelle passed the question on to María, who paused, then answered, "No quiero decir que"—I don't want to say it.

"The man has been dead for fifty years and she's afraid to say his name?"

When Michelle repeated my question in Spanish, María simply nodded.

"You said there was some good news," I reminded Michelle.

"Yes, María says that she and her nephew, who knows it really well, will take us to the cave on Cerro del Mono Blanco—White Monkey Mountain—where the first *brujo*, the teacher, worked and where he met with the Devil. They call it La Cueva del Diablo—the Devil's Cave."

Letting myself be guided to a place called the Devil's Cave by a woman I had just met and couldn't converse with might reasonably have been called reckless, but I knew I was going to do it. Michelle was convinced of María's good character, and whatever else might have been said of Michelle Gomez, she was a great reader of people. I had placed myself in a considerably greater number of dangerous situations than most persons, but not nearly so many as Michelle. She had survived and succeeded in large part by knowing who could be trusted and who could not be. I felt I had no choice but to place my faith in her. Plus, I needed to see that cave, now that I knew it existed. Otherwise, I might as well have stayed home.

We agreed to meet María in this same spot when she closed her stall at three o'clock, then said goodbye to her for now and walked up the stairs to the entrance of the basilica. It really was a lovely church, a white stucco blend of Baroque and Neoclassical design with a towering cupola covered in rolled gold that reached more than sixty-five feet high. The cool and dark interior seemed enormously spacious, especially at a time of day when there were only two other supplicants, an elderly couple, seated in the pews. The statue of the Virgin of Carmel stood inside a thick glass case on a raised platform behind the altar that could be approached by staircases on each side. She was a far cry, I thought, from Our Lady of Guadalupe. There was no prayerful pose, none of the gentleness and humility of the Guadalupe virgin. This Mary wore a splendid robe of crimson with gold trim and an enormous gold crown with a huge trailing veil of white lace. She was no Indian, but rather a porcelain-skinned redhead who wore an expression that was slightly imperious, at once sad and stunned, like a Queen of Heaven who was deeply disappointed in her subjects. The fact that this version of Mary—wherever it had come from—was so vastly different from the Guadalupe image had to signify something about this place, I thought, but I was in no position to suggest what that might be.

After wandering about the interior of the basilica and examining the stained glass windows surrounding the cupola that depicted the lives of Jesus and Mary, Michelle and I realized that the church office could only be approached by exiting the building and entering through a door at the back. When we did so, we were told by the two women seated at desks inside that the padre was out for the morning. Only after some hesitation were we invited to take a chair and wait for him. Michelle quickly struck up a conversation with the women, who both seemed a bit put off, though not at all surprised, when it was explained that we were in Catemaco to study the sorcerers. Immediately, the plump, dark-skinned woman who did most of the talking repeated almost exactly what María had told us: the *brujos*, the real *brujos*, the *brujos* who had made Catemaco famous, were long dead. Certain members of Gonzalo Aguirre's family were the only true link to them, the woman said. When I inquired through Michelle who those family members were, the woman seemed to grow even more uncomfortable and answered simply that we should ask someone else. Like María, she was reluctant to speak the name of the witch who had been Aguirre's teacher, but eventually came forth with the name: Manuel Utrera. She did not believe in *brujería*, the dark woman told Michelle, but she could not deny that Utrera had had certain powers, powers that could only have come from the Devil himself. It was difficult to get more information than that from the dark woman, other than it was very dangerous in Catemaco, especially for gringos, and that walking the streets after dark would be unwise.

I was quite distracted during this conversation by the other woman in the office, who had remained silent all during it. She was extraordinarily beautiful, with perfect creamed coffee skin, brilliantly white teeth, hair and eyes that were black and lustrous. I couldn't stop stealing glances at her. She knew it and appeared to be uneasy and appreciative in just about equal measure. She did not speak until the dark woman went into the back section of the office to answer a ringing telephone, then told Michelle while looking at me that if I really wanted to know about "these things" there was a man I should talk to. His name was Facundo Pereyra Cadena, known to all as Cundo. He was a kind of historian of Catemaco, and especially of the magicians who had made the town famous. His family was "part of all that," and there were at least a couple still alive who had known Manuel Utrera. Cundo shouldn't be difficult to locate, the woman said. He owned several buildings and businesses on the street that ran straight from the basilica off the *zócalo*.

It took just minutes to find one of Cundo's enterprises, where two men working between three walls open to the street were reupholstering the seats of wood chairs with squares of foam, sheets of vinyl, and brass tacks.

After Michelle explained what we wanted with Cundo, a cellphone call was made. Just minutes later a pickup truck pulled up in front of us and Cundo stepped out of it. He was a strapping, handsome fellow with a large black mustache, in his early forties, I reckoned, wearing a white polo shirt that was taut across his considerable belly. He opened a locked steel gate and insisted that we come upstairs to his home, which turned out to be a spacious apartment with a large terrace that stretched across the second floor above three different business enterprises operating at street level. Cundo's youngest child, a boy of about three or four, immediately leaped into my arms and hugged me tight, grinning with delight and refusing to be put down. The child's sweetness and affection as he clung to my neck created a sudden sense of joy and connection among us all. Cundo beamed as he motioned to his shy but smiling wife to take photographs, then posed with his son and me.

For a few moments it did not seem possible that I was there to talk about witches, black magic, and devil worship. When Cundo sat us all down, though, he immediately told Michelle that it was fortunate for me that I had been sent to him. Others I might have approached with the kinds of questions I was asking would have led me into danger if they could. I would have been robbed certainly and killed possibly. When Cundo said, "Do not go anywhere with anyone unless you know and trust them well," Michelle and I shared a glance, thinking of María and this nephew of hers that we hadn't met yet. He had numerous family members, mostly from the generation before his own, who were involved with the use of magic, Cundo said, some for the purpose of healing, some for "other reasons." He guessed I was not there to learn about the healers. When Michelle told him that I was interested in learning more about Manuel Utrera and his student Gonzalo Aguirre, Cundo's expression became serious. Gonzalo's daughter Isabel was the most powerful *curandera* in Mexico, he said. Some feared her, some did not, but he could testify that, unlike her father, she used her powers for good. If she would speak to me, I could learn much. He would see if that could be arranged. Manuel Utrera had not distributed his knowledge or his powers among his children, only among those few he chose as students, and they were required to serve him for years as the price of their lessons. Even those close to him had feared Utrera, Cundo said, "because he could do things that no one else could." The man had been dead for many years, and people still whispered his name when they spoke it aloud. His great uncle Dagoberto Pereyra had briefly been Utrera's student when he was young, Cundo said, and later was one of the few who could call Utrera a friend. He believed Dagoberto would speak to me, Cundo told Michelle, who added after she translated those words into English that she had a sense this Dagoberto might want money.

Michelle told Cundo that María who ran the stall closest to the entrance to the church had agreed to take us to the cave at the top of Mono Blanco. He nodded and said she was someone who could be trusted, and who would know the dangers to avoid.

After we returned from Mono Blanco we should ask María to send him a message, Cundo told Michelle, and he would meet us with Dagoberto at my hotel for an evening meal. Would we want to attend one of the Black Masses that would be held that night, for the Hour of the Witches? asked Cundo. I nodded when Michelle translated the question, then asked how many such ceremonies there would be. Many small ones in private, Cundo answered, three larger ones in public. The main event would be the one held by the lake, but that was really just a show for tourists, Cundo said. The worst danger there was pickpockets. The Black Mass held at Mono Blanco was the real thing, Cundo said, but that had been taken over by the cartel members, and he would not consider attending that. Neither should I. There would also be a Black Mass conducted under a cliff at the base of the San Martín volcano by the *brujo* that he personally considered the most powerful currently operating in Catemaco, Enrique Verdon, who was known as "The Italian" because of his mother, Cundo said. That one he might consider taking us to, Cundo said, after he spoke with Dagoberto. This could be decided when we met at the hotel. We shook hands on our agreement, then Cundo led us back down the iron stairs to the steel gate and let us out onto the street. "Do not wander at Mono Blanco," he said before sending us off. "Go only where María says to go."

MARÍA'S NEPHEW DANIEL, a slim young man of about twenty, inspired even more trust than she did. He was coming along on our exploration of Mono Blanco, it became clear, mainly to see that no harm came to his aunt. As his wariness subsided, he revealed a kind personality that extended his protection to Michelle and me. María seemed genuinely excited about the trip, telling Michelle that it had been years since she had hiked up the mountain and more years than that since she had seen the Devil's Cave. This was the busiest day of the year at Mono Blanco and the number of people made the trip safer, María told Michelle, so long as we were out of there before dark.

As María and Daniel crammed themselves into the tiny backseat of the Ikon, it occurred to me how unconsciously I was neglecting the warmth and generosity I had encountered so often in my earlier trips south of the border. Focusing on the strains of darkness in the Mexican national soul had hardened my heart and narrowed my mind without my even realizing it. We do the Devil's work for him, I thought, and he doesn't even appreciate it. For some reason this struck me as humorous, but when I chuckled, Michelle shot me a puzzled look. I shook my head in reply, not wanting to share a joke I doubted anyone else would find amusing.

It was not a long drive, perhaps twenty minutes up a road that was very wide at the bottom but narrowed steadily; there scarcely seemed room for two small cars to pass by the time we reached the top, and I couldn't imagine what I'd do if a truck was coming the other way. The parking lot María directed us to was adjacent to a tiny market that was the only building we'd seen since starting the climb. We were all startled to see several military vehicles, Jeeps and Humvees, parked alongside us. María said she had no idea why the *federales* would be here, but she seemed unconcerned, and said that perhaps it was to protect common people from the cartels.

The trail hike was much like the road, wide and easy at first, but narrowing rapidly as it descended, initially, toward the Laguna Encantada, which sat at the base of Cerro del Mono Blanco. Slippery with dust and tangled with tree roots, the trail was slow going, especially for María. I held her hand on the steepest part of the descent, but then began to get ahead of her and the others after the trail leveled and I let go. Behind me, I heard her speaking rapidly to Michelle, who called out that there were tarantulas in the low-hanging branches of the trees and coral snakes and scorpions in the rocks, so watch out. There were also puss caterpillars in the foliage that could kill a man in twenty minutes with the venom they injected from the tiny red hairs that cover their bodies, María told Michelle, and assassin bugs that could give you Chagas disease, an ailment similar in its effects to mesothelioma that could make a person's life agony for twenty years or longer. One must remain alert in the jungle.

It was a relief at first, then a delight, and finally something like ecstasy when the trail emerged into a meadow that sat right on the shore of the Laguna Encantada. This lake was less than half the size of Laguna Catemaco, but more than twice as beautiful, a body of water renowned for its purity and for the abundance of medicinal plants lining its shores. Flowering water lilies by the thousands grew among the rocks close to where I stood; beyond them I could see the rainforest and the sky above reflected with mirror-like clarity from the blue-black surface of the lake. The nearest large tree, the bottom of its trunk submerged in water, was literally filled with white parrots; it looked at first glance like a living cloud that had descended from the heavens.

Laguna Encantada more than justified its name, I was thinking, as I stooped to collect a palmful of cool water that I splashed on the back of my neck. At almost that moment, the others emerged into the meadow and I heard Michelle shout out in a panicked voice, "Randall, watch out for the crocodiles." I experienced a warping moment of disorientation when I realized that what I had seen at first as a gray-green rock was moving in the water about thirty feet from where I stood. "I didn't know there were crocodiles in Mexico," I heard myself say, as if that made some difference.

The crocodile was actually moving away from me, paddling toward the far shore of the lake. "Randall scared it off," María joked to Michelle when they arrived at the shore of the lake. I didn't especially enjoy the joke, but María got a chuckle from me when she added, "They are shy."

IT SHOULD HAVE OCCURRED TO ME earlier that my visit to Catemaco would pose the problem of natural evil. The theological discussions of natural evil that I'd read or heard had been particularly troubling to me. Jeffrey Burton Russell had described evil in general as anything that causes harm or suffering to a sentient being and, like most other students of theodicy, divided it into two categories: moral evil and natural evil. Moral evil was an easy concept to grasp, Russell had told me, because it required a perpetrator, a person who acted intentionally in disregard for or defiance of right and good. In Christian theology, the Devil bore ultimate responsibility for the existence of moral evil, although each human or angelic being that committed such evils was responsible as well. This added up and made sense. Natural evil, though, was another matter.

Natural evil was typically defined as an evil for which no "nondivine agent" could be held morally responsible. Included in this category was everything from brain cancer to earthquakes to being eaten by a crocodile. The monism of the ancients viewed all such catastrophes as the will of God, and it was pretty much the same in the Old Testament. God had brought "a flood of waters on the earth" (Genesis 6:17), had "sent thunder and hail, and fire" (Exodus 9:23), had produced the "great wind" that blew down Job's house, had promised Isaiah that "the earth will be shaken," and had warned Ezekiel that he would kindle a fire to "devour every green tree." Christian theologians, though, were determined to separate God from natural evil, and I had a difficult time buying what I understood of their arguments. Russell admitted to me that he couldn't ultimately accept the traditional separation of moral and natural evils, because it was clearly God's choice, if there was a God, to let natural evils occur. Atheists had been making that same point for centuries.

Russell at least had been able to offer succinct descriptions of the arguments by which the great minds in the history of Christianity had attempted to explain how a loving God could create a universe where bad things happen to good people. Perhaps the most commonly deployed answer to natural evil, Russell said, has been to assert that because God's plan is beyond human understanding, we are incapable of realizing that what appears to be evil is actually part of God's "benevolent divine scheme." Another Russell, Bertrand, had expressed a biting contempt for this argument, suggesting Christian theologians make it to the mother of a child dying of leukemia. Jeffrey Burton Russell answered with what I found to be a powerful retort: "Would you prefer to tell the mother that the child's suffering is meaningless, that there will be in all eternity no reward or justice for her child, or for her, or for any human being, because the universe is gratuitously cruel?" Still, Russell conceded, the it's-a-mystery argument was a simpleminded "pseudo-answer" in which he found no satisfaction. Neither did I.

The next most widely supported argument of theologians had been that natural evil was "the necessary by-product of an essentially good universe." Since only the infinite can be perfect, God, in creating the finite world we live in, had to include imperfections. He had created the best of all possible worlds, as close to perfect as he could make it. A corollary to this argument had been to remind those who doubted God that evil was only the absence of good, and there were inevitably pockets of this absence in the material world, pockets we perceived as evil.

This led to the only really comprehensive answer to natural evil that traditional Christian theology has produced: the Fall of Adam and Eve in the Garden of Eden had distorted not just human beings but all of creation. Therefore, the Devil, who had tempted Eve in the guise of a serpent, was the ultimate source of not only moral evil but natural evil as well. I was slightly shocked when Russell dismissed this as "a quaint, metaphorical relic of an anthropocentric age."

An argument that Russell did not make—at least to me—was that the creator was separate from his creation. Catholic theology asserts that the world we live in has real existence and nature operates according to inherent principles. Aquinas had used this as the basis of his argument that natural evil comes about, essentially, by happenstance. A good and useful thing like fire, for example, can operate so successfully that it causes another good thing to lose its form: "For instance, when on the form of fire there follows the privation of air or of water. Therefore, as the more perfect the fire is in strength, so much more the perfectly does it impress its own form, so also the more perfectly does it corrupt the contrary. Hence that evil and corruption befall air and water comes from the perfection of the fire; but this is accidental; because fire does not aim at the privation of the form of water, but at the bringing in of its own form, though by doing this it accidentally causes the other."

So if the crocodile had devoured me, I thought, it would have merely been doing what it was meant to do, and my death would have been, essentially, accidental. I found no consolation in this whatsoever, but at least it made sense.

On the opposite side of the meadow were trees in which I saw, as I approached, what appeared to be darting blots of black and yellow. Drawing closer, I saw that these were keen-billed toucans that moved in a flock from tree to tree in short bursts of flight, almost like long leaps. I veered off the trail toward the trees for a closer look and heard María speaking with some urgency to Michelle, who called out, "Randall, you don't want to go into the forest. There are jaguars."

Tarantulas, coral snakes, scorpions, puss caterpillars, assassin bugs, crocodiles, and now jaguars, I thought. What can possibly be next?

There were people in this region who feared another creature of the forest even more than all of the above. *Chaneques* were, in Aztec legend, sprite-sized beings described as looking like small children with the faces of old men and women. They were considered to be both elemental forces of nature and guardians of the rainforest, capable of attacking intruders and frightening them so terribly that the soul would abandon the body. Only by a complex ritual could the *chaneques* be appeased and return the soul to the body. If this was not done, the person would die. The advent of Catholicism in Mexico had altered the perception of *chaneques* from forces of nature to violent demons that preyed on persons who wandered into the country's forests and jungles. They were said to confuse people so they would become lost, then to prey on them in the nighttime and to eat those who failed to take protective measures, like turning one's shirt inside out and shouting "Juan!" three times.

Chaneques had been essentially a natural evil in precolonial times, I thought to myself as I followed the trail to the other side of the meadow and back into the jungle, but the priests had felt constrained to make them into moral ones. In Mexico, of course, such distinctions blurred. The *brujos* drew on the forces of nature, using plants and animals and water and air as mediums through which they contacted the Devil and his demons to draw on dark powers to become black magicians. Blood was considered to be by far the most powerful such medium, which was why animal—and human—sacrifices continued to be used in their rituals.

The branches of the trees and the vines hanging from them pressed lower on this part of the trail, forcing me to crouch as I moved forward, constantly on the watch for spiderwebs. After about another ten minutes I could hear the sound of splashing water, and soon after that, voices. We were approaching what was known as the

Arroyo Seco, which had been created in the 1930s when the Laguna Encantada fractured. It was a favorite picnic spot of local people on hot days, María had told us, because of the small waterfall that spilled into a pool of volcanic stone and provided a place for families to cool off.

That idyllic spot was being put to a different use on this special day of the year, though. I understood that the moment I climbed over a log that lay like a natural barrier at the top of a rise and found myself looking down on the pool, where people were swimming or sitting on rocks under the waterfall. Overlooking them were two enormous white sheets, hung from trees, that had been imprinted with giant images of Satan that I recognized as illustrations from a nineteenth-century edition of *Paradise Lost*, woodcuts made by the French artist Gustave Doré, each depicting Satan as a winged creature with short horns and a very human face. The images on both sheets showed a ten-foot-tall Devil perched on a large rock with a barren landscape in the background, his expression one of scheming hatred in one woodcut and of despairing rage in the other. To describe myself as startled at the sight of the silkscreened sheets would understate their impact: I was momentarily petrified with shock.

Off to one side was a long wooden table covered with candles and Santa Muerte statues of various sizes. Next to that was a stone altar topped by the largest of the Santa Muerte statues, wearing a long black cape that hung nearly to the ground. Across the small clearing, in front of the pond, was a makeshift animal pen filled with at least a dozen goats and another pen next to it where a pig rooted in the mud. Behind the pens were crates and cages filled with at least fifty chickens. All of the animals had been brought to be sacrificed in the Black Mass that would be held at midnight, María told us, a Black Mass to be attended only by people connected in some way to the cartel.

I realized after a moment that it was only women and children in the water; the men all stood on the near shore. The men had stopped whatever they were doing when I appeared on the log above them and were staring at me with blatantly hostile expressions. I felt a moment of panic, then saw the *federales*, seven or eight of them in olive drab uniforms, sitting under trees on the far side of the pool, beyond the waterfall, with automatic rifles cradled between their knees.

When my companions clambered up onto the log next to me, María nodded and through Michelle told me to keep going. I stepped off the log and down steps cut into the bank below into the clearing, then crossed it under the glares of the men and continued to where the trail began to rise steeply through rocks toward the peak of Mono Blanco. At a point about a half mile up the mountain I came face-to-face with a fissure between two large black boulders that was filled with thousands of rocks. There were unfamiliar symbols painted on the boulders. I was studying them when the others came up behind me. María spoke rapidly for a few moments, then Michelle turned to me with wide eyes. "María says that this was known as the Door to Hell," she told me. "Hundreds and hundreds of people came out here to seal it up about ten years ago. There was a ceremony and everyone prayed together." María spoke again, then Michelle said, "We have a ways to go to reach the Devil's Cave."

The trail became almost vertical past this point, and I was so absorbed in making my way up that I never looked back until I had cleared the final rise and I found myself about a dozen feet from the opening of what I knew must be La Cueva del Diablo. The entrance was perhaps five feet wide. I could see guttering candles and Santa Muerte statues lining the sides of the walls before they disappeared into darkness. I had to wait five minutes or so for the others to reach the top and was astonished to see María coming in front. She arrived breathing hard and sweating heavily, but also grinning triumphantly. Her nephew was right behind her.

Michelle came over the last rise a couple of minutes later, wearing an expression that was much more terrified than the one she had worn while telling me about the Door to Hell. "The *federales* are coming up behind us," she told me breathlessly. "They're going to kill us, Randall."

I had been listening to Michelle talk about how corrupt the *federales* were almost from the moment I arrived in Texas. She had dealt with them many times when she was working south of the border and said they were all crooked. "They're going to rob us and kill us," Michelle said. "We have to find a way out of here."

But there was no way out. The trail came to a dead end at the cave and there was no climbing further. The only possible descent other than going back down the trail was to jump off a cliff. I explained that to Michelle, then sat down on a rock. María and her nephew sat on rocks also, neither of them looking particularly alarmed. Michelle remained at the top of the last rise, peering down the trail. Only a few minutes passed before she said, "They're here."

I stood up, and so did María and her nephew. I was afraid but not that afraid. I had exchanged a glance with the *commandante* when we passed him and his men at the waterfall. He had nodded to me with an expression that was respectful, not menacing. There was intelligence in the man's eyes that I found reassuring.

The *commandante* came first as he led his men over the last rise. He was a husky man of about forty who looked to have little if any Indian blood in him, wearing a brimmed cap with a flat top, armed with an automatic pistol. His men, who walked in file behind him, looked far less European and all carried assault rifles. The *commandante* gave me another nod, then saw the expression on Michelle's face and smiled very slightly. He was looking me in the eyes as he spoke to Michelle, and he said that he and his men had not come up after us but rather were here to enter the cave. There were some among them who wished to ask for favors, which were said to be granted most freely on this day of the year, the *commandante* said. He stepped to the entrance to the cave, then paused and glanced over at me again. He had been told it was essential to bow three times before entering, the *commandante* explained, to show respect to the demons that lived inside. He did in fact make three deep bows before stepping into the cave, and each of his men did the same as they followed him inside.

The four of us did not need to speak to reach an agreement that we would remain outside the cave until the soldiers left. They came back out no more than ten minutes later. The *commandante*'s expression was almost jovial as he approached to ask Michelle where we were from. Michelle had been giddy with relief ever since the soldiers

entered the cave and began to babble to the *commandante*. My limited
Spanish was good enough to know she had told him I was an *escritor*
famoso who had written a magazine article about her that was now being developed as a television show by the company Lionsgate and
blah, blah, blah. The *commandante* caught me signaling to Michelle
to shut her mouth and seemed much amused, though not even slightly
impressed. I had Michelle ask if he and his men would be at the arroyo that night. The *commandante* shook his head and answered that
he was sorry, but there would be no "protection" here after dark. "You
should be gone by then," he advised, then led his men back down the
trail. Michelle stood watching them descend for several minutes before she was ready to enter the cave.

I went first again. The line of candles and statues continued for
about ten feet along the narrow entrance before the cave opened into
a cavern that was at least thirty feet broad and much deeper. Candles
had been placed in various spots at the edges of the cave but gave no
light where I was walking. I could feel rather than see the earth turning to thick sucking mud beneath my feet, and tried to move faster,
afraid that if I stood still I would sink to the ankles. Or deeper. María
had told us that the cave was the source of the water that flowed into
the Laguna Encantada. I don't know what I had imagined this meant,
but now I understood. It was sticky and in the upper eighties outside,
but the temperature was twenty degrees higher inside the cave and
the humidity twice what it was outside. How it could be hotter inside
than out, I had no idea. There was dripping condensation on the rocks,
and the air was so thick it barely seemed breathable. I had a tiny
Streamlight nano flashlight on a cord around my neck and was trying
to fish it out of my shirt when I conked my head on the ceiling of the
cave and was temporarily dazed. When I got the flashlight out and
pointed ahead with it I could see that the ceiling was lowering steadily
as it approached the back of the cave. When I pointed the light down,
I saw the black mud was even sloppier than where we entered. The
combination of my wounded head, the oppressive air, and the sucking mud made me feel confused for a moment. And there was a weird
clacking sound coming from somewhere that I couldn't identify. Sud-

denly, I felt truly afraid of whatever was in here with us. I began to whisper a prayer for protection as I moved forward, but I had the panicked thought that no prayers could be heard inside these rock walls. I was close enough now to see that at the back of the cave an altar of loose rocks had been constructed and covered with lighted candles. I crouch-walked up to within a few feet of it. There was a Santa Muerte statue, but the main figure behind the altar was a large stone mask that looked very old. It was a hideous, grinning face that I thought might be the Hummingbird Wizard, though I wasn't sure. I felt an abrupt and urgent need to get out of there. I turned around to see that Michelle and the others had all stopped fifteen or twenty feet behind me and were watching warily. Michelle, more than a foot shorter than me, was still standing upright, I noticed, which for some reason irritated me. That fleeting annoyance steadied me somehow, and I began to walk back toward the entrance to the cave. "Are we done in here?" Michelle said as I approached. "Yes," I told her, and kept going.

I had passed all three of them and was actually in the lead again by the time I reached the entrance to the cave and stepped outside into the blinding sunlight. I gasped for air like someone who had just made a long swim to the surface of deep water and noticed for the first time that I was literally drenched in sweat. I walked to the farthest rock at the edge of the cliff and sat on it, still trying to catch my breath. Michelle and María came out making jokes about me hitting my head on the cave's ceiling. Part of me knew that they were trying to calm their nerves, yet I still felt an overwhelming rage that I almost released in a snarled description of Michelle as a "midget primitive." I caught myself before the words were out, but I was breathing even harder than I had been a moment earlier. I stood up and started back down the trail without a word to the others. They came behind me, silently, as if they sensed my capacity for violence.

When we arrived again at the waterfall, I continued without hesitation across the stream flowing from the mountain into the clearing by the pool of water where women and children still splashed and played. This time, I glared back at the men who glared at me. While some part of my mind understood quite clearly that it would be suicide to get into it with one of these guys, I still felt an overwhelming desire to beat the hell out of someone. I didn't realize I had slowed to almost a stop until Michelle gave me a shove from behind and told me to keep going. Without a word back to her, I continued up the slope on the other side, over the fallen log, and back onto the trail into the jungle.

By the time we reached the meadow by the lake, I was under control and breathing normally. Now what scared me was how close I'd come to doing or saying something stupid. I inhaled deeply and exhaled slowly, trying to feel myself relax. I was fairly near the large chinini tree that was filled with those white parrots. I stared at the birds, mesmerized by their beauty and number, thinking almost dispassionately about how far away from home I was, and how vulnerable. Michelle and the others had stopped on the path and were staring at me, waiting. I looked at them for a moment, then continued down the trail, still in the lead.

Before we reached the other side of the meadow, a young man about Daniel's age stepped out of the forest coming our way. He was leading two goats with ropes around their throats, and smiled in a friendly way as he passed with the creatures he was about to offer in sacrifice to El Diablo. "I do not belong in this place," I whispered aloud. As if I believed someone listening spoke English and cared.

CHAPTER FOURTEEN

DAGOBERTO ESCOBAR PEREYA was a tall, trim, raffish fellow with a bit of red still showing in his thinning silver hair and beard. With the sash belt he wore, Dagoberto cut a rather dashing figure for a man of seventy-eight, other than that he was missing about half his teeth. Cundo had showed up at our hotel with his great-uncle while Michelle and I were trying to grab a quick meal. The two men seated themselves at our table and promptly ordered several plates of food. This was going to be a different situation, I knew, from the one with María, who had adamantly refused any payment to her or her nephew.

Dagoberto made it clear that he had liked and admired Manuel Utrera and would not be offering any of the "bad tales" we might hear from others. Those people were only repeating what they had been told. Unlike himself, said Dagoberto, who had known Don Manuel well and been close to him for a period of years. When I replied through Michelle that this was quite all right with me, Dagoberto studied me for a few moments, then nodded that he was prepared to continue.

He had met Don Manuel through his aunt, who was one of the famous *brujo*'s many girlfriends, Dagoberto said. Don Manuel was a "very handsome, happy man" who, when he was younger, had the reputation of a gigolo: "he liked to go out with all the women" long after he had married. He lived on a ranch on the far side of the lagoon. He had cattle and equipment, but only enough income to live a simple lifestyle. His family had practiced *curandismo* for generations, and all of them said Manuel was the most gifted. Sick people regularly came to his ranch to be healed. Then came some who were suffering because of curses or hexes. Don Manuel had proved he could cure those also. Word spread, and soon "people from the political sector and some famous Mexican actors came for the cures he was accomplishing," Dagoberto said.

"How did Manuel Utrera convert to *brujería* from just being a medicine man?" Michelle asked at my request.

I couldn't tell from his expression if Dagoberto's hesitation to answer was reluctance or uncertainty. Finally he said, "It happened gradually." In Dagoberto's telling, much of the blame, if that was the word, should be laid at the feet of those who came to Don Manuel for help. After a time, the famous and important people who sought him out were asking not just to be protected from curses but to have curses cast on various rivals. At first, Don Manuel was curious to see if he could contend with the *brujos* in Veracruz and Mexico City who were working for the opposition. But he had converted to black magic mainly "because he wanted to know how strong he could become," Dagoberto explained.

I had Michelle ask if it was true that the *brujos* drew their power from the Devil. This time there was no hesitation as Dagoberto nodded. "The *brujo* only works with evil," he said. "They must make a pact with the Devil to obtain their powers. It is the only way."

Did Dagoberto know anything about the circumstances of Utrera's pact with the Devil? I asked Michelle. She put the question to him, and Dagoberto answered that he could only say it had taken place originally and was renewed regularly inside the cave atop Cerro del Mono Blanco. He knew none of the details and Don Manuel did not talk about them. Don Manuel did take people to the Devil's Cave sometimes, Dagoberto said, when he was attempting something difficult and needed assistance. What sort of things would those be? I asked Michelle. Dagoberto gave me another of his measuring looks, then replied that it was only when Don Manuel intended to do harm to someone. "Not to the person he brought to the cave," Dagoberto hastened to add, "but to the enemy of that person."

Dagoberto then suddenly and without prompting attempted to explain the morality of *brujería*. It was almost as if he were replying to what I had heard all those months earlier from Antonio Zavaleta about the "ancient mentality" that prevailed in Mexico: "In life, as we all know, the creator made everything even and level-like: good and bad, day and night, sun and moon, light and water—everything has a level of place. Night and day have an even balance, just like hot and cold. God exists. But so does the Devil! One can draw power from either. And if one can, one will."

I waited for more, but that was all Dagoberto felt the need to say on the subject. I was tempted to suggest that he had told me nothing, but instead kept silent.

Michelle asked Dagoberto if he had seen Don Manuel practice *brujería*. Dagoberto nodded vigorously and replied that he would never forget the first time, which had occurred when Don Manuel was visiting his aunt: "A woman arrived having labor pains when she was only five months pregnant, and he checked her out. With his power. He advised her husband that *brujería* had been done to her, and that there was an animal inside her that was going to harm the baby. Don Manuel worked on her, then a few days later the animal inside her came out of her as if it were a child—dead. The animal was small and Don Manuel placed the animal inside a jar filled with alcohol. Four months later the woman had a healthy baby."

Dagoberto let us absorb that for a moment, then told us that on occasion Don Manuel had showed his power to his aunt, just to keep her in line. There had been an evening when his aunt had asked Don Manuel to go out dancing with her. Don Manuel had said he didn't feel like it and that she could go without him. "He told her to have fun, but he also told her that he wanted her back at the house right at twelve midnight, and not one minute later." Midnight came and his aunt had not returned, Dagoberto recalled. She showed up about a half hour later, shaking with fear and in great distress. "She told us she had begun to feel her panties tighten around her," Dagoberto said. "She said they began to feel as if they were made of steel, not cotton, and that she was being squeezed to death by them. She said it been terrifying, and that she had run out of the bar she was in and hurried home. The pain had continued right up to the moment she walked into the house. Don Manuel simply said, 'When I tell you to be some-place at a certain time, you will be there.' My aunt was in tears when she promised nothing like this would ever happen again. Don Manuel had showed her his power, and she knew now to fear it."

I had Michelle ask if Dagoberto could tell me the most impressive thing he had seen or heard of Utrera doing. The old man thought for only a moment before saying, "Don Manuel became a *nahual*." The term *nahual*, I knew, exists only in Mexico and parts of Central America, although there is some correlation to the Native American term "skinwalker." *Nahual* essentially means "shapeshifter," and refers specifically to a sorcerer who has the power to transform into an animal. Literally transform. The *nahual* concept was popularized in the books of Carlos Castaneda, who used it broadly to describe sorcerers who could leave their human form and pass into a realm of power or dreaming or whatever it was that great fraud called it. What books might have resulted, I couldn't help musing during my stay in Mexico, if Castaneda had actually done the field research he claimed, had come to Catemaco and placed himself under the tutelage of Don Manuel Utrera? Castaneda, though, had done his research in libraries and invented the sorcerer Don Juan. As a result, his books had obviated entirely the fact that *brujos* explicitly declare that they obtain their power from compacts with El Diablo. Only in Mexico did it occur to me that Castaneda's unremitting rejection of the Catholicism he had been raised in actually limited his ability to understand sorcery far more than a measure of respect for it would have.

Don Manuel had been a *nahual* in the traditional sense, as Dagoberto described it. "Don Manuel could also change other people into animals," Dagoberto asserted, with an expression that dared me to question him. He had seen it with his own eyes, Dagoberto said a moment later: "He turned a man he had helped and who had not paid him as promised into a chicken. The after-effects of this smelled like sulfur." The ceremony had taken place in the cave at Mono Blanco,

Dagoberto said. "That is where Don Manuel would change people into animals, inside La Cueva del Diablo. He needed the power of evil to do this."

The conversation digressed for a few minutes as Dagoberto and Cundo began to discuss the magical natures of the Laguna Encantada and Cerro del Mono Blanco. One of the unusual aspects of the lake, Cundo said, was that the water level dropped during the rainy season and rose when it was dry, exactly the opposite of what would be expected. Scientists had come many times to try to explain how this could happen, but none of them had been able to do so. Many local people claimed that there was a sunken city under the lagoon, Cundo went on; others said that UFOs entered it during the night. My attempt to deflect the conversation back to Don Manuel was brushed aside when Cundo and Dagoberto began to talk about a photograph of the lake taken by a man named Rogelio. "Monkeys were visible in the picture, as if they were dancing on the water," Cundo told me. Rogelio had nothing but bad luck after the picture was published in a magazine, Dagoberto observed a moment later, and eventually died of diabetes. The same thing had happened to each of his relatives who had inherited possession of the photograph, Cundo said; they got sick and died. He himself had seen the photograph and had seen the monkeys, which were more like the ghosts of monkeys, Cundo said. "But I wouldn't actually touch the photograph with my hand, because anyone who touches it gets ill. It is true! We have all seen it." Dagoberto nodded in affirmation.

I moved us back on topic by asking what kind of animals Don Manuel transformed himself into. Did he become a monkey? Most often he turned himself into a bird, Dagoberto replied, because when Don Manuel changed himself in this way, it was commonly for the purpose of conducting surveillance on those whom he suspected of working against him in some manner. Don Manuel also changed himself—though less often—into a horse, Dagoberto added: "He told me that the Devil had come to him on his ranch as a black horse and had granted him the power to become such a horse himself when he chose. He became a horse for the purpose of spying, also because as a horse he could get very close to people, get them to actually touch him." Don Manuel could cause harm in the form of a horse, Dagoberto said, "but if he truly wanted to hurt people, or to end their lives, he would come as a butterfly, and land on them. Don Manuel did his most evil magic in the form of a butterfly." Dagoberto smiled broadly at my expression of astonishment.

How much of Manuel Utrera's work involved causing harm to people? I asked Dagoberto, through Michelle. The old man was not pleased by the question but answered it, sort of. "He did such things, but only when he thought it needed to be done," Dagoberto said. "Don Manuel would not tolerate being disrespected. Everyone feared him. He did not demand it, but at the same time it was expected. But if a person tried to act as if they did not fear him, they would suffer for it."

But Don Manuel also took payment for causing harm, didn't he? I asked. For money, he caused people to get sick and to die; wasn't that right? Dagoberto gave me what I took to be a rather contemptuous look. "It was known that he did, but Don Manuel never discussed this subject with me," Dagoberto said. So Dagoberto didn't know how many? I asked. "No, I don't," he replied, in a way that made it clear this subject was closed.

For reasons of his own, Dagoberto seemed intent on emphasizing the trickster aspect of Manuel Utrera. "Don Manuel always liked to be out," the old man told me. "He would go to bars and drink a lot. When it was time to pay, he would fool the cashier and pay with orange peels, but to the cashier it looked like money. Only when Don Manuel was gone would the cashier realize what had happened."

Had Don Manuel instructed him in *brujería*? I asked Dagoberto. Again the man's expression darkened, but after a few moments of silence he nodded and said, "He instructed me in how to make a Santa Muerte, a true Santa Muerte, one that has the real power of evil in it." I nodded, encouraging him to go on. "To make a true Santa Muerte is very difficult," Dagoberto said, "but it is also very effective. It must be made of plastic, with a black tunic if one desires to use it for dark purposes. Then a coffin the size of the Santa Muerte must be made and the Santa Muerte must be placed inside. This has to be taken to

a Catholic church during the mass. When the wafers are being consecrated, you must lift the Santa Muerte into the air to receive the blessing. Then you must approach the father to receive communion and a
personal blessing. The priest will never bless a Santa Muerte, so you
must hide it under another saint and ask that this statue be blessed. But
when the father offers the blessing you must pull the Santa Muerte out
from under the saint so that the Santa Muerte will receive the blessing
instead. This is the most important part; the Santa Muerte must be
touched by holy water that is administered by a priest who has been
tricked into doing it. When the mass is over and you go home, you
must prepare a small table somewhat like an altar. Then you need to
make five offerings to five demons. Then you must prepare four lumi-
naries [candles inside paper bags] and light them. You must also place
two rosaries on the table. Then you prepare one cup of water and one
cup of oil. You drop one drop of oil in the water as you petition for
your request, and if all has been done as required, your request will be
granted."

Had he done all that, created a true Santa Muerte? I asked. And
if he had, for what purpose?

Dagoberto eyed me with amused disdain before replying, "I will
not tell you."

I shrugged, as if to suggest it was not important for me to know,
then asked when and how Manuel Utrera had died. Don Manuel had
died in the mid-1960s, Dagoberto answered; he couldn't remember
exactly what year. "How he died is not a subject I choose to discuss,"
he added, with a tone of finality.

"So he has been dead for fifty years," I said. "And yet I've noticed some people are still afraid to speak his name."

"Some people are afraid he might hear them," Dagoberto said,
which drew a hearty laugh from Cundo.

Could Dagoberto describe for me Don Manuel's appearance? I
asked. "He was not a large man, but he seemed large," Dagoberto
replied, and left it at that.

I was beginning to run out of questions I thought might be
answered.

"When Don Manuel taught you something—how to make a Santa Muerte, for instance—did you pay him?" I asked.

"Don Manuel never asked me for money," Dagoberto replied. "He asked for favors. That was common for him. Don Manuel was mainly interested in power, not money. He wanted to see what he could do, how powerful he could be. Wealthy people who came to him from far away, those he made pay. But a local person who was poor could pay him with a chicken or by working at his ranch. Gonzalo Aguirre was a man of money. He became a *brujo* to grow wealthy, and did so."

What was the relationship between Utrera and Aguirre? I asked. "Gonzalo was Don Manuel's apprentice," Dagoberto replied. "He studied with Don Manuel for many years before establishing himself as a *brujo*. He worked for Don Manuel, as his cab driver. He took Don Manuel wherever Don Manuel wanted to go. They spent much time together."

Were they friends? I asked. Or was it a father-and-son sort of relationship?

"I do not think they would be described as friends," Dagoberto said. "I was more of a friend to Don Manuel than Gonzalo was. Whether Don Manuel saw Gonzalo as a son, that is a question. Don Manuel had children of his own, but he did not teach any of them *brujería*. They complained about this. Whether Don Manuel's refusal was for their protection or his own I cannot say. But with Gonzalo Aguirre it was a student-teacher relationship. Don Manuel saw that Gonzalo was talented and that he was willing to do what it took to become a man of power. I myself was not willing to do all of those things. Few were."

I was about to ask what those things might be when Cundo interrupted the conversation to say it was time to leave. He had arranged for me to meet Gonzalo Aguirre's daughter Isabel, whom Don Gonzalo had taught and who was known to be the most powerful *curandera* in Catemaco, perhaps in all of Mexico.

"She's a *curandera*, not a *bruja*?" I asked.

"Correct," Cundo answered. "She does not perform black magic, but I think she knows how."

"Do you know why?" I asked.

Cundo shook his head slightly and smiled. "You can ask her for yourself. Come."

DURING THE HOURS between our return from Cerro del Mono Blanco and our meeting with Cundo and Dagberto at the hotel, Michelle and I had learned at least a bit about the business of witchcraft in Catemaco. And it was a business. "*Brujo* tourism," they called it locally.

It was made clear to me by several people we questioned that conditions had changed dramatically in Catemaco after the death of Manuel Utrera. While Don Manuel had never once given a reporter an interview, his successor as the great witch of Catemaco, Gonzalo Aguirre, used the media shamelessly. After a couple of articles about Aguirre's fearsome powers had appeared in Mexican magazines, the first television crews ever to visit the town had descended on Catemaco. Though he was best known in the press as "the Devil's representative on earth," Aguirre also had become the first in Catemaco to hold the city's unofficial office of *brujo mayor*, a title that for more than three decades now had been handed down annually. Aguirre also had been the central figure of the first National Congress of Sorcerers, held on the first weekend in March ever since the first one in 1970. The gathering of witches gradually became a major tourist attraction and the biggest yearly economic event in Catemaco.

The title of *brujo mayor* had become highly coveted after Aguirre's death in the early 1980s, ensuring as it did a substantial increase in both profit and prestige. Among the first to follow Don Gonzalo in the position had been Nicolás Chagala, who claimed (and there was some dispute about it) to have been Aguirre's apprentice. Gilberto Rodríguez Pereira had attempted to seize Aguirre's mantle by calling himself "the Devil" and developing a business entirely dedicated to casting spells against enemies or crafting "protections" from the spells of other *brujos*. Héctor Betaza, "the Raven," won the title of *brujo mayor* in 2009, and when a reporter from the newspaper

Zócalo Saltillo had showed up in Catemaco to interview Betaza, the reporter had been stunned to be kept waiting by a contingent of federal deputies who had come seeking amulets and other "protections" from curses and hexes they believed were being cast in their direction by the Gulf Cartel. Veracruz state governor Fidel Herrera won the lottery for a second time that same year, and deflected questions with the claim that blessings from the Raven were the source of his good luck. Shortly before this, Governor Herrera had begun to allocate money to support a Catemaco-based group called the International Congress of Witches, Fellowship of Magicians of the Region of Los Tuxtlas. In 2008, the state of Veracruz advanced 300,000 pesos toward the staging of a "black mass of white witches" in Catemaco.

The Gueixpal clan had turned witchcraft into a flourishing family business. *Brujo mayor* Julián Gueixpal had been succeeded by son Tito ("the Black Power") and grandson Apolinar ("the Leaping Tiger"). Another grandson, Pedro Gueixpal Cobix, began charging tourists as much as 3,000 pesos apiece to take them to the cave at Mono Blanco after he was named *brujo mayor*.

No family had been more financially successful, though, than the Aguirres. Don Gonzalo's descendants became by far the most affluent family in Catemaco, owners of much of the city's prime real estate, and of a chain of drugstores and clinics spread throughout the region. Some of Don Gonzalo's grandchildren had actually obtained medical degrees to supplement their healing businesses.

By the 1990s there were numerous stories in the Mexican mainstream media about the athletes, actors, and singers who were visiting Catemaco to seek blessings, amulets, and other protections. It was whispered that more than a few of them had also sought hexes and curses against those they considered rivals. Whenever reporters came to Catemaco to prepare a story about the new *brujo major*, the interview was held in an office where the walls were filled with the photographs of various celebrities who had consulted the witch.

Catemaco's attempt to position itself as a year-round tourist destination had resulted in the development of a resort on the eastern shore of Laguna Catemaco called Nanciyaga, where Mexican movie stars regularly went to stay in "rustic" cabins, enjoying mud facials and mineral baths by day and consulting with witches after dark. US film-makers had discovered Catemaco by then, beginning with the pro-duction of the 1992 Sean Connery movie *Medicine Man*, which had taken place mostly within the rainforests surrounding Laguna Catemaco. In 2005, Mel Gibson had brought the cast and crew of his film *Apocalypto* to the Catemaco area, renting the entire resort of Nan-ciyaga during production.

In the early twenty-first century, stories began to appear in the Mexican media about national politicians who had sought the help of Catemaco's *brujos*; among those widely reported to have received such assistance were former Mexican presidents José Lopez Portillo, Car-los Salinas de Gortari, and Ernesto Zedillo Ponce de Léon. It had been a big story in the newspapers when it was discovered in 2001 that Marta Sahagín de Fox, the wife of Mexico's new president, Vicente Fox, had imported Santerian priests to conduct "occult rituals" in the official presidential residence, Los Pinos. The only real scandal in the minds of many citizens, however, was that the first lady had gone outside the country rather than using one of the *brujos* from Catemaco. By the time Fox's term as president was coming to an end, journalists from Mexico City and other major cities were regularly consulting Catemaco's witches about which politicians they favored. It was na-tional news when Isabel Aguirre, easily the most famous person in Catemaco after her father's death, had stated that rivals were plotting with black magicians against Andrés Manuel López Obrador, the lead-ing anti-corruption politician in Mexico, to stymie his campaign for the presidency. Many stories mentioned Doña Isabel's remarks when they reported that López Obrador had lost the election by one-half of 1 percent after a series of attacks on him through the courts and other civil bodies controlled by President Fox, who was determined to usher in his handpicked successor, Felipe Calderón.

Contests between the various witches who competed for the ti-tle *brujo mayor* became increasingly intense and often violent; one *brujo* had been beaten so badly by the associates of a rival that he spent the rest of his life in a wheelchair. Complaints about the enormous fees charged by certain *brujos* produced several local scandals, and a number of lawsuits were filed by clients who claimed this or that witch had defrauded them.

The rise of the cartels, though, and in particular the Zetas' seizure of control in the Catemaco region, had not only suppressed but nearly eradicated the *brujo* tourism industry, I was told; it was why a recent *brujo mayor* named Antonio Vázquez Alba had packed up his office and moved to Tijuana. Yet private jets continued to land regularly at the one-runway airport in the nearby town of Tuxtla, and most of those who deplaned were headed for a single destination: the former home of Gonzalo Aguirre, now occupied by his daughter Isabel.

When we arrived there at about nine o'clock on that Thursday evening, Cundo pointed to a house that had been tiny once but expanded at least fourfold by additions that took up almost an entire block. The structure's most striking feature was the marble statue of Don Gonzalo perched at the edge of a terrace above the garage. When we parked out front, Cundo and Dagoberto told us that "many" neighbors claimed to have seen the statue descend from the roof to the street and walk back and forth out front, as if it were alive. When Manuel Utrera had moved from his ranch into town, he had lived in a house almost directly across the street, said Dagoberto, pointing, but it had been torn down after Don Manuel's death. The lot was occupied now by a *supermercado*, owned by the Aguirres.

Cundo told us to wait at the car while he went to the front door to make sure we would be welcome. He stepped back out onto the sidewalk a minute or two later and waved us toward the porch. Doña Isabel stood at the door. Gonzalo Aguirre's daughter was a tiny seventy-five-year-old woman with twigs for arms and legs who made my four-foot-eleven-inch, ninety-nine-pound companion Michelle look like an Amazon by comparison.

Doña Isabel was wearing a dark green skirt and blouse, with what appeared to be a small purple blanket pinned about her neck in a manner I'd never seen before, flat and folded tight on one shoulder, loosely draped over the other. I felt like an alien giant looming over her when we were introduced, but Doña Isabel's gaze brought me up short. It was piercing and unblinking, but there was also a deep melancholy in it that suggested some irreplaceable loss.

The interior of the house was startling also. A living room that might have seemed spacious was crammed with heavy leather furniture and an abundance of religious iconography. There were at least four or five Our Lady of Guadalupe statues and paintings, but what was truly overwhelming was the dozens of images of Jesus suffering on the cross or bleeding under his crown of thorns. The entire focus of the room seemed to be on the agony Christ had experienced during his Passion. It wasn't what I had been expecting to find in the home of a famous Catemaco witch. She was a devout Christian, Doña Isabel said, and she owed her father for that. I tried not to look surprised.

Her father had chosen faith at the end, Isabel said. You see, Don Gonzalo had obtained a time limit when he made his pact with El Diablo as a young man. This was common. People who came to Catemaco at this time of year, in fact, usually negotiated a one-, two-, or three-year deal with the Devil during the Hour of the Witches, depending on the magnitude of their request, Isabel's daughter Chevala told us later; Satan hoped that people would violate the terms of their agreement so that he could claim their souls. Gonzalo Aguirre, though, had wanted much and had promised much in return—to serve the Devil without fail until his sixtieth birthday. This he had done, according to both his daughter and granddaughter. Terrible events, including deaths and sicknesses, had resulted. But on the day he turned sixty in the summer of 1982, Don Gonzalo had declared that his contract with El Diablo was satisfied and that he intended to try to save his soul. There was little time, though, Doña Isabel said her father told her, because he was going to die in exactly ninety days. This was a condition he had accepted, Don Gonzalo said, and he did not wish to explain further.

What had followed this announcement was a period of spiritual drama that no one who had been living in Catemaco would forget. Don Gonzalo had made his confession for eighty-nine consecutive days. Priests came from all over the region, and then from all over Mexico, to hear those confessions, because no one cleric could absorb it all. People told us later that they had seen one priest after another emerge from the Aguirre house ashen-faced and exhausted. Everyone in town, they said, had been speculating on what those priests must be hearing. And then, on September 21, 1982, just as he said he would, Gonzalo Aguirre passed. It was only then people realized that Don Gonzalo's death had occurred on the very same date that Manuel Utrera's had, thirteen years earlier. There was a connection, of course, Doña Isabel told us, but even she was not certain what it had been.

I didn't entirely believe her about that but tried not to give any indication of my thoughts. From the moment I'd stepped through the door, I'd known with piercing certainty that meeting this tiny, hesitant old woman was the purpose of my visit to Catemaco. And yet I had no sense of what it was I wanted from her, other than as much of her father's story as she would share. Doña Isabel motioned, then directed us into a short hallway that led to one of the additions to the house, and pointed to a photograph of her father hanging on the wall. It was a black-and-white photo, more than thirty years old, faded and grainy, but clear enough. I had seen a lot of human faces in my life, hundreds of thousands at least, and not one—save perhaps Lawrence Bittaker's—that came close to disturbing me so deeply. There was something beyond sadness or even despair in Gonzalo Aguirre's face. What I saw, though, was not obvious malevolence. Rather, it was as if every atom of joy had been stripped from the man, without the slightest chance of him ever getting any of it back. I may have described his expression later as empty or blank, but that wasn't accurate. Something showed in the man's face; I just couldn't say what it was. The only word that came to mind was "knowledge." Don Gonzalo Aguirre had the face of a man who *knew* that he was beyond hope. Looking into that face, I felt hopeless also.

And yet his daughter Isabel had loved Don Gonzalo deeply. She choked up and her voice throbbed as she spoke of how much she adored her father. As I was thinking of how to frame a question about what it was she had loved, Doña Isabel began to tell a story:

My father taught me all that I know of healing knowledge. He taught me about plants and how they may be used. He taught

me how to prepare potions for many purposes. He taught me
how to harness the power of nature and taught me things that
he had learned from Don Manuel or that he had acquired by
his application of that knowledge. But he did not teach me
brujería. He told me that one could only receive the powers
of *brujería* directly from the Devil. He told me that people
who said otherwise were ignorant or lying. He told me, "Isabel, I will teach you *curandismo*. I will teach you to heal. Be a
healer. But do not be a *bruja*." But he said I should know the
Devil, or at least know *of* the Devil. He told me, "God exists,
Isabel. So does the Devil. You must know them both, but only
choose God." So he took me to the tree at the spring, Arroyo
Agrio, on Los Animas [Manuel Utrera's former ranch, now
owned by the Aguirres], where he had first made his own pact
with the Devil, and where he went to renew it once each year.
We arrived and my father spoke and repeated certain words.
My father did not call the Devil El Diablo; he called him
Adonai. My father was renewing his pact with the Devil and
promising to serve him for another year. Then he got to make
his request, to say what he wanted from the Devil for his pledge
of loyalty. He told the Devil that he wanted me, his daughter
Isabel, to know him, to know that he existed. And he asked the
Devil to make himself known to me. I was very afraid, thinking
that the Devil was about to appear before me. But it did not
happen like that. A minute passed, nothing occurred. Then
there was a slight breeze, out of nowhere, and a single leaf fell
from the tree right into the palm of my hand. I looked at the
leaf, and it was a perfect triangle. A *perfect* triangle, a shape that
nature does not make. I knew it was the Devil making himself
known to me, but my father did not think I knew well enough.
So he asked the Devil to show me again. And a second leaf fell
from the tree into the palm of my hand. It was a perfect square.
And then I knew well enough. The Devil wanted me to serve
him, but my father said no. He said the Devil had him, but
could not have me.

Doña Isabel was studying my face to see if I believed her story. She saw that I did.

Cundo chose that moment to say we must leave now if we were going to attend the Black Mass on the Volcán de Santa Martha. I refused to budge until we had secured a promise that I would be welcome to return to Doña Isabel's the next day. Cundo negotiated that, then pulled me by the elbow, saying, "We must go now!" Doña Isabel followed us to the front door. Through Michelle, I asked Gonzalo Aguirre's daughter if she would participate in any of the ceremonies being held that night or the next day. She shook her head. What would her father make of the *brujo* industry that had developed in Catemaco during the thirty-three years since his death? I asked Isabel. "He would laugh," she replied. "No one here has known *brujería* as he and Don Manuel did. These others, they are imitators. The Devil may use them, but they do not know him."

CUNDO, BEHIND THE WHEEL of his truck with Dagoberto in the seat next to him, led the way north into the foothills of the volcano. Before we left the restaurant, Cundo had insisted that I take off the T-shirt I had on and turn it inside out and backward before putting it back on. "For your protection!" he had vehemently told me. I was still wearing it that way.

Alone with me in our little Ikon as we followed Cundo's truck up a series of climbing gravel roads, Michelle made it clear that she had been every bit as impressed by Doña Isabel as I had, and was equally convinced that Gonzalo Aguirre's daughter had not been entirely truthful about the distance she kept from *brujería*. The tiny old woman emanated profound loss and exhausted humanity so palpably it was an aura. I had sensed resignation as much as deep sadness when I looked into her eyes. "She's done some black magic for sure, Randall. I could feel it," Michelle said.

I hadn't told Michelle about my conversation with Cuban Joe, the young man who had accompanied us on our adventure in Louisiana. Joe had grown up in New Orleans as the son of a devoutly Catholic Cuban mother and a Black father who was one of the city's most notorious gangsters, absent during most of his childhood because of prison sentences. Joe himself was trying to find a straight path, struggling to maintain connection to his mother's religious faith at the same time he was working security for various rappers. He was armed with a Glock and resolute seriousness as we searched for the fugitive Michelle was after, explaining to me along the way that he was doing this for her to repay an unspecified favor. Joe had seen my disappointment when Michelle broke a promise made in my presence. She and I had both made pledges to the associate of the fugitive who gave him up to us. Mine had been that I would not use the man's real name in the magazine article I was writing if he told me the whole truth about his relationship with the fugitive. I kept that promise. Michelle had sworn to the same man that if he gave her the information she needed to locate the fugitive, she would not reveal his identity to the authorities or mention to them other crimes she knew the man had committed. After we found the fugitive aboard his yacht, docked next to a plantation on the Bayou Teche, Michelle summoned the police to take him into custody, then immediately broke her promise and told the cops the informant's name. Afterward, Michelle defended herself to me by saying that lying to criminals was part of her job, but I hadn't liked what she had done and told her so. Later that same day, when we were alone, Joe had advised me that I should be careful in my dealings with Michelle. She was not a Christian, he said, then told me that he knew for a fact that Michelle was more than a dabbler in the occult, that she lit candles to ungodly spirits and could probably be described as a witch. That conversation had been replaying in my head at intervals during the trip to Catemaco. At this point, though, I had no choice but to trust Michelle, and no real reason not to. So far she had performed splendidly in Catemaco, connecting with the people there, especially the women, in ways I could never have, even if I spoke Spanish. I had decided not to mention the conversation with Joe.

The road to the Black Mass ended at a long paved driveway where the line of parked cars stretched far out into the street. We watched Cundo's truck park halfway into a drainage ditch. Another vehicle immediately pulled up close behind our car, its headlights flooding the Ikon. Michelle, who had never shown me even the slightest sign of fear before this trip, for the third time since our departure from Veracruz seemed to panic. "They've led us into a trap, Randall! We need to get out of here!" As at the top of Mono Blanco, though, there was nowhere to go; we were at the end of the road and the way back was blocked. I pulled over behind Cundo's truck and parked at the edge of the ditch.

Cundo was the same smiling friendly fellow he had been since the moment I met him when he climbed out of his truck. The vehicle behind us had parked also. Several young people got out and walked past us with barely a glance. I looked at Michelle, who breathed out and said, "I guess it's okay."

It wasn't that okay, I decided when we walked up the driveway to the terraced villa where the Black Mass would be staged. To be admitted, one was required to walk counterclockwise through a labyrinth of stones carved with Nahualist symbols. Smoke from small fires of sage and rue that burned in stone basins filled the labyrinth and added to the eerie atmosphere. I hesitated at the entrance to the labyrinth, wondering what I might be doing to myself if I entered. There was no other choice, though, if I wanted to see what was happening behind the smoke. It was an acute moment in which I found myself admitting I believed there most likely was a Devil and that I most certainly feared there was. I reached inside my shirt to clasp the cross I was wearing (at the suggestion of Antonio Zavaleta) and silently but fervently repeated a "Hail Mary" as I shuffled through the smoky maze under the watchful gaze of two costumed young women who stood at the end of it.

Those minutes of making my way in turned out to be the scariest part of the Black Mass. Doña Isabel's visceral contempt for the satanic ceremonies that were the residue of what her father and Manuel Utrera accomplished in Catemaco had instilled me with a confidence that Enrique Verdon's Black Mass was nothing to be tremendously frightened by. These new *brujos mayores*, Doña Isabel had said, did not really know the Devil. I believed her, because at that moment I believed she really *did* know the Devil.

The hours I spent outside the phosphorescent circle under the fires burning on the cliff above had been uncomfortable, even distressing, but not terrifying. My trust in Michelle had actually increased when I saw how shocked she was by the animal sacrifices. And she had stayed outside the circle, too. Still, I had made one more concession to belief that the Devil existed when I refused to enter what the *brujo* called the Black Cave at the end of the ceremony. If I went inside, a small voice inside me warned, I *would* be in danger.

Michelle and I had both been taken aback when the *brujo*, Verdon, had lifted the large bowl filled with the collected blood of the murdered goats and chickens, then walked with it around the perimeter of the circle, demanding that all present insert a finger and daub the blood on their foreheads. He glared at me with a hateful expression when I refused. Cundo had long since withdrawn to a safe distance, but Dagoberto stood with Michelle and me, and he shocked us when he dipped his forefinger deep into the blood, exchanging nods with the *brujo*.

Dagoberto didn't even surprise me, though, when, through Cundo, he asked to be paid for the assistance he had provided. He actually asked me to buy him a new engine for his car. Instead I gave him about $80 in pesos. Cundo seemed to think that was fair, if not generous. He clasped my shoulder as we said goodbye and through Michelle told me he hoped he had been of help. He leaned forward and told me in almost a whisper, "Doña Isabel is real."

MICHELLE AND I RETURNED to Isabel Aguirre's home the next afternoon. The lady of the house was not available at the moment, her daughter Chevala told us at the door. A wealthy woman with cancer had flown in by private jet from Miami and come directly here from the airport at Tuxtla. Her mother might work with her for an hour, two hours, four hours, or six, Chevala said. Which turned out to be just as well. Doña Isabel's daughter was more talkative than her mother, and willing to disclose some information I might have left Catemaco without if Michelle and I hadn't gotten Chevala alone.

I was riveted as Chevala described how Gonzalo Aguirre had staged the first public Black Masses in Catemaco, beginning in the early 1970s, soon after Manuel Utrera's death in 1969. Her grandfather's original description of those ceremonies had been "interviews with the Devil," Chevala said. He had staged them at his ranch, at the tree near the spring by the shore of Laguna Catemaco, the same place where he met privately with the Devil. Only those who had been invited could attend, but there were as many as two thousand there by the end of Don Gonzalo's tenure as *brujo mayor*.

People said that it was her grandfather who had chosen the first Friday in March, though that was not strictly true, Chevala said. Adonai, as her grandfather addressed the Devil, had instructed him that this was the date by which he commemorated his fall from heaven and the creation of his own empire in hell. Don Gonzalo had taken his responsibilities very seriously, his granddaughter told us; he practiced fasting and abstinence for a full week before officiating at the annual Misa Negra, or Black Mass, and would eat only vegetables on the day of the event.

At the midnight gathering, Don Gonzalo had opened the same way each time, renewing his pact with the Devil and offering his soul to eternal damnation in return for greater powers. El Diablo "went into the tree," as Chevala put it; she made it sound as if the Devil had taken possession of the tree the way demons were said to take possession of persons. "Everyone could feel it happen," Chevala said. It was explained to those who wished to make a request of El Diablo that they must pledge their souls, and that this pledge must be made in a document written in their own blood. Always, Chevala said, there were at least a few willing to do so.

These documents were signed not at the ranch but rather at Don Gonzalo's office, which he called "Lion's Leap." Lions and tigers were both very important to her grandfather, Chevala said. Don Gonzalo actually had many more statues of tigers than of lions; some were up on the rooftop terrace here.

The office was set up so that Don Gonzalo could offer two types of "treatments," Chevala said. In the front was the altar where Don Gonzalo offered what he called "the white" and far less effective treatment, his granddaughter recalled. Scapulars and pictures of various saints hung on the wall behind an altar that was decorated with a crucifix featuring a one-legged Christ. She did not know why the Christ figure in her grandfather's office had only one leg, Chevala said.

Behind a curtain in the back of the office was where Don Gonzalo offered "the black" treatment, which he more often described as "the infallible," his granddaughter said. The altar there was decorated with images of Adonai, a grotesque red devil that had been carved from the trunk of a mangrove tree.

Chevala would describe the difference between Manuel Utrera and Gonzalo Aguirre in almost the same words that Dagoberto had, and yet portrayed that difference in highly divergent terms. When Dagoberto had told us that Don Manuel was motivated not by money but by acquiring greater powers, he had made it sound as if Utrera was somehow nobler than Aguirre, a man driven by the desire to become wealthy.

It was true that her grandfather's goal in becoming a *brujo* was to make money, Chevala said, but in her telling that made him much more sympathetic than Don Manuel, for whom accumulating power was a purpose unto itself. Don Gonzalo had grown increasingly rich and famous during the 1970s, Chevala said. When she was a little girl, he was easily the wealthiest and most influential person in the Los Tuxtlas region. People were in awe when movie stars, pop singers, and political leaders began to show up in Catemaco, drawn by what they had heard of the great Gonzalo Aguirre. Stories of the vast sums these people paid for an hour of Don Gonzalo's time were whispered all over Los Tuxtlas.

As he approached his sixtieth birthday, though, her grandfather began to waver in the stoic acceptance of damnation he had shown in the past, Chevala said. He increasingly wanted to do good with his wealth, donating large amounts of money to various school boards in the region and to hospitals to build clinics with the Aguirre name

on them. He was especially prone to donating statues to various institutions on Mother's Day. He was trying to "settle his account,"
Don Gonzalo told his family.

It had come as a shock, though, when on the first day of summer in 1982 Gonzalo Aguirre had told his family he had just ninety
days to live. Don Gonzalo had made his confession every day for the
rest of his life because he was determined to redeem his soul from the
pact he had made with the Devil, Chevala said. Her mother was convinced he had succeeded, said Chevala, without revealing whether she
believed this herself. And of course, her grandfather had died on exactly the day he had said he would. The official cause of death was
cerebrovascular disease, but who could possibly know that they were
going to die of a massive stroke on a certain day that was months away?

Only when I asked about the circumstances of Manuel Utrera's
death did Chevala seem to hesitate. All she knew, Chevala said, was
what her grandfather had told them. What had he said? I asked. "He
told us that Don Manuel had broken his pact with the Devil, that
he had refused to do something he had been asked to do, and that the
Devil was going to take his life. He told us this just a week or two
before Don Manuel's death." Did she know what Don Manuel had
been asked to do? I inquired of Chevala. She shook her head: "I think
my grandfather knew, but he would not tell us." How had Don Manuel died? I asked. Chevala avoided my eyes when she answered that
Manuel Utrera had been found hanging in a closet at his house directly across the street from this one. "It was not called a suicide," she
said, "because everyone knew he had not taken his own life. The Devil
had taken it."

CHAPTER FIFTEEN

MY RECOGNITION THAT MEETING Isabel Aguirre had taught me all I really needed to know dawned on me gradually. During the drive back to Veracruz, the day and night we spent there, and even on the flights to Mexico City and San Antonio, Michelle and I had been giddy with relief at having survived the trip to Catemaco. That passed, of course, and as it did was replaced by a realization that Doña Isabel had proved something to me. This wasn't that the Devil existed. It was that *I believed* the Devil existed. And what I believed was what mattered. For the first time, I wasn't pushing back against the idea that there was a supernatural force of evil working against the good in me, and in the world. The shift in perspective this concession produced was comprehensive. I found myself looking at almost anything that took place around me—or far away for that matter—in terms of the battle between good and evil.

Affirmation of a formerly vague notion that Mexico was the epicenter of the Devil's power on earth came from places I least expected. At the suggestion of Father Benedict Groeschel, the Benedictine monk who had become the most renowned arbiter of the supernatural in Catholicism and who in 2010 had offered himself as my advisor,* I had been studying what he described as "the most famous and the best-documented" exorcism in American history. It had been performed on a woman named Emma Schmidt in Earling, Iowa, in 1928. The daughter of German immigrants, Emma Schmidt had begun

* Father Groeschel died in 2014, six months before my trip to Catemaco.

showing signs of demonic possession as early as age fourteen, but she was forty-six when she was brought to Iowa from her home in Wisconsin for an exorcism that would last four months. Emma was a tiny woman whose formal education had ended in the eighth grade, according to church records. As a teenager, the formerly pious child began to tell a series of pastors that inner voices were telling her to do "vile and disgusting things" that involved combinations of biological functions and sexual acts. She was so tormented by her perverse "lusts," the girl said, that she wanted to hang herself.

Several times she was witnessed growling, barking, shrieking, writhing on the ground, and foaming at the mouth when she attempted to enter the local Catholic church. A rumor spread that the girl's aunt Mina, reputed to practice witchcraft, had put cursed herbs in the girl's food.

The local bishop did not believe Emma was possessed and did not want to authorize an exorcism; he insisted instead that the young woman be monitored and counseled. So she was, for more than a decade. Only after several priests advised the bishop that they believed this was a true case of demonic possession—mainly because Emma had demonstrated an understanding of several foreign languages and was suddenly fluent in Latin—would he agree to an exorcism.

The ritual would be performed by Theophilus Riesinger, a Capuchin priest from Bavaria. The Franciscan convent in Earling was chosen as the location because it provided privacy, because Riesinger's friend Father Joseph Steiger was the town pastor in Earling, and, especially, Reisinger said later, because he had been so impressed by the mother superior of the convent, who agreed that she and the other nuns would assist in the exorcism.

Riesinger was sixty years old at the time, but he was described by those who had worked with him as a tall, strapping fellow who seemed much younger and projected enormous self-confidence. He would look his age and then some by December.

Emma Schmidt was transported by train to Earling on August 17, 1928. The crew of the train arrived in Iowa visibly shaken by the ferocity with which the tiny woman had cursed and spat at them during the trip. Two of the nuns who met her at the station and escorted her to St. Joseph Church said in sworn statements that Emma had attacked and attempted to strangle them.

The mother superior said she had selected her "four strongest" nuns to assist the priests, Riesinger and Steiger, during the exorcism. They were barely strong enough. Minutes after the exorcism ritual began on the morning of August 18, according to the sworn statements of all four nuns and both priests, Emma, moving with startling speed and strength, had broken the grasp of all four nuns as she "rose" from the bed and "attached" herself to the wall above the door, feet on the ceiling, hands on the wall, posing upside down on all fours in a defiance of gravity that terrified the nuns and Steiger. Father Riesinger remained calm, the others said afterward, ordering them to pull the woman down—which they did "with great difficulty"—and to place her back on the bed. This time, the four nuns kept a tight grip on the woman, even as she thrashed and cursed them, copiously spewing vile-smelling green vomit that covered them. Then suddenly there was an immensely loud and shrill voice that filled the room with curses and strange guttural sounds that seemed to be coming not directly from the woman but from someplace "far off." They were all shaking uncontrollably by then, the nuns and Steiger admitted in their sworn statements. Riesinger, still showing no outward sign of fear, shouted in a loud and commanding voice, "Silence, Satan!" according to the nuns and Steiger, but the noises in the room only grew louder. It sounded as if "a pack of hyenas" had been set loose in the room, Steiger would say.

As the exorcism continued, day after day for more than a week in this first of three sessions, the nuns said, the worst part became dealing with the incredible amount of vomit that came out of Emma Schmidt. It did not seem possible, given that she was not eating—the only nutrition they could get down her was an occasional teaspoonful of milk or water, the nuns said. Yet somehow she managed to produce gallons of spew, so much that they had to carry it out of the room to the toilet down the hallway in pitchers or pails as often as twenty times a day. The smell was nearly unbearable, according to the nuns, who said that what they carried away sometimes looked like green macaroni and at other times like sliced and chewed tobacco leaves.

Emma Schmidt's body began to bloat incredibly, according to the sworn statements of the nuns. Her head swelled also, and her face became bright red. Her eyes bulged horrifyingly in their sockets and—this part seemed to frighten the nuns most—her lips grew to more than twice their normal size. In some moments, the woman's body seemed to try to float up from the bed, the nuns said, then at other times it became so heavy that they literally could not budge her.

The toll on these first four nuns became too great, and two other teams of four nuns each began to rotate in to provide relief. Father Steiger often collapsed with exhaustion, but Father Riesinger stayed at it, day after day, from dawn to dusk. On the second day of the exorcism, according to the sworn statements, Riesinger had asked if Emma was possessed by one or more demons. A voice that again did not seem to come from the woman on the bed answered, "There are many."

Riesinger was wearing a pyx (a small round container used to carry a consecrated host) on a chain around his neck during the exorcism, and when he took the wafer out of the pyx, according to the other witnesses, Emma, or the demons inside her, as the nuns put it, began to bark, then howled mournfully. She bellowed and moaned and then began to foam at the mouth, and to spit the foam at the nuns and priests surrounding the bed, soaking them with the spray.

All of this I had read before leaving for Catemaco. Only after returning home did I dig deeper into the pile of documents on my desk and discover that, beginning on the fourth day of the exorcism of Emma Schmidt, Rev. Reisinger had entered into a "dialogue" with the demons who possessed the woman.

At first it was just one voice that spoke, a "head demon," who gave his name as Beelzebub. According to the witnesses, when Riesinger asked, "Am I speaking to Lucifer, the prince of devils?" the reply was, "No, not the prince, but one of the leaders," a former member of the "seraphic choir."

Riesinger asked the demon what he would do if God offered him a chance to "atone."

"Are you a competent theologian?" was the sneering reply.

A demon who identified himself as Judas Iscariot said the purpose of the possession was to "bring her to despair, so that she will commit suicide and hang herself. She must get the rope! She must go to hell!"

Did everyone who committed suicide go to hell? Riesinger asked. No, but it increased the likelihood, depending on the person's level of "volition," was the answer.

Eventually two new voices spoke, one belonging to Emma Schmidt's father, Jacob, who said it was he who had put the curse on his daughter, at age fourteen, after she refused to have sex with him. Then a voice that identified itself as Mina spoke. This voice was very different from the others, according to the witnesses, so high-pitched it sounded almost like a falsetto. She had been sent to hell not for her adultery with Jacob, Mina told the priests, but for the murders she had committed.

"Who did you murder?" Riesinger demanded.

"Little ones," the voice answered, according to the two priests. It took some lengthy probing before Mina admitted the "little ones" were her own children. When Riesinger asked how many she had murdered, Mina answered that there had been three, according to the priests, then corrected herself—"actually four."

These conversations between Riesinger and the voices took place over a period of a week, but this was not some sort of constant back-and-forth, as the exorcist recounted it, because it was interrupted by hours and hours of howling and screeching. There were more, many more, entities inhabiting Emma than the four who had spoken to him, Riesinger was informed at one point. He began to recognize the demons before they spoke, Riesinger said, because they distorted Emma's features in different ways. The demon who caused the woman's eyes to look as if they might explode out of her head was a different entity than the one who made her lips grow to "the size of hands." As the days passed, the body of Emma, a woman so thin she had appeared almost emaciated when they first encountered her, the nuns said, became inflated to the point that it lost all shape and the skin seemed stretched to the point of splitting. The woman's abdomen and extremities became hard as stone, according to the nuns, and her weight seemed to increase exponentially; at times she was so heavy that the iron slats that supported the mattress began to bend and so did the iron rods that served as bedposts. What they all found most frightening, the nuns said, was the pea-sized lump that moved constantly under the woman's skin, like a living thing inside her.

Eventually, near the end, Riesinger recounted, he heard a new voice, one even harsher and more mocking than the others. He believed it to be Satan himself, the exorcist would write later, though the voice never actually identified itself.

According to both priests, when Steiger demanded to know how this demon (or the Devil, if Riesinger was correct) imagined he might challenge the power of Jesus Christ, the answer was, "Do you know the history of Mexico? We have prepared a nice mess for Him there. . . . He will learn to know us better."

I continued reading, but in a state of distraction. The exorcism had accelerated rapidly toward a conclusion in the middle of December. The "lesser demons" left one after another, Riesinger said, until only the four "meanest," one being the entity he identified as Satan himself, remained. Those four would moan and howl whenever he read the prayers of the Holy Trinity in his increasingly hoarse voice, Riesinger remembered.

Emma Schmidt began to emerge from unconsciousness more and more often as the days passed. She described the "dreams" she was having of a terrible battle between the forces of good and the forces of evil, as both Riesinger and Steiger recalled it. Even as the lesser demons left her, countless evil spirits continued to arrive, Emma told the priests, and good angels in equal number were also coming, most of them seated on white horses, led by St. Michael.

One evening, the nuns and the housekeeper, Steiger's sister, said they had seen a cluster of white roses form on the ceiling of the room, directly above the bed where Emma lay. When the woman on the bed regained consciousness again, she told them she had been visited by Thérèse of Lisieux; the Little Flower had told her not to lose courage, and that she must tell Father Steiger not to lose hope, because the end was at hand.

Riesinger told Steiger and the nuns he knew this was true, because the demons had begun to beg to be banished to another place, or into another creature, rather than be sent back to hell. They were becoming weaker and more docile, Riesinger said, no longer cursing or threatening him, but simply moaning; their despair was palpable. He knew the four still inside Emma were beaten, Riesinger said, when they agreed to call out their names as they departed the woman's body.

A little more than two days before Christmas, at about nine o'clock on the evening of December 22, according to the sworn statements of seven witnesses, Emma Schmidt, moving with astonishing speed, wrenched free of the nuns at her bedside and stood erect on the bed, with only her heels touching the mattress. Fearing that she was about to be hurled against the ceiling, Riesinger shouted at the nuns, "Pull her down!" Almost in that moment, though, Emma's body went limp, and she slumped back to the bed. This time, she lay there without the stiffness they had seen in her body almost from the moment the exorcism began. Emma looked almost relaxed, the nuns would say. They wanted to relax as well, but they were terrified back to attention by an eruption of piercing shrieks that were the worst sounds they had heard since it began, the nuns said, followed by four names screamed in hideous strangled voices: "Beezlebub . . . Judas . . . Jacob . . . Mina," then the words "Hell! Hell! Hell!" The room filled with the vilest of the many grotesque odors they had breathed during the twenty-three days of the exorcism, the nuns said, but in the same moment Emma Schmidt opened her eyes, seemed to smile slightly, then cried out, "My Jesus, mercy!" She looked at Riesinger, the nuns said, told him, "God bless you," then fell into a coma-like sleep that lasted until the sunrise of the following day.

The woman, who looked like a different person from the one who had showed up back in August, according to the nuns, was on a train home the next day. They had changed as well, the nuns said. During the next several months, each of them would ask for a transfer to

another convent, hoping it would help them forget the horror of what
they had witnessed.

I went back through the "dialogue" several times, making sure
that the only "challenge" to the power of Christ that any of the voices
had made was the "situation" in Mexico, where the entity Riesinger
thought to be the Devil promised to "make the kettle hot and heavy."

I was still digesting the Emma Schmidt documents when, barely
three weeks after returning from Catemaco, I read of the "mass exorcism" held in the central interior of Mexico, at the Cathedral of San
Luis Potosí, an event intended to "banish demons from an entire
country," as London's *Telegraph* described it. That Cardinal Juan San-
doval Iñiguez presided over a ritual attended by tens of thousands of
Mexicans was less impressive to me than that Pope Francis himself had
not only approved but actually encouraged the event. Just weeks
earlier, Francis had proclaimed that Mexico was being punished "by
the Devil for its criminal violence." Many of the pope's fans in Europe
and the United States had been startled by that pronouncement. Francis was supposed to be the progressive pontiff, the one who doubted
that homosexuality was a mortal sin and seemed open to the idea of
married priests and women celebrating the Eucharist. That he would
embrace the most atavistic thread of Christian theology, the one that
placed a being of supernatural evil at the center of the struggle for salvation, was unthinkable.

For most of the twentieth century, the Roman Catholic Church
had done its best to deemphasize the Devil, to make him into a sym-
bolic or even mythological figure. There had been an uproar in 1985
when the head of the Congregation for the Doctrine of the Faith, Cardinal Joseph Ratzinger, answered a question from a reporter in a way
that suggested the Devil was an actual being, specifically a fallen angel. The degree of scorn and ridicule that was heaped upon Ratzinger, from both outside the Church and inside, had startled and
shaken the Vatican. The pope himself, though, stood by the cardinal.
While John Paul II had permitted the Church's transition from de-
fining the Devil less as an evil spirit than as a spirit of evil, there was
widespread belief that he was not entirely comfortable with the change.

After the furor over Cardinal Ratzinger's remarks, John Paul had been the only member of the Roman curia to publicly support the future Pope Benedict in his affirmation of the Devil's existence. During a visit to the Sanctuary of St. Michael the Archangel in May 1987, John Paul declared, "The battle against the Devil, which is the principal task of Saint Michael the archangel, is still being fought today, because the Devil is still alive and active in the world. The evil that surrounds us today, the disorders that plague our society, man's inconsistency and brokenness, are not only the results of original sin, but also the result of Satan's pervasive and dark action."

John Paul and Benedict were conservatives, though, clinging to the past, while Francis was cast as the pope who would usher the church into the brave new world of the twenty-first century. On the subject of Satan, however, Francis was every bit the traditionalist his predecessors had been. As Jorge Mario Bergoglio, the archbishop of Buenos Aires, he often had spoken publicly about Satan moving among the peoples of the planet. In his 2010 book *On Heaven and Earth*, Bergoglio had devoted the entire second chapter to the Devil, echoing Baudelaire when he wrote: "Perhaps [the Devil's] greatest success in these times has been to make us think that it doesn't exist, that everything can be traced to a purely human plan."

As pope, Francis had encouraged the training of exorcists, and in early 2014, a year after being installed as pontiff, he had prayed over a young man in a wheelchair who had been presented to him in St. Peter's Square by the most famous (many would say notorious) exorcist in Rome, a priest named Gabriele Amorth. The Vatican downplayed the event, insisting that Francis had simply prayed for the young man—who, it turned out, was Mexican—and had not performed any part of the exorcism ritual.

When the pope finally visited Mexico in early 2016, however, he would confound his intermediaries by once again publicly insisting on the existence of the Devil. At the biggest event of his five days in Mexico, Francis would preside over a mass held in the criminally violent suburb of Mexico City called Ecatepec, and during his homily warn the crowd that even the "white" magic of *curandismo* was seeded with corruption: "With the Devil there is no dialogue. He will always win."

THERE WAS ANOTHER LINE from the pope's admonition to the crowd at Ecatepec that I took more personally. After urging the faithful to continue resisting the murderous *narcotraficantes*, Francis asked people to remember that resignation "is the Devil's favorite weapon."

The resignation I had in mind involved giving up on the solution to a mystery. To do so, I had been thinking since my return from Mexico, costs more than most people are willing to admit. Our sighs of surrender are invariably preceded by concessions to futility that take something vital out of us. Redemption becomes less possible, deliverance more unlikely. The common response is to reduce the weight of words like "redemption" and "deliverance" until they are light enough to float away.

What alternative do we have, besides a stubborn push forward, groping blindly for answers that were already disappearing into the passage of time before we thought to look for them? It may be a pitiful option, but it's the one I've most often chosen.

Brenda Rowland understood why. "To just let things go, to try to tell yourself, 'Hey, bad things happen,' it don't give you no peace. It just makes you numb," she had told me on the morning of July 4, 2014. We were attempting to push through the thicket that had overwhelmed Boxer's Corner in the quarter century since Tate Rowland was found hanging there. At Brenda's insistence, I was carrying her pistol, because of concern that we might run into the wild hogs that were said to be living in the weeds. In the end, without the horse apple tree to give us a target, we arrived only in the vicinity of where Tate had died, with no certainty that we were at the actual spot.

Dredging things up was a risk also, Brenda agreed, and so was trying at what had already failed. But you *had* to try if the opportunity presented itself. And she saw the glimmer of such an opportunity in the summer of 2008. On July 26, Brenda had posted what was intended to be both a lament and a solicitation on her Facebook page to mark the twentieth anniversary of her stepson's death. There were people out there who knew "what really happened to Tate," Brenda had written, and she was appealing to them, or to anyone who knew them, to make contact with her. Probably the last person she had in mind was that girl from Lockhart she had heard about (but whose name she didn't know), Brenda told me. She was stunned at first, and then excited, to learn that the Lockhart girl, now a woman of thirty-seven, had grown up to be an investigator who was highly sought after for her ability to find people who had tried to disappear, Brenda told me, and that the younger woman was nearly as haunted by Tate's death as she was. "It seemed almost like somethin' that was meant to be."

SHE HADN'T BEEN OF MUCH HELP to Brenda Rowland in the months after they first connected in 2008, Michelle admitted. She was too busy raising her daughter as a single mother while working full-time as a skip tracer to devote more than an occasional evening to the Tate Rowland case. In the first email she sent to Brenda, on August 10, 2008, a week or so after they spoke on the phone, Michelle had declared, "I need to confront Mary Reyna after all these years that have passed; it still bothers me that she knew too much . . . too much detail."

Finding Mary had proven to be more difficult than expected, however. She'd left Texas a few months after returning home to Childress from Lockhart in 1988, Michelle discovered, and there was no clear indication of where she'd landed. More than a year passed before she determined that Mary's last name now was Trones. She'd married a much older man who had made a career in the air force and had moved repeatedly when her husband was transferred to one base after another. She thought she'd found Mary in San Diego, Michelle said, but by the time she got an address and phone number, Mary's husband had retired from the air force and they were again nowhere to be found. It was only a post on a Facebook page maintained by one of Mary's relatives that led her to the discovery that the woman she was looking for had returned to Texas and was living in

Denton, a town about forty miles north of Dallas. Within an hour of learning that, she had obtained a phone number and was placing a call to someone she still remembered as a teenage girl dressed all in black. It turned out to be a short conversation.

"I said, 'Mary, this is Michelle.' And she said, 'Michelle who?' I said, 'Michelle from Lockhart, your backyard neighbor. I know you remember me.' And she goes, 'Oh, you. How can I help you?' And I said, 'Well, I'm investigating the Tate Rowland case and I need to talk to you.' The silence after I said that was so long that I wasn't sure if she was still on the line. But then she finally spoke: 'That happened a long time ago. You all need to bury that, just like he's buried.' And then she hung up."

The tone of Mary's voice had been "so cold and flat," Michelle said. "It sounded more like she was making a threat than making a statement. I knew she wasn't going to talk to me, but I called a couple more times. She never picked up. I thought about driving up there and showing up at her front door, but I was busy and time passed. I followed Mary through her contacts on Facebook for a while, but then I stopped doing even that. I just sort of let her—and it—slip away. I checked in on Brenda a couple of times, because I felt guilty but, basically, I accepted that whatever happened to Tate was, like Mary said, buried."

I couldn't fault Michelle for seeing it that way. Confronting Mary Reyna was likely pointless and possibly dangerous. And her interest in the Tate Rowland case had lost some steam as conditions on the ground changed in Childress. I felt somewhat responsible for that; I hadn't been the cause, but I was a catalyst. After my separate conversations with Brenda Rowland and Kevin Overstreet, the two began to compare notes over the telephone. One thing led to another, and now Brenda was living with Kevin in Lubbock, Jimmie Rowland left behind with his bottle and his bad memories. Again, I could find no fault: Brenda had endured more than twenty-five years with Jimmie as he obliterated his pain with whiskey; Kevin stood back all that time out of respect for Brenda's marriage. The two of them had made more effort to get to the bottom of Tate Rowland's death than any other people alive. And this was a last chance for each of them to be happy.

Before leaving town, Brenda had done all she could to compel further investigation of Tate's hanging. The Childress County Sheriff's Department maintained that it *had* investigated further and stood by its original finding of suicide. "We have packaged up all the evidence and filed it away and it's never to be brought out again," a representative for the sheriff's department told me over the phone in 2017. No one, including me, was going to be allowed to look through that evidence: "The case is closed."

I let years pass after that conversation, but an itchy unease came back to me every time I thought about Tate's death. During her earlier investigation, Michelle had learned that nearly all of the young people who were named as those involved in a Childress-based satanic cult back in the 1980s had since died. "It was a dozen people," Michelle recalled when I asked her about this, "and it seemed strange that ten of them were now dead. And it seemed *really* strange that only one of them had died of natural causes. There were three suicides and two deaths by drug overdose. What are the odds of that? There were also a couple of car wreck deaths and two or three that had died under circumstances that weren't clear. It was curious."

Aside from Mary Reyna, the only one on her list of names who was still alive was Chad Johnston. I ignored that information for a long time, concluding that the story of Tate Rowland's death was of evil's ubiquity and evasiveness. The Devil was everywhere and nowhere at once. The people who said the Devil didn't exist had a good argument, just not as good as those that said he did. "What the Devil does best," I remarked to a friend, "is keep us guessing." I imagined that those might be the last words of this book.

Still, the one and only person I was certain knew what had happened out at Boxer's Corner in the late afternoon of July 26, 1988, had been Chad, who was either fourteen or fifteen at the time—different sources said different things about that. He'd be forty-nine years old now. Tate would have been fifty-one if he'd lived.

I finally asked Michelle to see if she could locate Chad. It didn't take her long to report that she had; he was living in Fort Worth and, she thought, working on oil rigs, though she never confirmed that last bit to my full satisfaction. It had to be him, though, Michelle said, born on July 28, 1973, meaning he would have been two days from his fifteenth birthday on the day Tate Rowland died. There were other Chad Roy Johnstons in Texas, Michelle said, but no other who was anywhere near to the right age.

On her own initiative, Michelle had obtained this Chad Johnston's phone number and called him one morning in December 2022. More than a week passed before she reported the conversation to me. Afterward, she had felt compelled to comb through her search results, Michelle explained, "to make absolutely certain it couldn't be anybody but him. And I am certain." But she had been unable to get him to admit he was the Chad Roy Johnston she was looking for, Michelle told me. The man she spoke to did say something that startled her, though. "He said he had been contacted by people over the years who mistakenly thought he was connected to a murder in West Texas," Michelle told me. Not a death in West Texas or even a hanging in West Texas; a "murder" in West Texas.

That sounded like a tell to me, and it was enough to convince me that I should follow up. My call was answered on the second ring, and in that short span of time I decided to do something that was either bold or stupid or both. "Tate?" I asked when the man on the other end said hello. There was a long, very long, pause before the voice said, "No."

"I'm sorry, Chad," I said. "Tate's been on my mind lately."

There was another long pause before Chad asked who I was. I told him my name and said that "my investigator," Michelle Gomez, had spoken to him some days earlier and that I wanted to follow up with a few questions of my own. He at once denied he was the Chad Johnston I was looking for. I said I understood that was what he had told Michelle, and that he had mentioned being contacted in the past by people who mistakenly thought he was the Chad Johnston connected to a murder in West Texas. He thought about this for a few moments, then said I had the story wrong, that what he had described was being "pulled over" in 1991 or 1992 by a police officer who thought he was the Chad Johnston who was wanted for "some crime" that had been committed in West Texas.

"I see," I said. "So you're not the Chad Johnston who was living in Childress in 1988?"

"No, sir, that is not me. And I really don't have more time to waste on this. You should know that there are other people with my name in Texas."

"There are three other Chad Roy Johnstons in Texas," I agreed. "But, see, my problem, Chad, is that you're the only one who was fourteen years old in 1988."

He went quiet. I waited maybe half a minute, then said, "I know it's you."

"You do, huh?" he asked. "Well, I'm sure you also know where I live. Why don't you come to my front door and we can settle this once and for all?"

Shooting an uninvited stranger on your porch would be a defensible crime in Texas, I supposed. "That sounds like a threat," I said.

"You're finally listening to me," he replied, then ended the call.

I sat listening to the empty silence for a few moments, feeling an uneasiness that would increase over the next several days. Chad Roy Johnston sounded more convincing each time I replayed my conversation with him, the indignation and exasperation in his voice increasingly genuine. Finally, I called him back. He immediately apologized for how our previous conversation had gone, said he hadn't meant to lose his temper, that it wasn't like him, but he had been dealing with people calling him and accusing him of being somebody he wasn't for almost twenty years, beginning back in 1995. It had gotten hard to take.

I told the man on the other end of the call that I was sorry if I'd been given wrong information. "You don't need to be sorry," he said. "I understand that this person y'all are lookin' for may be a very bad person, who was involved in some kind of cult murder or somethin', and I'd help you if I could."

I was finding it difficult to doubt him. There was a resonance
of decency in the man's voice. "I'm going to try to figure this out," I
told him.

"I hope you can," he replied, and we said goodbye.

I phoned Michelle, who said she still felt certain this was the
guy. I didn't challenge her, but I did begin to sift through all the
notes and documents I'd accumulated over the years, scanning dozens and dozens of pages until I came upon one that stopped me short.
It was the "Voluntary Statement" Chad had given to Deputy Sheriff
David Morris on the afternoon after Tate Rowland's death, the one
in which he'd provided the first of his several differing descriptions
of what had happened out at Boxer's Corner during the late afternoon and early evening of July 26, 1988. The first thing that struck
me was that Chad had given his age as "fifteen." The birth date of the
Chad Roy Johnston I had spoken to on the phone was July 28, 1973,
meaning he would not have turned fifteen until the day after he gave
his statement to Deputy Morris. Maybe he had fudged his age by a
day, but the discrepancy gave me pause. Then I read that during his
statement the witness had identified himself as Chad Jeremy Johnston. Not Chad Roy.

I went into a mild state of shock. I had read or heard the name
Chad Roy Johnston at least a dozen times. But now it occurred to me
that this had been in either my conversations with Michelle and
Brenda Rowland or in email exchanges between the two of them that
I had copies of. Somehow, I'd missed the name Chad Jeremy Johnston
in the one document I had where it appeared.

I read the "Voluntary Statement" Chad Jeremy Johnston had
given on July 27, 1988 with eyes refreshed by a jolt of consternation,
and only then did it occur to me that, even if the boy had been telling
the truth at that time, he was admitting at least a measure of complicity in Tate's death. Chad had acknowledged talking Tate through his
wish to hang himself and doing little or nothing to stop it from happening. His recounting of what had taken place out at the horse
apple tree was highly implausible, in particular his claim that in the
"about three minutes" it took Chad to step around the corner to

urinate, then return to the tree, Tate had somehow managed to remove a ski rope from the trunk of his car, tie it into a noose, string it over a limb, put it around his neck, climb up onto the hood of his car, then step off and hang until dead. Chad's description of seeing Tate's body dangling at the end of the rope with his left foot touching the bumper was chilling, especially given that, by his own account, Chad had done nothing to lift Tate's feet back up onto the car hood or to free him from the rope but had simply climbed into the car and driven back to the Rowlands home.

According to Kevin Overstreet, Chad had changed his story in a variety of ways when confronted with contradictory information, such as the two sets of rope burns on Tate's neck, but he had never really denied what was at a minimum tacit involvement in Tate's death, nor had he ever admitted any direct involvement.

After reading and rereading Chad's statement to Deputy Morris, I sat in my office and pondered why I had felt compelled to search Chad Johnston out and to question him. I had known it would be futile; it was absurd to imagine that Michelle or I were going to get Chad on the phone and that he would at last tell the truth and nothing but the truth about what had happened to Tate Rowland all those years ago. If he had any criminal exposure—and I was in no position to say he did—Chad was not going to admit it to the likes of us. But solving the case was not really the point. There was some other kind of resolution I was after, and it took me a while to acknowledge what it was: I wanted to excuse myself from pursuing this matter further.

I couldn't quite do that, at least not yet. With a little help from Michelle, I found a Chad Jeremy Johnston who had turned fifteen in May of 1988 and was now fifty years old and living in a small town northeast of Dallas. Soon after that, I obtained what I was certain was his cell phone number. Over the next week, I placed at least twenty calls at varying times of day, morning, afternoon, and evening. Each time, I heard five rings and then a Verizon wireless voice mail message.

It was likely, I knew, that he was never going to pick up. Leaving a voice mail message, though, probably would ensure that no call from my number would ever be answered. So I persisted, punching out the 817 area code number every couple of days. Listening to the same five rings and the eventual voice mail message, I realized I was learning something. It was that I felt more relief than disappointment when my calls went unanswered. A dead end was what I needed to bring me to a halt.

Eventually, though, deciding there was no alternative, I made one last attempt to reach Chad Jeremy Johnston, leaving a voice mail at the number I had for him:

"Hello Chad. My name is Randall Sullivan. At the request of the family, I've been looking into the death of Tate Rowland in Childress back in July of 1988. They're hoping, and so am I, that you'd be willing to tell us once and for all what really happened that day out at Boxer's Corner. I understand that you'd rather leave it all in the past, well behind you, but I'm asking you to consider it from the Rowland family's point of view. They've had to live for decades convinced that they don't know the whole truth about how Tate's life ended. You could give them some relief from the terrible pain they've suffered if you'd take the time to tell the whole truth about what took place. Maybe you'd find some relief yourself.

"Please call me back at (my telephone number). The name, again, is Randall Sullivan, and I'd very much appreciate your call. Good day."

I was astonished when Chad Johnston—*the* Chad Johnston— did call me back. He was angry and suspicious, demanding to know what my "angle" was; at one point I thought he might be accusing me of being a blackmailer. After a minute or two of hot conversation, though, he seemed to accept that I was who I claimed to be, but then said abruptly, "I have nothing to say to you," and told me goodbye. He didn't hang up, though. "My family and me were harassed out of Childress, unfairly," he said after a few moments. "And when I heard your phone message I felt like I was harassed again."

I said I was sorry if it felt that way, but that I just wanted to be able to go back to Brenda Rowland with the truth about what had happened to Tate. Chad's voice was thick when he answered, "Brenda is gonna have to learn to move on. A terrible thing happened to my friend. I've had to live with that terrible thing. Brenda and Tate's family will have to live with it too."

He said goodbye again, but I kept him talking by replying with a series of new questions. The one and only moment when he seemed to soften and waver came when I pointed out the several varying versions of his story he had given to law enforcement in a span of about four years during the late 1980s and early 1990s. After a long silence, Chad declared that just "a few years ago" he had made another statement to the Childress Police Department that I apparently did not know about, one in which "I told them the whole story and was cleared." When I asked what the whole story was, though, what exactly he had told the Childress police, Chad refused to say. "You'll have to get it from them," he told me. "Good luck with that." I tried to get in another question, but Chad said, "Don't ever bother me again," and ended the call.

I was able to confirm with Childress PD's one and only detective, Ronnie Bentley, that the interview Chad described had taken place at what was then his home in Fort Worth. Bentley wouldn't say a word about what Chad had told him, though, and when I asked to see his report, or any transcription of the interview that might exist, he flatly refused. He would only say that he believed Chad, and he believed also that "Chad has suffered enough about all this." He had personally "taped up" the entire Tate Rowland case file, including all of the records from the sheriff's department's investigation, and put it in the basement of the police station, Bentley told me, "where it will never be opened or even touched again."

When I said I imagined that only a judge would have the authority to seal evidence in the investigation of a person's death, Bentley snorted. "*I* have the authority," he said.

Brenda Rowland told me she wasn't "about to take Bentley's word for anything." She called the detective, who refused to let her see Chad Johnston's signed statement or the record of his interview with Chad, either. "I don't see how he can tell you no," I told her. "You should have an attorney write him a letter."

Brenda didn't reply. After several moments of silence, I suggested that maybe Chad's original description of what had happened out at the horse apple tree had been at least largely true. Brenda said she still didn't believe it.

I repeated my suggestion that she hire a lawyer. Brenda was quiet again for a time, then said, in a far-off voice, "It seems like we're not supposed to ever know exactly what really happened to Tate out there that day." I could hear it: She was done with this.

Then so was I. In what felt like the space between one breath and another, I admitted to myself that I had reached the end of the essential inquiry years earlier. I might not ever be able to say for certain what had happened to Tate Rowland, but I had long since decided that there *is* a Devil, a force of evil that human beings can best comprehend by personifying it, and that this force of evil had somehow, some way, been involved in the boy's death, and in all that had transpired in that small Texas town in the weeks and months and years afterward. The Devil had gotten away with it, I thought, as the Devil always seems to, escaping into the cover we provide with our fear, our denial, our rationalizations, our deluded sense of enlightenment and subsequent dismissal of his existence, and if all that fails, our resignation. I had come to believe—and at least partially to understand—that all the discord, calumny, and sheer hatred that drive the world were descended from the first break with God that the Devil had made before there was any time to count, let alone human beings to corrupt or redeem. It was all a product of this original separation. Yet no matter who or what the Devil was, believing in his or its existence didn't make me feel any less responsible for my own numerous failings and countless sins.

I *believed* the Devil was to blame, but I *knew* I was. And only because I knew my own guilt had I arrived at a conclusion that was truly terrible: I did indeed hold the door ǝH hides behind. And the one thing worse than throwing it open was leaving it closed.

Appendix A

WITH THE EXCEPTION of some shade thrown in 1979 by the anthropologist William Arens, whose work has since been shown to be riddled with fallacies, there is no doubt among serious scholars that the Aztecs, among other Mesoamericans, practiced human sacrifice and cannibalism.

The evidence has been abundant for nearly six centuries, yet the subject remains fraught, for reasons that have almost nothing to do with historical or scientific data.

Bernal Díaz del Castillo's *The Conquest of New Spain*, written in 1568, remains the primary historical source. Attacks on the work from various revisionist quarters have never come close to impeaching it. Díaz was in Mexico even before Cortés, and his is by far the most comprehensive eyewitness account of what the Spanish encountered on their approach and entry into Tenochtitlan. He and his fellow soldiers passed through more than one town, Díaz wrote, where men, women, and children were held in wooden cages before being slaughtered and eaten. Before their first big battle with the Spaniards, Díaz wrote, the Aztecs were so sure of victory that they began to prepare large pots with salt, peppers, and tomatoes where the bodies of the slain conquistadors would be cooked before being eaten. Inside the main temple in Tenochtitlan, Díaz added, the Spaniards found large pots where the flesh of sacrificed prisoners was cooked to feed the priests.

Díaz's account was corroborated by a number of other Spaniards who arrived in the region during the sixteenth century. In his *History of Tlaxcala*, written in 1585, Diego Muñoz Camargo wrote that the tribe kept public "butcher shops" for human flesh "as if it were of cow or sheep." It was Juan Bautista de Pomar who in his 1582 book *Relación* described how, after the Aztec priests performed a ritual of human sacrifice, the body of the victim was given to the warrior responsible for the capture, who cut it into pieces to be given as gifts to important persons, who would offer gifts and slaves in exchange. In his *Historia general*, Bernardino de Sahagún, the sixteenth-century Franciscan friar often described as the world's first anthropologist, included an illustration of a man being cooked in a pot, as an example of the dangers faced by those who traded with the Aztecs.

All efforts to cancel this considerable body of evidence have been based in some way on the claim that the accounts of Díaz, Muñoz Camargo, Pomar, and others were nothing more than an attempt to justify the Spanish campaigns of conquest and colonization. In the absence of any competing accounts—the description of the mass sacrifice under the direction of Tlacaelel comes from an Aztec witness—the revisionist histories are no more than ad hominem arguments. The best-known and most obviously specious case against Aztec cannibalism was made by Arens in his book *The Man-Eating Myth*.

It was Mexico's National Institute of Anthropology and History, though, that for decades served as the main agency for denying the historical accounts of sacrifice and cannibalism among Mesoamericans. As late as 2008 the institute derided missionary accounts of cannibalism among the Xixime people as "myth." By 2011, though, in the face of overwhelming physical evidence, the institute's director, archeologist Jose Luis Punzo, conceded that, yes, the Xiximes had practiced cannibalism.

The institute still resisted "stories" of Aztec cannibalism until 2020, when its archeologists made what *Smithsonian* magazine would describe as a "horrifying" discovery at the Zultepec-Tecoaque site in what is today Mexico City. What the archeologists had found were the remains of the members of a 1520 Spanish convoy that had arrived from Cuba carrying provisions for Cortés and his soldiers. Captured by the Aztecs shortly after stepping ashore, the captives included fifty women and ten children, who had been held alongside the men in doorless cells and "fattened up" for six months before being sacrificed, cooked and eaten, their heads strung up afterward on towering skull racks. Now the National Institute of Anthropology and History knew why, in the Nahuatl language, Tecoaque means "where they ate them."

With the question of whether the Aztecs practiced cannibalism no longer in question, those determined to defend the native peoples of Mexico from the cultural imperialism of Europeans have turned their attention to *why* the Mesoamericans ate people. This began right around the time Arens published *The Man-Eating Myth*, when two other anthropologists, Marvin Harris and Marshall Sahlins, went at each other in the pages of the *New York Review of Books*. Harris, who advocated "cultural materialism," argued that the Aztecs were driven to cannibalism by a shortage of other food sources in their region. Sahlins countered with the insistence that the Aztecs' consumption of human flesh was a result of their "culture." Even if his refusal to use the word "religion" was comically obtuse, Sahlins had all the evidence on his side. Recognizing this, the revisionists have circled their wagons around a defense of the beliefs that compelled the Aztecs to ritual sacrifice and cannibalism. An unintentionally amusing recent example is the paper written by a consulting scholar at the University of Pennsylvania Museum of Archeology and Anthropology, Jill Leslie McKeever Furst, titled "Food for the Gods." "While there is no doubt that the Aztecs were cannibals—they readily admitted it to Spanish chroniclers—they had strict rules about when human flesh could be eaten, who could be consumed, and who were to be the guests at the banquets that occurred in the annual cycle of agricultural rituals. They did not practice a culinary free-for-all in which anyone could unexpectedly end up as the piece de resistance. Nor did they gluttonously inhale every single morsel of the body."

Oh, yes, the Aztecs had rules. And as the paper observes in the following paragraphs, it is true that the sacrifices they made were to their gods. Not for McKeever Furst to ask what kind of deity would require that men, women, and children be taken captive, held in cages, force-fed until they were suitably plump, then murdered and eaten.

But it is for me. I have no illusions about the motives of the conquistadors; I don't doubt that conquest and plunder were at the forefront of more Spanish minds than was bringing word of the One True God. Nevertheless, their descriptions of Huitzilopochtli and Tezcatlipoca as infernal will get no argument from me, and I won't disagree, either, with those who have described the Aztecs as devil worshippers.

Bibliography

Preface

Sullivan, Randall. *The Miracle Detective*. New York: Atlantic Monthly Press, 2004.

Chapter One

Ahern, M. B. *The Problem of Evil*. Vol. 1. Oxford, UK: Routledge, 2012.

Albright, William Foxwell. *Yahweh and the Gods of Canaan*. University Park, PA: Eisenbrauns, 1990.

Becker, Ernest. *The Structure of Evil*. New York: Free Press, 1976.

Cavendish, Richard. *The Powers of Evil*. New York: Dorset Press, 1993.

Fromm, Erich. *The Anatomy of Human Destructiveness*. New York: Holt, 1992.

Hick, John. *Evil and the God of Love*. New York: Springer, 2010.

Homer. *The Iliad and The Odyssey* (boxed set). Translated by Robert Fagles. New York: Viking, 1990, 1996.

Kapadia, Shaporji Aspaniarji. *The Teachings of Zoroaster*. Paris: FV Editions, 2020.

Kreeft, Peter. *Philosophy 101 by Socrates*. South Bend, IN: St. Augustine's Press, 2012.

Langton, Edward. *Essentials of Demonology*. Eugene, OR: Wipf and Stock, 2014.

———. *Satan: A Portrait*. London, UK: Skeffington, 1945.

Mascaro, Juan, trans. *The Upanishads*. New York: Penguin Classics, 1965.

Metzger, Bruce M., and Michael D. Coogan, eds. *Oxford Companion to the Bible*. New York: Oxford University Press, 1993.

Russell, Jeffrey Burton. *The Devil*. Ithaca, NY: Cornell University Press, 1977.

Sontag, Frederick. *The God of Evil*. New York: Harper and Row, 1970.

Taylor, Richard. *Good and Evil*. New York: Prometheus Books, 1970.

Online Sources

Long, Vincent L. "Scenes from a Mexican Black Mass." *Vice*, August 19, 2015. https://www.vice.com/en/article/bnpv9a/scenes-from-a-mexican-black-mass

Chapter Two

Ahern, M. B. *The Problem of Evil*. Vol. 1. Oxford, UK: Routledge, 2012.

Albright, William Foxwell. *Yahweh and the Gods of Canaan*. University Park, PA: Eisenbrauns, 1990.

Bamberger, Bernard. *Fallen Angels*. Melrose Park, PA: Jewish Publication Society, 2006.

Gellner, Ernest. *The Devil in Modern Philosophy*. Oxford, UK: Routledge, 2003.

Holy Bible, New International Version. Grand Rapids, MI: Zondervan, 2002.

Kreeft, Peter. *Angels (and Demons)*. San Francisco: Ignatius Press, 1995.

Langton, Edward. *Satan: A Portrait*. London, UK: Skeffington, 1945.

Pagels, Elaine. *The Origin of Satan*. New York: Random House, 1995.

Plantinga, Alvin. *God, Freedom and Evil*. Grand Rapids, MI: Eerdmans, 1989.

Rohr, Richard. *Job and the Mystery of Suffering*. Chestnut Ridge, NY: Crossroad, 1998.

Russell, Jeffrey Burton. *The Devil*. Ithaca, NY: Cornell University Press, 1977.

———. *Satan*. Ithaca, NY: Cornell University Press, 1981.

Sontag, Frederick. *The God of Evil*. New York: Harper and Row, 1970.

Trachtenberg, Joshua. *The Devil and the Jews*. New Haven, CT: Yale University Press, 1943.

Wilson, Edmund. *Israel and the Dead Sea Scrolls*. New York: Farrar, Straus and Giroux, 1978.

Chapter Three

Barnard, Leslie W. *Athenagoras: A Study in Second Century Christian Apologetic* (boxed set). Paris: Beauchesne, 1972.

Broadie, Alexander. *Aquinas, St. Thomas*. Oxford, UK: Oxford University Press, 1999.

Brown, Peter. *Augustine of Hippo*. Berkeley: University of California Press, 2013.

Chadwick, Henry. *The Early Church*. New York: Penguin, 1993.

Colgrave, Bertram, ed. and trans. *The Earliest Life of Gregory the Great*. Cambridge, UK: Cambridge University Press, 1985.

Dante Alighieri. *The Divine Comedy*. Translated by John Ciardi. New York: Berkeley, 2003.

Grant, Robert M. *Gnosticism and Early Christianity*. New York: Columbia University Press, 1959.

Groeschel, Benedict J. *Augustine: Major Writings*. Chestnut Ridge, NY: Crossroad, 1995.

Kreeft, Peter. *I Burned for Your Peace: Augustine's Confessions Unpacked*. San Francisco: Ignatius Press, 2016.

———. *A Shorter Summa*. San Francisco: Ignatius Press, 1993.

Kung, Hans. *The Great Christian Thinkers*. New York: Continuum, 1994.

McManners, John, ed. *The Oxford Illustrated History of Christianity*. New York: Oxford University Press, 1992.

Metzger, Bruce M., and Michael D. Coogan, eds. *The Oxford Companion to the Bible*. New York: Oxford University Press, 1993.

Miller, Robert J., ed. *The Complete Gospels*. San Francisco: Polebridge Press, 1992.

Pagels, Elaine. *The Gnostic Gospels*. New York: Vintage, 1989.

Russell, Jeffrey Burton. *Lucifer*. Ithaca, NY: Cornell University Press, 1984.

———. *Satan*. Ithaca, NY: Cornell University Press, 1981.

Sullivan, Randall. *The Miracle Detective*. New York: Atlantic Monthly Press, 2004.

Urban, Linwood. *A Short History of Christian Thought*. New York: Oxford University Press, 1995.

White, John Wesley. *The Devil: What Scriptures Teach about Him*. Wheaton, IL: Tynedale House, 1977.

Chapter Four

Anshen, Ruth Nanda. *The Reality of the Devil*. New York: Harper and Row, 1972.

Behringer, Wolfgang. *Witches and Witch Hunts*. Cambridge, UK: Polity Press, 2004.

Carroll, Warren H. *Isabel: The Catholic Queen*. Front Royal, VA: Christendom Press, 1991.

Cavendish, Richard. *The Powers of Evil*. New York: Dorset Press, 1993.

Dante Alighieri. *The Divine Comedy*. Translated by John Ciardi. New York: Berkeley, 2003.

Flint, Valerie. *The Rise of Magic in Early Medieval Europe*. Princeton, NJ: Princeton University Press, 1991.

Klaits, Joseph. *Servants of Satan*. Bloomington: Indiana University Press, 1985.

Russell, Jeffrey Burton. *Lucifer*. Ithaca, NY: Cornell University Press, 1984.

——. *Witchcraft in the Middle Ages*. Ithaca, NY: Cornell University Press, 1972.

Smith, Damian J. *Crusade, Heresy and Inquisition in the Lands of the Crown of Aragon*. Leiden: Brill, 2010.

Sullivan, Randall. *The Miracle Detective*. New York: Atlantic Monthly Press, 2004.

Chapter Five

Anderson, R. F. *Hume's First Principles*. Lincoln: University of Nebraska Press, 1969.

Arthur, Richard T. W. *Leibniz*. Cambridge, UK: Polity Press, 2014.

Besterman, Theodore. *Voltaire*. London, UK: Longman, 1969.

Boyer, Carl. *A History of Mathematics*. Princeton, NJ: Princeton University Press, 1985.

Clarke, Desmond. *Descartes: A Biography*. Cambridge, UK: Cambridge University Press, 2006.

Copleston, Frederick. *A History of Philosophy* (boxed set). New York: Image, 1993.

Cullen, Patrick. *Infernal Triad*. Princeton, NJ: Princeton University Press, 2016.

Davidson, Ian. *Voltaire: A Life*. London, UK: Profile Books, 2010.

Ellwood, Roger. *Prince of Darkness*. Norwalk, CT: C. R. Gibson, 1974.

Holl, Adolf. *Death and the Devil*. New York: Seabury Press, 1976.

Israel, Jonathan. *A Revolution of the Mind*. Princeton, NJ: Princeton University Press, 2010.

Kant, Immanuel. *Introduction to the Critique of Pure Reason*. Edited by Paul Guyer and Alan W. Wood. Cambridge, UK: Cambridge University Press, 1998.

Kenyon, John Philipps. *The History Men*. Pittsburgh: University of Pittsburgh Press, 1984.

Leibniz, Gottfried Wilhelm. *Leibniz: Selections*. Edited by Phillip Weiner. New York: Scribner's, 1951.

Nadler, Steven M. *A Book Forged in Hell: Spinoza's Scandalous Treatise and the Birth of the Secular Age*. Princeton, NJ: Princeton University Press, 2011.

Voltaire. *Candide*. Translated by David Wooten. London, UK: Hackett, 2000.

Chapter Six

Barzun, Jacques. *From Dawn to Decadence*. New York: Harper Perennial, 2001.

———. *Romanticism and the Modern Ego*. Boston: Little, Brown, 1943.

Blanning, Tim. *The Romantic Revolution*. New York: Modern Library, 2012.

Byron, George Gordon, Samuel Coleridge, John Keats, Percy Bysshe Shelley, and William Wordsworth. *Five Great English Romantic Poets* (boxed set). Mineola, NY: Dover, 1993.

Drummond, Walter. *Philosopher of Evil: The Life and Works of the Marquis de Sade*. New York: Regency Books, 1962.

Eisler, Benita. *Byron: Child of Passion, Fool of Fame*. New York: Vintage, 2000.

Ellwood, Roger. *Prince of Darkness*. Norwalk, CT: C. R. Gibson, 1974.

Goethe, Johann Wolfgang. *Goethe's Faust*. Translated by Walter Kaufman. New York: Anchor, 1962.

Gray, Francine du Plessix. *At Home with the Marquis de Sade*. New York: Simon and Schuster, 1998.

Masson, David. *The Three Devils; Luther's, Milton's and Goethe's*. Charleston, SC: Biblio-Bazaar, 2009.

Masters, Anthony. *The Devil's Dominion: The Complete Story of Hell and Satanism in the Modern World*. Auckland: Castle Books, 1978.

Milton, John. *Paradise Lost*. Edited by John Leonard. New York: Penguin Classics, 2003.

Moore, Thomas. *Dark Eros: The Imagination of Sadism*. Washington, DC: Spring Publications, 1998.

Praz, Mario. *The Romantic Agony*. New York: Oxford University Press, 1978.

Russell, Jeffrey Burton. *Mephistopheles*. Ithaca, NY: Cornell University Press, 1986.

———. *The Prince of Darkness*. Ithaca, NY: Cornell University Press, 1988.

Newspapers

Pendergast, Martin. "The Catholic Church Learns to Love Oscar Wilde." *The Guardian*, July 17, 2009.

Taylor, Jerome. "The Vatican Wakes Up to the Wisdom of Oscar Wilde." *The Independent*, July 17, 2009.

Willsher, Kim. "How 555 Nights in Jail Helped to Make Paul Verlaine a 'Prince of Poets.'" *The Guardian*, October 17, 2015.

Periodicals

Bernhard, Thomas. "Jean-Arthur Rimbaud." *Die Zeit*, May 14, 2009.

Bordwell, Harold. "Late Conversion: Was Rimbaud a Saint?" *Commonweal*, May 8, 2008.

McCracken, Andrew. "The Long Conversion of Oscar Wilde." *New Oxford Review*, September 1998.

Stavrou, Constantine N. "Milton, Byron, and the Devil." *University of Kansas City Review*, 1955.

Chapter Seven

Baldick, Robert. *The Life of J.-K. Huysmans*. Sawtry, UK: Dedalus, 2006.

Baudelaire, Charles. *Flowers of Evil*. Translated by Jacques Leclercq. New York: Peter Pauper Press, 1958.

Huysmans, Joris-Karl. *Against Nature (À Rebours)*. New York: Oxford University Press, 2009.

———. *The Damned (Là-Bas)*. New York: Penguin Classics, 2002.

Masters, Anthony. *The Devil's Dominion: The Complete Story of Hell and Satanism in the Modern World*. Auckland: Castle Books, 1978.

Praz, Mario. *The Romantic Agony*. New York: Oxford University Press, 1978.

Rimbaud, Arthur. *I Promise to Be Good: The Letters of Arthur Rimbaud*. Translated by Wyatt Mason. New York: Modern Library, 2004.

———. *A Season in Hell/The Illuminations*. Translated by Enid Rhodes Peschel. New York: Oxford University Press, 1973.

Russell, Jeffrey Burton. *Mephistopheles*. Ithaca, NY: Cornell University Press, 1986.

———. *The Prince of Darkness*. Ithaca, NY: Cornell University Press, 1988.

Weir, David. *Decadence and the Making of Modernism*. Amherst: University of Massachusetts Press, 1996.

Wheatley, Dennis. *The Devil and All His Works*. London, UK: Hutchinson, 1971.

White, Edmund. *Rimbaud: The Double Life of a Rebel*. London, UK: Atlas Press, 2008.

Chapter Eight

"Albert Pike." In United Daughters of the Confederacy, Arkansas Division, *Historical Arkansas*. Little Rock, AR: Democrat Printing and Lithographing Company, 1992.

Allsop, Fred. *Albert Pike: A Biography*. Whitefish, MT: Kessinger, 1997.

Brown, Walter. *A Life of Albert Pike*. Fayetteville: University of Arkansas Press, 1997.

Davis, Susan Lawrence. *Authentic History: Ku Klux Klan 1865–1877*. Scotts Valley, CA: CreateSpace, 2014.

Duffy, Eamon. *Saints and Sinners: A History of the Popes*. New Haven, CT: Yale University Press, 1997.

Ellis, Bill. *Raising the Devil*. Lexington: University Press of Kentucky, 2000.

Garrard, Graeme. *Counter Enlightenments*. London, UK: Routledge, 2006.

Gerrish, Brian A. *A Prince of the Church: Schleiermacher and the Beginnings of Modern Theology*. Eugene, OR: Wipf and Stock, 2001.

Gilman, Richard M. *Behind "World Revolution": The Strange Career of Nesta H. Webster*. Ann Arbor, MI: Insights Books, 1982.

Hawthorne, Nathaniel. *Young Goodman Brown and Other Tales*. New York: Oxford University Press, 2009.

Knight, Peter. *Conspiracy Theories in American History*. Bridgeport, CT: ABC-Clio, 2003.

Lester, J. C., and D. L. Wilson, with introduction and notes by Walter L. Fleming. *Ku Klux Klan: Its Origin, Growth and Disbandment*. n.p.: Project Gutenberg, 2010.

Livingstone, David. *Terrorism and the Illuminati: A Three-Thousand Year History*. San Diego: Progressive Press, 2011.

Masters, Anthony. *The Devil's Dominion: The Complete Story of Hell and Satanism in the Modern World*. Auckland: Castle Books, 1978.

Melville, Herman. *The Confidence Man*. New York: Penguin Classics, 1991.

Miller, Edith Starr. *The Occult Theocrasy*. Scotts Valley, CA: CreateSpace, 2009.

Pipes, Daniel. *Conspiracy: How the Paranoid Style Flourishes and Where It Comes From*. New York: Free Press, 1997.

Poe, Edgar Allan. *The Unabridged Edgar Allan Poe*. Philadelphia: Running Press, 1983.

Porter, Lindsay. *Who Are the Illuminati? Exploring the Myth of the Secret Society*. Glasgow, UK: Pavilion Books, 2005.

Quardt, Robert. *Master Diplomat: From the Life of Leo XIII*. Translated by Ilya Wolson. New York: Alba House, 1964.

Russell, Jeffrey Burton. *Mephistopheles*. Ithaca, NY: Cornell University Press, 1986.

———. *The Prince of Darkness*. Ithaca, NY: Cornell University Press, 1988.

Schneider, Heinrich. *Quest for Mysteries: The Masonic Background for Literature in 18th Century Germany*. Whitefish, MT: Kessinger, 2005.

Sibley, W. G. *The Story of Freemasonry*. Whitefish, MT: Kessinger, 1996.

Smith, Dean F. "Albert Pike." In *Historical Times Illustrated History of the Civil War*, edited by Patricia L. Faust. New York: Harper and Row, 1986.

Twain, Mark [Samuel Clemens]. *The Mysterious Stranger and Other Stories*. New York: Signet, 2012.

Newspapers/Wire Services

"Protesters Topple Confederate General Statue in Washington D.C. and Set It on Fire." Associated Press, June 20, 2020.

Smith, Drew A. "Albert Pike's Legacy in Arkansas." *Arkansas Democrat-Gazette*, June 22, 1920.

Online Sources

"Albert Pike—Hero or Scoundrel?" The Smithsonian Associates Civil War E-Mail Newsletter 5, no. 1. https://civilwarstudies.org/articles/Vol_5/pike.shtm

"Albert Pike Letter to Mazzini: The Illuminati Plan for 3 World Wars." August 15, 1871. Internet Archive. https://ia601900.us.archive.org/16/items/albert-pike-letter-to-mazzini/Albert%20Pike%20Letter%20to%20Mazzini.pdf

Anderson, Kevin. "Conspiracy Theories and the Canadians Who Love Them." Active History, November 16, 2020. https://activehistory.ca/blog/2020/11/16/conspiracy-theories-and-the-canadians-who-love-them/

"Complete Confession of Leo Taxil." Freedom Ministries International, posted May 2, 2006. https://www.freedom-ministries.com/catalog/confession-leo-taxilm-and-albert-pike.html

Evans, Richard. "Edith Starr Miller, Martyr to a Cabalist Conspiracy." henrymakow.com, January 25, 2012. https://www.henrymakow.com/unsung_heroine_--_illuminati_d.html

Exorcism Prayer to St. Michael by Pope Leo XIII." Marian Apostolate, posted December 9, 2012. https://marianapostolate.com/2010/12/09/original-exorcism-prayer-to-st-michael/

Westmoreland, Ingrid P. "Pike, Albert." Oklahoma Historical Society. Accessed October 5, 2022. https://www.okhistory.org/publications/enc/entry?entry=PI006

Periodicals

Chaitkin, Anton. "Why Albert Pike's Statue Must Fall: The Scottish Rite's Ku Klux Klan Project." *Fidelio* 2, no. 1 (Spring 1993): 4–13.

Lee, Martha F. "Nesta Webster: The Voice of Conspiracy." *Journal of Women's History* 17, no. 3 (Fall 2005): 81–104.

Chapter Nine

Lane, Brian, and Wilfred Gregg. *The New Encyclopedia of Serial Killers*. London, UK: Headline, 1996.

Lewis, C. S. *The Screwtape Letters: With Screwtape Proposes a Toast*. New York: HarperCollins, 2001.

Marksman, Ronald, and Dominick Bosco. *Alone with the Devil: Psychopathic Killings That Shocked the World*. London, UK: Warner Books, 1990.

Online Sources

"Lawrence Bittaker." Murderpedia. https://murderpedia.org/male.B/b/bittaker-lawrence.htm

"A Matter of Obedience." Facing History and Ourselves, May 12, 2020. https://www.facinghistory.org/resource-library/matter-obedience

"The Psychology of Evil." TED Talk by Philip Zimbardo, March 12, 2014. https://www.ted.com/talks/philip_zimbardo_the_psychology_of_evil?language=en

Periodicals

Zimbardo, Philip. "When Good People Do Evil." *Yale Alumni Magazine*, January–February 2007.

Television Programs/Podcasts

Barajas, Joshua. "How the Nazi's Defense of 'Just Following Orders' Plays Out in the Mind." *PBS NewsHour*, February 19, 2016.

Dunning, B. "What You Didn't Know about the Stanford Prison Experiment." *Skeptoid Podcast*, Skeptoid Media, May 27, 2008.

Zimbardo, Philip. "The Psychology of Evil." *Eye on Psi Chi* 5, no. 1 (Fall 2000).

Chapter Ten

Lane, Brian, and Wilfred Gregg. *The New Encyclopedia of Serial Killers*. London, UK: Headline, 1996.

Marksman, Ronald, and Dominick Bosco. *Alone with the Devil: Psychopathic Killings That Shocked the World*. London, UK: Warner Books, 1990.

Romm, Cari. "Rethinking One of Psychology's Most Infamous Experiments." *The Atlantic*, January 28, 2015.

Waxman, Olivia B. "Lessons of the Gruesome Case behind One of America's Last Legal Executions by Hanging." *Time*, January 5, 2018.

Newspapers

Prokop, Jessica. "Child Killer Westley Allan Dodd Hanged 30 Years Ago." *Columbian*, January 5, 2023.

Online Sources

"Westley Allan Dodd." Murderpedia. https://murderpedia.org/male.D/d1/dodd-westley-allan.htm

Periodicals

Blass, Thomas. "The Man Who Shocked the World." *Psychology Today* 35, no. 2 (March–April 2002).

———. "The Milgram Paradigm after 35 Years: Some Things We Now Know about Obedience to Authority." *Journal of Applied Social Psychology* 29, no. 5 (1999): 955–978.

Chapter Eleven

Arens, William. *The Man-Eating Myth*. New York: Oxford University Press, 1980.

Carroll, Warren H. *Our Lady of Guadalupe: And the Conquest of Darkness*. Front Royal, VA: Christendom Press, 2004.

Díaz del Castillo, Bernal. *The Conquest of New Spain*. Harmondsworth, UK: Penguin Classics, 1973.

Harris, Marvin. *Cannibals and Kings*. New York: Vintage, 1991.

Prescott, William H. *History of the Conquest of Mexico and History of the Conquest of Peru*. New York: Cooper Square Press, 2000.

Smith, Jody Brant. *The Image of Guadalupe*. Garden City, NY: Image Books, 1984.

Newspapers/Wire Services

"Mexico Archeologists Reveal Tale of Cannibalism and Retaliation from Conquest." Associated Press, January 21, 2021.

Rensberger, Boyce. "Experts on Cannibalism Deny Withholding Cannibalism 'Facts.'" *New York Times*, March 3, 1977.

Online Sources

Gershon, Livia. "After Aztecs Cannibalized Spanish Convoy, Conquistadors Retaliated by Killing Innocents." Smithsonian Daily Report, January 21, 2021.

Lenchek, Shep. "The Aztecs Speak—An Aztec Account of the Conquest of Mexico." MexConnect, 2008. https://www.mexconnect.com/articles/682-the-aztecs-speak-an-aztec-account-of-the-conquest-of-mexico/

Roos, Dave. "Human Sacrifice: Why the Aztecs Practiced This Gory Ritual." History Channel, October 11, 2018. https://www.history.com/news/aztec-human-sacrifice-religion

Periodicals

Harner, Michael. "The Enigma of Aztec Sacrifice." *Natural History*, April 1977.

Leslie McKeever Furst, Jill. "Food for the Gods." *Expedition* 45, no. 2 (2003).

Chapter Twelve

Castañeda, Angela N. "The African Diaspora in Mexico: Santería, Tourism, and Representations of the State." In *The African Diaspora and the Study of Religion*, edited by Theodore Louis Trost, 131–150. New York: Palgrave Macmillan, 2007.

Newspapers/Wire Services

Allen, Nick. "Mexico's 'Most Sadistic' Drug Kingpin's Reign Ends without a Shot." *Daily Telegraph*, September 4, 2010.

Castillo, Eduardo. "Even More Brutal Leader Takes over Mexico's Zetas." *Brownsville (TX) Herald*, March 7, 2011.

———. "War between Gulf Cartel, Zetas Marks Year Anniversary." *Brownsville Herald*, March 7, 2011.

Garcia, Diana. "Many Go Missing on Mexican 'Highway of Death.' Their Families Continue to Search for Them." *Arizona Republic*, November 18, 2021.

Iliff, Laurence. "Mexico: Battling Drugs and Crime." McClatchy Newspapers, July 18, 2008.

Lacy, Marc. "In Drug War, Mexico Fights Cartel and Itself." *New York Times*, November 7, 2008.

Roebuck, Jeremy. "Violence the Result of Fractured Arrangement between Zetas and Gulf Cartel, Authorities Say." *Brownsville Herald*, March 9, 2010.

Rosenberg, Mica. "Bustling Mexico Port New Front in Drugs War." Reuters, September 22, 2011.

Tuckman, Jo. "Tortured Mexican Kidnap Victim Says: 'I Would Sit There Wondering How People Could Be That Bad." *The Guardian*, September 4, 2010.

"Two Cartels Dominate in Veracruz Drug War." *Lubbock Avalanche-Journal*, October 1, 2011.

"'Veracruz Is an Enormous Mass Grave': 250 Skulls Found in Hidden Graves on Mexico's Gulf Coast." Associated Press, March 14, 2017.

"Victims of Mexico's Drug War: Tracing the Missing." *The Economist*, June 14, 2014.

Vulliamy, Ed. "The Zetas: Gangster Kings of Their Own Brutal Narco-State." *The Guardian*, November 14, 2009.

Wilkinson, Tracy. "Girl's Killing Spurs City to Face Fears." *Los Angeles Times*, July 18, 2008.

"Zetas Hit Man Arrested over Marine Torture-Slayings." *Tucson Sentinel*, May 12, 2012.

Television Programs/Online Sources

"All Tamaulipas a War Zone." *Borderland Beat* (blog), April 22, 2010. https://www.borderlandbeat.com/2010/04/all-tamaulipas-war-zone.html?m=1

"'A Brutal Complicity': The Roots of Violence in Veracruz." Mexico Violence Resource Project, November 23, 2020. https://www.mexicoviolence.org/post/a-brutal-complicity

Bunker, Robert J. "Santa Muerte: Inspired and Ritualistic Killings." Federal Bureau of Investigation bulletin, February 5, 2013.

"Five Most Dangerous Roads in Mexico." Dangerous Roads. https://www.dangerousroads.org/north-america/mexico/10085-the-five-most-dangerous-roads-in-mexico.html

Grant, Will. "Mexico's Zetas Drug Gang Split Raises Bloodshed Fears." BBC News, September 11, 2012.

"Gulf Cartel vs. Los Zetas ... One Year Later." Borderland Beat, February 26, 2011. https://www.borderlandbeat.com/2011/02/cdg-vs-zetas-one-year-later.html

Kahn, Carrie. "Highway 101: A Trip Down One of Mexico's Most Dangerous Roads." *Morning Edition*, NPR, June 6, 2016.

Lorentzen, Lois Ann. "Santa Muerte: Saint of the Dispossessed, Enemy of Church and State." Hemispheric Institute, vol. 13, no. 1, 2016. https://hemisphericinstitute.org/en/emisferica-13-1-states-of-devotion/13-1-essays/santa-muerte-saint-of-the-dispossessed-enemy-of-church-and-state.html

"Mexican Troops Kill Zetas Cartel Founder Mellado." BBC News, May 12, 2014.

"Mexico Arrests over La Santa Muerte Cult Killings." BBC News, March 31, 2012.

"Mexico Highway Slaughter Seen as Challenge to Zetas Cartel." Fox News, December 12, 2016.

"Mexico Navy Smashes Zetas Cartel Communications Network." BBC News, September 8, 2011.

Ramsey, Geoffrey. "Video: 'Highway of Death' Runs Past Mass Graves in Northern Mexico." InSight Crime, April 14, 2011. https://insightcrime.org/news/analysis/video-highway-of-death-runs-past-mass-graves-in-northern-mexico/

Tucker, Duncan. "Santa Muerte: The Rise of Mexico's Death 'Saint.'" BBC News, November 1, 2017.

Ware, Michael. "Los Zetas Called Mexico's Most Dangerous Drug Cartel." CNN, August 6, 2009.

Chapter Thirteen

Booklets

Catemaco: Tierra de Ensonacion. San Andrés Tuxtla, Veracruz, 1992.

Newspapers

McKinley, James C. "In the Town of Catemaco, Witches Are Taken Seriously." *New York Times,* March 28, 2008.

Television Programs/Online Sources

Garcia-Navarro, Lulu. "Mexican Town Hosts Annual Congress of Witches." *Day to Day,* NPR, February 28, 2007.

Long, Vincent L. "Scenes from a Mexican Black Mass." *Vice News,* August 19, 2015. https://www.vice.com/en/article/bnpv9a/scenes-from-a-mexican-black-mass

Matthews, Roberto. "Catemaco: A Hideout of Wizards and Witches in Veracruz, Mexico." Bridgehead Media, March 14, 2018. https://www.bridgeheadmedia.com/catemaco-a-hideout-of-wizards-and-witches-in-veracruz-mexico/

Tuckman, Jo. "Witchcraft and Capitalism Hit Mexican Town." *Salon,* March 7, 2004. https://www.salon.com/2004/03/07/witchcraft/

Chapter Fourteen

Ebon, Martin. *The Devil's Bride.* New York: Harper and Row, 1974.

MacNutt, Francis. *Deliverance from Evil Spirits: A Practical Manual.* Grand Rapids, MI: Chosen Books, 1995.

Martin, Malachi. *Hostage to the Devil: The Possession and Exorcism of Five Contemporary Americans.* New York: Harper and Row, 1976.

Olson, Alan M., ed. *Disguises of the Demonic: Contemporary Perspectives on the Power of Evil.* New York: Association Press, 1975.

Peck, M. Scott. *Glimpses of the Devil.* New York: Free Press/Simon and Schuster, 2005.

Shetler, Joanne. *And the Word Came with Power.* Portland, OR: Multnomah Press, 1992.

Vogl, Carl. *Begone Satan: A Soul-Stirring Account of Diabolical Possession in Iowa*. Translated by Celestine Capsner. Charlotte, NC: TAN Books, 1994.

Young, Francis. *A History of Exorcism in Catholic Christianity*. London, UK: Palgrave Macmillan, 2016.

Television Programs/Online Sources

Kryt, Jeremy. "The Pope, Dope, and Mexican Satanic Cults." *Daily Beast*, April 13, 2017. https://www.thedailybeast.com/the-pope-dope-and-mexican-satanic-cults

Lynch, Dennis. "Pope Francis and Exorcism: How He's Brought the Practice Back to the Modern Catholic Church." *International Business Times*, April 15, 2016. https://www.ibtimes.com/pope-francis-exorcism-how-hes-brought-practice-back-modern-catholic-church-1884000

Schneible, Ann. "Resignation Is from the Devil, Pope Warns Mexico Priests, Religious." Catholic News Agency, February 16, 2016. https://www.catholicnewsagency.com/news/33432/resignation-is-from-the-devil-pope-warns-mexican-priests-religious

Stefco, Jill. "An Exorcism in Earling, Iowa." Suite 101, September 21, 2005.

Wire Services

"The Devil Is Punishing Mexico with Violence, Says Pope Francis." Reuters, March 13, 2015.

"Exorcist Says Pope Helped 'Liberate' Man." Associated Press, May 21, 2003.

"Pope Warns against Devil in Hardscrabble Mexico City Suburb." Associated Press, February 14, 2016.

Winfield, Nicole. "Pope Warns Vatican Staff an 'Elegant Demon' Lurks among Them." Associated Press, December 22, 2022.

Childress/Tate Rowland Hanging/Satanic Panic

Brands, H. W. *Lone Star Nation*. New York: Anchor, 2005.

Hechler, David. *The Battle and the Backlash: The Child Sexual Abuse War*. New York: Macmillan, 1989.

Raschke, Carl. *Painted Black: From Drug Killings to Heavy Metal; The Alarming True Story of How Satanism Is Terrifying Our Communities*. New York: HarperCollins, 1990.

Victor, Jeffrey S. *Satanic Panic: The Creation of a Contemporary Legend*. Chicago: Open Court, 1993.

Documents

Authority to Perform an Autopsy: Authorization of Dr. Sparks Veasey, Justice of the Peace Dottie S. Bettis, July 29, 1991.

Inquest Record: Tate Rowland Death, Decision of Justice of the Peace Dottie S. Bettis, Childress County Courthouse, July 27, 1988.

Interview of Michelle Gomez, In Re: Mary Rena, for Childress P.D. Lockhart Police Department, Criminal Investigation Division, March 23, 1989.

Offense Report, Juvenile Arrest, Unauthorized Use of Motor Vehicle, Ray Wilks, November 6, 1988.

Order on Motion to Disinter, Justice of the Peace Dottie S. Bettis, July 29, 1991.

Vermilion Parish Schools Grade and Attendance Report: Tate Janson Rowland, June 2, 1988.

Voluntary Statement: Chad Johnston. Childress County Sheriff's Department, July 27, 1988.

Newspapers/Wire Services

Applebome, Peter. "Midlothian Journal: Where City Meets County, a Killing." *New York Times*, October 29, 1987.

"As Indictment Nears Anxiety Is Mounting." *Childress (TX) Index*, October 29, 1991.

Bohanan, Sonny. "Erdmann: Bruises Caused by Embalming." *Amarillo Globe-News*, October 26, 1991.

———. "Police Chief Says Trosper's Death Not Seen as Murder." *Amarillo Globe-News*, October 27, 1992.

———. "Questions about Deaths Draw Varied Reactions." *Amarillo Globe-News*, September 4, 1992.

———. "Testimony Begins in Trosper Death." *Amarillo Globe-News*, September 1, 1992.

———. "Witness 'Afraid' of Telling about Alleged Suffocation." *Amarillo Globe-News*, September 2, 1992.

"Bradford Bond Set at $100,000." *Childress Index*, March 9, 1992.

Brown, Chip. "Murder of Youth, 17, Brings Horror Films to Life in Texas Town." Associated Press, November 4, 1990.

Burchell, Anna. "Bradford Trial Set to Begin Monday in Carson County." *Childress Index*, August 11, 1992.

———. "Change of Venue for Bradford Trial?" *Childress Index*, August 9, 1992.

———. "One Jailed in Trosper Murder." *Childress Index*, March 8, 1992.

———. "Tate Rowland Death Remains Big Mystery." *Childress Index*, September 3, 1992.

Burchell, Anna, and Steve Clements. "29-Year-Old Held in Trosper Death." *Wichita Falls Times Review*, March 8, 1992.

"Childress Stories Top '91 Headlines." *Amarillo Globe-News*, December 12, 1991.

DeMay, Daniel. "The Most Liberal and Most Conservative Cities in the U.S." *Connecticut Post*, December 17, 2015.

"Erdmann Ends Medical Career." Associated Press, August 23, 1992.

Goleman, Daniel. "Proof Lacking for Ritual Abuse by Satanists." *New York Times*, October 31, 1994.

Hutchison, Russell L. "Students Tell about Cult Ritual at Grave." *Amarillo Daily News*, November 2, 1988.

Jones, Brett. "Jury Says Bradford Is Guilty." *Childress Index*, September 3, 1992.

———. "Lewis Gives 'Damaging' Testimony . . ." *Childress Index*, September 1, 1992.

Reinhold, Robert. "The Longest Trial—A Post-Mortem: Collapse of Child Abuse Case: So Much Agony for So Little." *New York Times*, January 24, 1990.

"Ricky L. Bradford Will Begin Life Sentence Tuesday." *Childress Index*, September 6, 1992.

Sharbutt, Jay. "Caldron Boils over Geraldo's 'Devil Worship': 'Satan' Wins Ratings, Loses Advertisers." *Los Angeles Times*, October 27, 1988.

Stevens, David. "Family's Grief Mixed with Anger as Officials Continue Investigation." *Amarillo Globe-News*, October 26, 1991.

———. "Suspect Arraigned in Trosper Death." *Amarillo Globe-News*, November 2, 1991.

———. "Suspect Arrested in Trosper Death." *Amarillo-Globe News*, March 8, 1992.

"Tales of Satanism Mark Molestation Cases." Associated Press, December 13, 1987.

"Veasey Describes Bruises as Recent." *Amarillo Globe-News*, October 26, 1991.

Yoachum, Gene. "Amarillo Youth Minister Believes Satanic Cults Are Present in Area." *Amarillo Globe-News*, October 23, 1991.

———. "District Attorney Says Case Nears Indictment." *Amarillo Daily News*, October 28, 1991.

———. "Family Reports Woman's Body to Be Exhumed." *Amarillo Daily News*, October 22, 1991.

———. "Pathologist Stands by Original Autopsy of Childress Woman." *Amarillo Globe-News*, September 3, 1992.

———. "Questions Follow Childress Teen's Death." *Amarillo Globe-News*, October 20, 1991.

———. "Tate Rowland Talked about 'Satanists' after Paducah Arrest." *Amarillo Daily News*, October 11, 1991.

———. "Those Who Knew Childress Teen Don't Believe He Killed Himself." *Amarillo Globe-News*, October 21, 1991.

———. "Trosper Death Investigated as Homicide." *Amarillo Daily News*, October 26, 1991.

Online Sources

"Child Abuse and Day Care." Testimony of K. MacFarlane before Subcommittee on Oversight, Committee on Ways and Means, Select Committee on Children, Youth and Families, House of Representatives, September 17, 1984. http://law2.umkc.edu/faculty/projects/ftrials/mcmartin/macfarlanetestimony.html

"Childress." Texas Handbook of Texas Online, Texas State Historical Society. https://www.tshaonline.org/handbook/entries/childress-tx

"City of Childress: Your Government." Official city website. https://www.cityofchildress.com/government

Noss, Reed. "Western Shortgrass Prairie." One Earth. https://www.oneearth.org/ecoregions/western-shortgrass-prairie/

"Rolling Plains Ecological Region." Texas Parks and Wildlife Commission. https://tpwd.texas.gov/landwater/land/habitats/cross_timbers/ecoregions/rolling_plains.phtml

"Rolling Red Plains." United States Department of Agriculture. https://www.nrcs.usda.gov/plant-materials/news/cover-crop-seeding-rates-in-the-texas-rolling-red-plains

"Western Short Grasslands." World Wildlife Fund. https://www.worldwildlife.org/ecoregions/na0815

Periodicals

Bottoms, Bette L., and Suzanne L. Davis. "The Creation of Satanic Ritual Abuse." *Journal of Social and Clinical Psychology* 16, no. 2 (June 1, 1997): 112–132.

Cavenaugh, Lou. "The Devil in Childress County." *Detective Files*, May 1993.

Flenniken, Donna. "Death Stalks a Small Town." *Accent West*, October 1991.

———. "Out of the Night . . . A Killer Walked." *Accent West*, May 1991.

Hollandsworth, Skip. "Possessed by the Devil." *Texas Monthly*, July 1992.

Kent, Stephen. "Deviant Scripturalism and Ritual Satanic Abuse." *Religion* 23, no. 3 (1993).

Putnam, Frank W. "The Satanic Ritual Abuse Controversy." *Child Abuse and Neglect* 15, no. 3 (1991): 175–179.

Rubin, Frank. "The Homicide That Almost Slipped Away." *National Law Journal*, September 28, 1992.

Stowers, Carlton. "Crime Satanic Curses." *D Magazine*, June 1989.

Index